Today's World
Select Readings of Chinese Spotlight News

今日世界面面观
汉语焦点新闻选读

上册

王颖　王志军　徐丽莎　◎编著

北京大学出版社

图书在版编目（CIP）数据

今日世界面面观：汉语焦点新闻选读. 上册 / 王颖，王志军，徐丽莎编著. —北京：北京大学出版社，2016.12

ISBN 978-7-301-27623-5

Ⅰ.①今… Ⅱ.①王… ②王… ③徐… Ⅲ.①汉语—阅读教学—对外汉语教学—教材 Ⅳ.①H195.4

中国版本图书馆CIP数据核字（2016）第237015号

书　　名	今日世界面面观：汉语焦点新闻选读（上册） JINRI SHIJIE MIANMIANGUAN: HANYU JIAODIAN XINWEN XUANDU (SHANG CE)
著作责任者	王颖　王志军　徐丽莎　编著
责任编辑	孙　娴
标准书号	ISBN 978-7-301-27623-5
出版发行	北京大学出版社
地　　址	北京市海淀区成府路205号　100871
网　　址	http://www.pup.cn　　新浪微博：@北京大学出版社
电子信箱	z@pup.cn
电　　话	邮购部 62752015　发行部 62750672　编辑部 62753374
印 刷 者	北京宏伟双华印刷有限公司
经 销 者	新华书店
	889毫米×1194毫米　16开本　16印张　180千字 2016年12月第1版　2021年1月第3次印刷
定　　价	160.00元（含课本和练习本）

未经许可，不得以任何方式复制或抄袭本书之部分或全部内容。
版权所有，侵权必究
举报电话：010-62752024　电子信箱：fd@pup.pku.edu.cn
图书如有印装质量问题，请与出版部联系，电话：010-62756370

前言

本书是为美国大学及其在华中文项目编写的一套新闻时事课教材，同样适用于包括加拿大、英国、澳大利亚、新西兰等在内的其他英语国家。全书共分上下两册，各八个话题，每个话题又分主副两篇课文。一般来说，上册适用于美国大学中文项目的三年级下学期或者四年级上学期，美国外语教学委员会（ACTFL，the American Council on the Teaching of Foreign Languages）设定的"中级－高"（Intermediate-high）到"高级－低"（Advanced-low）水平的学习者；下册适用于美国大学中文项目的四年级上学期或者下学期，美国外语教学委员会设定的"高级－中"（Advanced-mid）到"高级－高"（Advanced-high）水平的学习者。

以报刊新闻作为高级汉语的教材具有诸多优点：语料真实、时效性强、实用性强、结合现实生活紧密、话题性强、便于学以致用等。但是受新闻本身求"新"求"快"特点的制约，不论是报纸上还是网络上登出的新闻原始材料大多是"急就章"，文字疏于仔细推敲和反复锤炼。另外，极强的"即时性"也使得不少新闻刚成为热点又迅速地"冷却"下来，昨日的新闻旋即成为今日的"旧闻"，不再引起读者的关注。本套教材本着"与时俱进""细选精编"的原则，力图发挥新闻材料的优势，同时克服和弥补其弱点。具体说来，这套教材具备以下一些特点：

在话题方面，选材虽来源于各大新闻网络，但文字都经过我们反复增删、加工和修改。教材的主要内容都是既体现了新闻的时效性又受到了大众持续关注的热门话题；既关注到中国和美国的焦点话题，又做到一个话题多个视角，突显问题的多元性和文化交叉的层面；既提供精读课文，又选有泛读或者扩展阅读材料。比如，环境污染问题是一个受到持续关注的话题，在这个话题下，我们选编的主副课文分别聚焦于近期在北京的雾霾和太平洋出现的白色污染——"塑料岛"上，而反映北京雾霾的主课文还讨论、比较了英国雾都伦敦的空气污染问题和历史。又如，枪支政策是美国长久以来一直"吸引眼球"的热点。在这个话题下，我们选编的主课文报道、评论了近年来美国校园频发的枪击案件，而副课文则重点讨论了美国民众对控枪政策的不同态度。由于同时关注中美两国时事，"时效性"和"持续性"兼顾，主副课文并存，做到了内容丰富、视角多广、观点深刻，便于在课上深入讨论和在课下延展学习。

在语言方面，教材将选词标准设定在汉语水平测试丙级以上，词频800以上。每课的主课文后都带有词汇和句法注释，旨在帮助老师教授和学生了解新闻阅读的难点和重点。词汇讲解从最小的语素单位开始，逐步过渡到书面语和口语表达，成语、四字格和虚词的使用等。句法分析则侧重在新闻书面语的长句上。

另外值得一提的是，教材的课文和生词都配有录音，便于学生掌握正确的发音、声调、轻重音，以及适当的停顿。为方便老师和学生使用，教材中所有的课后练习均单独成册，我们甚至考虑到了教材数字化的可能性。比方说，练习本中的练习大部分可以放到校园课件网上采用机改的方式。使用这套教材的老师也可以在麻省五校联盟的网上（https://commons.mtholyoke.edu/video/）找到一些我们选编的有关新闻话题的视频。我们计划继续增加和完善这方面的资料，提供给选择我们这套教材的师生使用。

王颖、王志军、徐丽莎
2015年10月于美国麻省先锋谷

PREFACE

This is a set of books designed for a newspaper reading class offered by Chinese programs in the United States and American study-abroad language programs within China. They can also be used by learners in other English-speaking countries such as Canada, United Kingdom, Australia, and New Zealand. The whole set includes two volumes; each volume contains eight topics, and each topic has a main text and a supplementary text. Generally speaking, the target users of this set of books are students who have completed two and half years of Chinese (or those who have completed the first semester of third-year Chinese) in a regular Chinese program from an American or any other English-speaking university. Volume 1 of this set of books is designed for intermediate-high to advanced-low learners according to ACTFL (the American Council on the Teaching of Foreign Languages); Volume 2 is designed for advanced-mid to advanced-high learners.

Using newspapers as instructional materials for advanced Chinese learning has several recognizable merits, including the authenticity, up-to-datedness, topicality, and practicality of newspaper language and information as well as its close connection and applicability to everyday life. However, because of the "newness" and swift turnaround that characterize newswriting, original publications in printed newspapers or online sources are all compositions created in a short timeframe and therefore lack careful deliberation and refinement. This time constraint and need for immediacy can quickly render hot topics cool; yesterday's breaking news becomes today's old news and no longer attracts readers' attention. Based on the principles of "keeping pace with the times" and "careful selection and editing," this set of books aims to make full use of the merits of newspaper materials while remedying their defects. Specifically, the content and form of the books demonstrate the following features.

The materials for these books have been selected from various major newspapers and online sources, but have been repeatedly and meticulously mended, revised, and refined by the editors. In material selection and content, this set of books not only reflects the transient nature of news reports, but also grasps long-lasting "hot topics"; it not only focuses on pressing issues for both China and the United States, but also brings forth diverse perspectives and cross-cultural aspects of these issues. Additionally, it not only provides careful and thorough reading of texts, but also includes extensive reading materials for each selected topic. For example, environmental pollution has been a long-time news topic. For this topic, we selected a main text that focuses on the air pollution in Beijing in recent years and a supplementary text that deals with "white pollution" in the Pacific—specifically, the ocean's "plastic island." Furthermore, within the main text, we compared Beijing's current air pollution with London's similar pollution problems in the past. Another issue that has continuously attracted readers' attention is the policy of owning private guns in the United States. For this topic, we reflected in the main text on the recent and frequent gun shootings that have happened on American campuses while discussing in the supplementary text the different attitudes Americans have toward gun control. Because of the dual focus on China and the United States, the consideration given to both the transiency and continuity of news issues, and the inclusion of both main and supplementary texts, this set of textbooks is rich in content, inclusive in perspective, and thought-provoking in its views. It is highly useful for deep and extensive discussion and study both inside and outside the classroom.

The vocabulary of this set of textbooks is set at the third level of the HSK (Chinese Proficiency Test) with a word frequency of 800 and above. To help instructors and students understand difficult and important points of vocabulary and grammar, vocabulary and sentence-pattern explanations are provided for each main text. The vocabulary section includes an explanation of morphemes, written and oral expressions, idioms, four-character phrases, and function words, while the sentence pattern section analyzes the long sentence structure of written news reports.

What is also worth mentioning is that the texts and vocabulary lists are accompanied by audio-recordings to assist with pronunciation, tones, stress, and pauses. For the convenience of our users, each volume provides a workbook. We have even considered the possibilities of digital adaptation of these materials and the incorporation of online resources. For example, a large portion of the vocabulary and grammar exercises can be adapted to an online format using learning management systems on campus. Users of this set of books can also find several related news videos on the website of the Massachusetts Five College Consortium (https://commons.mtholyoke.edu/video/). We plan to continue to increase and enhance the online materials and provide them to our users freely.

Ying Wang, Zhijun Wang, Lisha Xu
October, 2015 at Pioneer Valley, Massachusetts, USA

目录

第1课　看《非诚勿扰》知现代婚恋观　/1

主课文
/1　　看《非诚勿扰》 知现代婚恋观

词语注释
/7　　⊙语素：-观，-式，-度，-率，闪-，试-
/8　　⊙四字格和成语：非诚勿扰/非~勿~，令人担忧，以貌取人，语惊四座
/10　　⊙虚词及句型：以……方式，只是……而已，仅仅，宁愿……也不，即，不由得，而（1），令

副课文
/14　　"闪婚闪离"80后

第2课　职场上的"90后"　/19

主课文
/19　　职场上的"90后"

词语注释
/27　　⊙语素：-场，择-/-择，增-，维-，注-/-注，-偿/偿-，-强/强-（1），-展/展-
/28　　⊙四字格和成语：人满为患，门庭冷落
/29　　⊙虚词及句型：以……（为）……，被，于，根本，倒（倒是），乃至（乃至于），尽管

副课文
/33　　美国大学生中国"淘金"潮

第3课　华裔虎妈教女严 中西争论起"硝烟" /39

主课文

/39　华裔虎妈教女严 中西争论起"硝烟"

词语注释

/45　⊙ 语素：-述/述-，-行/行-，引-，-定，-自/自-，强-（2），关-，-从，-督/督-

/46　⊙ 四字格和成语：越俎代庖，唯命是从，随心所欲

/48　⊙ 虚词及句型：曾（曾经），到底，仍然（仍旧、仍），只有……才/还……，不论（无论）

副课文

/50　"成人青少年"——美国新一代啃老族

第4课　多元文化冲击 "圣诞节"世俗化 /55

主课文

/55　多元文化冲击 "圣诞节"世俗化

词语注释

/61　⊙ 语素：-化，-额，商-，-味，-裔，-予，同-

/62　⊙ 虚词及句型：随着，基本上，然而，而（2），由于，尚且，如此

副课文

/67　中国情人节 发帖租女友

CONTENTS

第5课 　你是"低头族"吗 /73

主课文

/73　你是"低头族"吗

词语注释

/78　⊙ 语素：-族，-网/网-，-时，-微/微-，-信/信-，-热/热-，获-/-获，-感，-面，-圈/圈-，-症

/81　⊙ 四字格和成语：毋庸置疑，自我~~，迫不及待，得不偿失，每时每刻，无~不~

/84　⊙ 虚词及句型：以及，而(3、4)，再也没/不……（了），甚至，从而，其，并且，进行 + 表示过程的双音节动词

副课文

/89　风靡一时的"自拍奥运会"

第6课 　女性维权非小事 社会关注人人知 /94

主课文

/094　女性维权非小事 社会关注人人知

词语注释

/102　⊙ 语素：严-，逐-，-侮/侮-，唤-/-唤，-称/称-，褒-，-护/护-

/103　⊙ 四字格和成语：小题大做，耿耿于怀，大有人在，随处可见，举不胜举

/105　⊙ 虚词及句型：就，通过，即使（即便），受到，至于

副课文

/108　从《爸爸去哪儿》看现代男性在家庭中的角色转换

第7课 北京与伦敦：雾都治霾浅议 /113

主课文

/113　北京与伦敦：雾都治霾浅议

词语注释

/119　⊙ 语素：-源，-物，-性，-产，超-

/120　⊙ 四字格和成语：令人注目，令人压抑，令人窒息，铺天盖地

/121　⊙ 虚词及句型：与……有关，使，大大，称……为……，之，虽然……却，难以，此外，则

副课文

/127　太平洋里的"塑料岛"

第8课 美国校园为何枪击案频发 /131

主课文

/131　美国校园为何枪击案频发

词语注释

/137　⊙ 语素：-案/案-，-满，-力/力-，-者，-视

/138　⊙ 四字格和成语：人手一～，～～不休，层出不穷，比比皆是，耳濡目染，密不可分

/141　⊙ 虚词及句型：其中，据，加上，为，为此，加以

副课文

/144　美国人如何看枪支管制

/148　**生词索引**

/184　**专名索引**

略语表 Abbreviations for Parts of Speech

abbr.	abbreviation	n.	noun
adj.	adjective	n.p.	noun phrase
ad.p.	adverbial phrase	num.	numeral
adv.	adverb	pr.	pronoun
attr.	attributive phrase	prep.	preposition
aux.	auxiliary word	r.f.	reduplicated form
b.f.	bound form	v.	verb
conj.	conjunction	v(c)	verb-complement compound
intj.	interjection	v.o.	verb-object compound
f.e.	fixed expression	v./n.	dynamic of multi-category
m(n)	measure word for noun		words (verb & noun)
m(v)	measure word for verb	v.p.	verb phrase

看《非诚勿扰》
知现代婚恋观

第1课

来晚一步　　　　　　　　新华社发　蒋跃新 作

主课文 Main Text

　　《非诚勿扰》是江苏卫视的婚恋交友节目，年轻人在这个电视节目上找到自己的另一半。每一期节目有二十四位单身女性与每位上场的男嘉宾交流互动。她们根据对上场男嘉宾的印象，以亮灯或者灭灯的方式来决定男嘉宾的去留。如果某个女嘉宾为男嘉宾留灯到最后，并且男嘉宾喜欢她，那么就算牵手成功，两个人一起离开舞台。

　　《非诚勿扰》播出以来，在收视率和观众关注度方面，已经成为当今中国最红的相亲节目。那么，《非诚勿扰》展示了什么样的婚恋观呢？

　　首先，选择恋爱对象时，多数男女嘉宾"以貌取人"。男嘉宾在短短的一两分钟内，没有任何交流和了解就选心动女生，那么选的只是漂亮的脸蛋而已。还有，女嘉宾留灯或者灭灯，也都是凭男嘉宾外表穿着来判断的。女嘉宾留灯的多是"高富帅"，男嘉宾选的都是"白富美"。这不仅仅是这些登上《非诚勿扰》节目的男女嘉宾的问题，它反映的是在浮躁喧哗的今天，

"以貌取人"已成为现代很多青年男女的普遍倾向。

其次，在婚恋交友中过分追求物质，谈恋爱等于谈条件。节目中的红人马诺的雷人语录最集中地体现了这种婚恋观。她说："宁愿坐在宝马车里哭，也不坐在自行车上笑。"这反映了现代青年婚恋观中很现实的一面，即金钱等物质因素成为恋爱婚姻的基本条件，有房有车才能谈婚论嫁。在女青年看来，"干得好，不如嫁得好"，理想对象是"高富帅"；在男青年看来，"拼自己不如拼爹"，中意的女孩子是"白富美"。有一项相关调查显示：有近半数的80后和90后女性表明愿意嫁"富二代"，这样自己就可以少奋斗很多年。很多男性青年也很在乎女方的收入和家庭经济背景。这种现象不由得令人担忧。

最后，"快餐式"婚恋受捧。节目短短几十分钟就促成几对男女牵手，但是牵手后又很少有人走入婚姻。其实这样的"闪牵"并不奇怪。近些年，"闪婚""闪离""试婚""试离"这种快餐式的婚姻方式正是现代人婚恋观的体现。几秒钟可以爱上一个人；几分钟可以谈一场恋爱；几小时就可以确定婚姻伴侣，两个人仅仅因为"看对眼了"就草草地闪婚……如此盲目而快速地寻求伴侣的方式，使得婚恋过程就像吃快餐一样。

因为《非诚勿扰》节目在中国具有相当多的观众，它展示的婚恋观必将影响很多年轻人的恋爱择偶标准、婚姻家庭观念和伦理道德观。所以，主持人、特邀嘉宾的正确引导显得极为关键。同时，参与嘉宾的正确婚恋观也会给观众一些好的启示。例如，在某期节目中哈佛的高才生安田向到场女嘉宾提出了一个关于价值观的问题。他说："如果中了一千万美元，你会怎么处理？"三位留灯女性的回答都没有得到安田的认可。因为她们都想的是自己怎么花掉这些钱，而安田的回答是："要是我，就会选择成立一个基金，或者照顾一些孤儿，做一些慈善。做人，必须要有为人民服务的精神！"安田的一席话语惊四座，令人深思。由此看来，电视相亲节目在娱乐的时候，也应该注意节目的教育意义。

Lesson 1
看《非诚勿扰》知现代婚恋观

讨论题 Discussion

根据课文内容回答下列问题
(Please answer the following questions based on the text)

1. 你对《非诚勿扰》这样的电视相亲节目有什么看法？
2. 你会去这样的节目寻找你的另一半吗？为什么？
3. 对《非诚勿扰》节目中展示的现代中国年轻人的婚恋观，你有什么看法？
4. 说说你们国家年轻人的婚恋观。
5. 如果你中了一千万美元，你会怎么处理？

生词 New Words

1	诚	誠	chéng	adj.	honest, sincere
2	勿		wù	adv.	do not, never
3	扰	擾	rǎo	v./b.f.	to harass, to disturb, to bother
4	知		zhī	b.f./v.	to know, to realize, to be aware of
5	婚		hūn	b.f.	to wed, to marry; marriage, wedding
6	恋	戀	liàn	b.f.	to love, to long for, to feel attached to
7	观	觀	guān	b.f./n.	outlook, concept, notion
8	卫视	衛視	wèishì	n.	satellite television
9	交友		jiāoyǒu	v.	to make friends
10	年轻人	年輕人	niánqīngrén	n.	young people, youth
11	单身	單身	dānshēn	attr./n.	unmarried or single person

3

12	女性		nǚxìng	n.	female sex, woman
13	上场	上場	shàng chǎng	v.o.	to enter, to appear onstage
14	嘉宾	嘉賓	jiābīn	n.	honored guest, distinguished guest
15	互动	互動	hùdòng	v./n.	to interact; interaction
16	某个	某個	mǒugè	attr.	certain, some
17	算		suàn	v.	to consider, to regard as, to count as
18	舞台	舞臺	wǔtái	n.	stage, arena, footlights
19	播出		bōchū	v(c)	to broadcast
20	收视率	收視率	shōushìlǜ	n.	audience rating
21	关注	關注	guānzhù	v.	to follow (an issue) closely, to pay close attention; concern, focus
22	当今	當今	dāngjīn	n.	current, present, nowadays
23	相亲	相親	xiāng qīn	v.o.	to have a blind date
24	展示		zhǎnshì	v.	to reveal, to show, to demonstrate
25	以貌取人		yǐ mào qǔ rén	f.e.	to judge people by outward appearance
26	心动	心動	xīndòng	adj.	heart-touching, heart-tempting
27	脸蛋	臉蛋	liǎndàn	n.	cheeks, face
28	而已		éryǐ	part.	That's all, nothing more, nothing but
29	凭	憑	píng	prep.	depend on, go by, base on
30	外表		wàibiǎo	n.	outward appearance, surface
31	浮躁		fúzào	adj.	impetuous, impulsive, flighty and rash
32	喧哗	喧嘩	xuānhuá	v.	to make an uproar; confused noise, uproar
33	倾向	傾向	qīngxiàng	n./v.	tendency, inclination; to prefer
34	物质	物質	wùzhì	n.	materials
35	谈恋爱	談戀愛	tán liàn'ài	v.o.	to be in a love relationship, to court
36	红人	紅人	hóngrén	n.	a public personality, favorite person by sb. in power, a popular person

37	雷人		léirén	adj.	thundering (cyber word that indicates an unexpected and shocking effect)
38	语录	語錄	yǔlù	n.	recorded utterance, quotation
39	体现	體現	tǐxiàn	v.	to embody, to reflect; realization
40	宁愿	寧願	nìngyuàn	conj.	would rather, preferably, prefer
41	一面		yímiàn	n.	one aspect, one side (of an object)
42	金钱	金錢	jīnqián	n.	money
43	谈婚论嫁	談婚論嫁	tán hūn lùn jià	f.e.	to talk about getting married
44	嫁		jià	v./b.f.	(of a woman) marry (a husband)
45	拼		pīn	v.	to fight or compete to the bitter end
46	爹		diē	n.	father, dad
47	中意		zhòng yì	v.o.	to be to one's liking, to catch the fancy of
48	半数	半數	bànshù	n.	half (the number)
49	男性		nánxìng	n.	male sex, man
50	在乎		zàihu	v.	(oft. used in the negative) to care about, to mind, to take to heart
51	女方		nǚfāng	n.	(oft. used on marriage-related occasions) bride's side, wife's side
52	背景		bèijǐng	n.	stage setting, backdrop, background
53	不由得		bùyóude	adv.	can't help, cannot but
54	令		lìng	v.	to cause, to make
55	担忧	擔憂	dānyōu	v.	to worry, to be anxious; anxiety
56	快餐		kuàicān	n.	quick meal, snack, fast food
57	促成		cùchéng	v(c)	to facilitate, to help to bring about, to effect
58	试婚	試婚	shì hūn	v.o.	to have a trial marriage
59	现代人	現代人	xiàndàirén	n.	modernist, modern people, neoteric
60	秒钟	秒鐘	miǎozhōng	m(n)	second (of time)

61	伴侣		bànlǚ	n.	mate, partner, husband or wife
62	草草		cǎocǎo	adv.	carelessly, hastily, hurriedly
63	盲目		mángmù	adj.	blind, aimless, lacking insight or understanding
64	快速		kuàisù	adj.	fast, in a high speed
65	寻求	尋求	xúnqiú	v.	to seek, to pursue, to look for
66	使得		shǐde	v.	to make, to cause
67	必		bì	adv.	certainly, necessarily; must, have to
68	择偶	擇偶	zé ǒu	v.o.	to choose a mate
69	观念	觀念	guānniàn	n.	notion, idea, concept
70	伦理	倫理	lúnlǐ	n.	ethics, moral principles
71	道德观	道德觀	dàodéguān	n.	morality, ethics, moral outlook
72	主持人		zhǔchírén	n.	host, anchor, emcee
73	特邀		tèyāo	v.	to be specially invited
74	引导	引導	yǐndǎo	v./n.	to guide, to lead, to instruct; guidance, instruction
75	极为	極為	jíwéi	adv.	extremely, exceedingly
76	参与	參與	cānyù	v.	to partake, to participate in, to have a say in
77	启示	啟示	qǐshì	n.	inspiration, revelation, implication
78	高才生		gāocáishēng	n.	top student, gifted student
79	到场	到場	dàochǎng	v.o.	to turn up, to show up, to be present
80	认可	認可	rènkě	v.	to accept, to approve; approval, acceptance, recognition
81	基金		jījīn	n.	fund, endowment
82	孤儿	孤兒	gū'ér	n.	orphan
83	慈善		císhàn	adj.	benevolent, philanthropic, compassionate
84	做人		zuò rén	v.o.	to conduct oneself, to behave
85	席		xí	m (n)	used for speech or talk

86	语惊四座	語驚四座	yǔ jīng sì zuò	f.e.	one's words electrify his listeners
87	深思		shēnsī	v.	to think deeply about, to ponder deeply over
88	由此		yóucǐ	conj.	from this, thus, therefrom
89	娱乐	娛樂	yúlè	v./n.	to give pleasure to, to amuse; entertainment, recreation

专有名词 Proper nouns

1	江苏	江蘇	Jiāngsū	Jiangsu province
2	马诺	馬諾	Mǎ Nuò	a person's name
3	宝马	寶馬	Bǎomǎ	the Chinese translation of BMW car
4	哈佛		Hāfó	Harvard (University)

词语注释 Vocabulary and Grammar Explanations

语素 (morphemes)

-观： 对事物的认识或看法。(concept, notion, idea)

> 例 婚恋观 择偶观 人生观 价值观 宇宙观 伦理道德观

-式： 样式，前面有形容词、名词等修饰语，中间不加"的"。(style, type)

> 例 中式 西式 欧式 新式 旧式 老式 现代式 快餐式 日本式 美国式

-度： 程度。(extent, degree, scope, range)

> 例 难度 强度 浓度 酸度 弯度 纯度 长度 广度 亮度 精度
> 关注度 能见度 灵敏度 精密度

-率：比值。(rate, ratio, proportion)

> 例　收视率　频率　出生率　死亡率　效率　速率　比率　利率

闪-：突然出现，快速进行。(flash, quick)

> 例　闪婚　闪离　闪牵　闪击　闪现　闪入　闪过

试-：试验，尝试。(try, test)

> 例　试婚　试离　试笔　试问　试销　试想　试看　试用　试行　试穿
> 　　试跳　试读　试唱　试飞

● 四字格和成语 (four-character expressions and idioms)

• 非诚勿扰 / 非~勿~

固定搭配，一般是四字格，来自古汉语。非：不是；勿：不要。《非诚勿扰》意思是"如果没有诚意就不要来打扰"。

(This is a fixed expression, and must be in four characters. It comes from classical Chinese. 非 means "is not; if it is not"; 勿 means "don't". 《非诚勿扰》 means "don't bother if you are not sincere".)

> 例　(1)《非诚勿扰》是江苏卫视的婚恋交友节目，年轻人通过上电视节目找到自己的另一半。
> 　　(2) 我跟人谈生意的态度是非诚勿扰，真诚对我来说非常重要。
> 　　(3) 美国恐怖电影《非礼勿视》在中国市场上获得了出人意料的成功。
> 　　(4) 李经理的门上写着"非请勿进"四个字，所以别人不能随便打扰。

- **令人担忧**

    让人担心忧虑。(to make people worried and concerned)

     (1) 这种现象不由得令人担忧。
    (2) 北京的交通问题确实令人担忧。
    (3) 互联网虽然给我们的生活带来了很多方便，但是其引发的社会问题也令人担忧。
    (4) 我国的食品安全问题一直令人担忧。

- **以貌取人**

    根据外貌来判别一个人，忽略了他品质和才能。

    (to judge a person solely by his appearance, but ignore his character and ability)

     (1) 这不仅仅是这些登上《非诚勿扰》节目的男女嘉宾的问题，它反映的是在浮躁喧哗的今天，"以貌取人"已成为现代很多青年男女的普遍倾向。
    (2) 我们不要以貌取人，因为往往有些人其貌不扬却能够做出一番事业来。
    (3) 美貌只是表面现象而已，以貌取人靠不住。
    (4) 在看脸时代的职场上，以貌取人已经成为大众的常态。

- **语惊四座**

    所讲的话让周围在座的人都感到震惊。形容说话、观点与众不同，有分量。

    (one's words electrify one's listeners; one's remarks astound everyone)

     (1) 安田的一席话语惊四座，令人深思。
    (2) 一个9岁的美国女孩希望废除标准化考试。她的这席演讲语惊四座。

(3) 美国总统大选时，候选人都希望自己的演讲能够**语惊四座**。

(4) 他一开始就说了一句**语惊四座**的话。

● 虚词及句型 (function words and sentence patterns)

● 以……方式 in the manner of...; by means of...

固定搭配，意思是"用……方法或方式"，多用在动词前做状语。

This is a fixed expression, meaning "用……方法/方式" (in the manner of... by means of…). It usually occurs before a verb and functions as an adverbial phrase.

(1) 她们根据对上场男嘉宾的印象，**以**亮灯或者灭灯的**方式**来决定男嘉宾的去留。

(2) 网络影视作品正**以**不同以往的**方式**改变人们的生活。

(3) 有人认为手机是**以**安全的**方式**传递信息，其实不然。

(4) 每个人想**以**自己喜欢的**方式**生活，可在现实中这很难做到。

● 只是……而已 only; nothing but

固定搭配，表示限定范围，前后常有说明情况或者进一步解释的词语。相当于"仅、仅仅、仅仅是、不过是"。

This is a fixed expression indicating a limitation, and other words often occur either before or after this expression to provide further explanations. It is similar to "仅, 仅仅, 仅是, 不过是".

(1) 男嘉宾在短短的一两分钟内，没有任何交流和了解就选心动女生，那么选的**只是**漂亮的脸蛋**而已**。

(2) 我没什么好生气的，只是有点儿难过而已。

(3) 他只是说说而已，不会认真的。

(4) 这是我人生中第一次参与足球活动，不过也只是看热闹而已。

- **仅仅 only**

"仅仅"是"仅"的重叠，意义和用法与"仅"基本相同，只是语气更重，表示限于某个范围。"仅仅"既可用于书面语，也可用于口语，而"仅"多用于书面语。

This is the reduplication of "仅", and its meaning and usage are basically the same as "仅". It is a stronger form of "仅" and indicates that the item mentioned is within the limits of a certain scope or quantity. "仅仅" can be used in both spoken and written language, while "仅" can only be used in written form.

例 (1) 这不仅仅是这些登上《非诚勿扰》节目的男女嘉宾的问题，它反映的是在浮躁喧哗的今天，"以貌取人"已成为现代很多青年男女的普遍倾向。

(2) 几小时就可以确定婚姻伴侣，两个人仅仅因为"看对眼了"就草草地闪婚。

(3) 虽然仅仅是一份最简单的套餐，老板做得却很是用心。

(4) 我并不懂音乐，仅仅是喜欢音乐。

- **宁愿……也不 would rather...than...**

固定搭配，表示在比较利害得失之后所做的一个选择。"宁愿"可用于动词前，也可用于主语前。

This is a fixed expression indicating a better option after comparing the advantages and disadvantages (of something). "宁愿" usually occurs before a verb and can also be used before a subject.

>
> (1) 宁愿坐在宝马车里哭，也不坐在自行车上笑。
> (2) 宁愿我多干一点儿，也不能让你累着。
> (3) 我宁愿早到半个小时，也不迟到一分钟。
> (4) 我宁愿站着死，也不跪着生。

- **即　that is**

动词，用作插入语，解释或者说明前面的部分，相当于"是"或"就是"。

This is a verb used as a parenthesis, explaining or illustrating a previous point. It is equal to "是" or "就是" (that is).

>
> (1) 这反映了现代青年婚恋观中很现实的一面，即金钱等物质因素成为恋爱婚姻的基本条件，有房有车才能谈婚论嫁。
> (2) 我刚来中国那一年，即一九八二年，陪父亲游览了黄山和庐山。
> (3) 在我的家乡，即江西，山上到处是竹子。
> (4) 越来越多的下岗职工从事第三产业，即服务业。

- **不由得　cannot help; cannot but**

副词，表示由不得自己，不由自主，不禁，用在动词前。

This is an adverb, meaning "things are not controlled by oneself and one cannot help but…"; it is used before a verb.

>
> (1) 这种现象不由得令人担忧。
> (2) 老师一说要听写，我就不由得紧张起来了。
> (3) 看着这些快乐的孩子，我不由得想起了自己的童年。
> (4) 见到日思夜想的亲人，孩子们不由得泪流满面。

- **而（1） and**

    连词，表示互相补充。相当于"又"或"而且"，用于连接并列的形容词。

    This is a conjunction word that is used to connect two complementary expressions. It is equal to "又" or "而且".

    (1) 如此盲目而快速地寻求伴侣的方式，使得婚恋过程就像吃快餐一样。
    (2) 他的文笔简练而生动，很有吸引力。
    (3) 十天紧张而充实的训练，使我们学到了很多东西。
    (4) 经验和才干才是一个人可靠而长远的资源。

- **令 make; let**

    动词，意思是"致使、使得"，有很强的被动意味，表示由于某种原因、事件、行为，或者条件引起一种心理状态。不能单独做谓语，后边常带兼语"人"，不能带"了""着""过"，不能带补语，不能重叠。

    This is a verb that means "to cause" or "to result in" and has a strong sense of passivity. It indicates that a person's feelings and/or reaction are caused by a certain reason, event, action, or condition. It can function as a predicate and usually be followed by the pivotal pronoun "人". It cannot take particles "了", "着", or "过"; cannot take complements; and cannot be reduplicated.

    (1) 安田的一席话语惊四座，令人深思。
    (2) 校长的做法令人讨厌，引起全体老师的反对。
    (3) 令人惊讶的是，数学课被选为他们最喜欢的科目。
    (4) 电视真人秀《爸爸去哪儿》被评为今年最令人失望的电视节目之一。

副课文 Supplementary Text

"闪婚闪离"80后

几年前,"闪婚"还是一个时髦的名词,而如今已经被"闪离"所代替。近年来,许多80后的年轻人结婚和离婚都过于迅速,成为社会学家关注的问题。一般来说,这样的婚姻长的不到三年,短的只有两三个月。"80后的年轻人离起婚来很'痛快',让人觉得不可思议。"一位婚姻登记处的工作人员对记者说,"来办理离婚的年轻人,有的坦然得像朋友,还用手机拍照留作纪念。有的虽然有了孩子,但双方提前写好了离婚协议,工作人员连规劝的话都插不上一句,他们就办完手续离开了。"

"闪婚闪离"为哪般

数据表明:涉及80后的离婚案件中,有90%的小夫妻都是独生子女。独生子女曾被称为最幸福的一代,他们享受着衣食无忧的生活,享受着来自父母、祖父母的种种疼爱,从小被当成"小皇帝""小公主",很难懂得珍惜与感恩。与六七十年代出生的人相比,80后在婚姻生活中不够宽容和忍让,导致了他们的婚姻稳定性下降。调查显示:在已婚的独生子女家庭中,有30%雇小时工做家务,20%由父母帮助整理房间,80%长期去父母家吃饭。而与此同时,这代人对婚姻质量的要求却更高,对平淡生活不愿意"凑合",由生活琐事引发的离婚也就越来越多。

也有人认为,离婚率高不完全出于独生子女的个性。因为80后年轻人的文化背景跟他们的父母不同,他们少了传统的婚姻观念,接受了社会上一些新的思想,对婚姻的态度没有父母那么慎重。他们的想法是:合则聚,不合则散。一位网友说:"错误的婚姻,勉强在一起才是不幸,对两个人都一样。结婚了发现性格不合,然后离婚,这没什么,难道要让错误一直继续?"值得注意的是,对一些年轻人的"闪婚闪离",家长们是支持的态度。因为家长不想让孩子在婚姻中受委屈,不是教育孩子互相包容,而是要求孩子不让步。

不如惜取眼前人

一位心理咨询师说："闪电结婚听起来时髦，其实痛苦只有当事人知道。"好几次，他面对刚结婚不久的年轻妈妈抱着几个月大的孩子来咨询离婚，感到非常痛心。他说："在婚姻中，结婚动机、彼此的了解、对婚姻的认识以及如何经营婚姻，这些方面都需要相当长的一段时间才能达成共识。幸福的家庭应来自对质朴生活的理解。结婚仅仅是开始，在婚姻中学习和成长才最重要。"他引用英国诗人蒲柏的话"一切皆可努力而获得，惟妻子是上天的恩赐"，希望青年男女珍惜眼前人。

有人建议想离婚的夫妻先"试离婚"。因为有的年轻人离婚后比较后悔，想复婚，复婚后又觉得不合适，还想离婚，"试离婚"可以尽量减少由于一时冲动造成的损失。

讨论题 Discussion

根据课文内容回答下列问题
(Please answer the following questions based on the text)

1. 什么是"闪婚"和"闪离"？
2. 为什么在80后的年轻人中容易发生"闪婚"和"闪离"？"闪婚"和"闪离"与独生子女的个性有关系吗？
3. 中国的独生子女有什么特点？美国的独生子女呢？你觉得形成独生子女个性特点的原因是什么？
4. 家长对"闪婚"和"闪离"的态度怎么样？为什么？
5. 为什么"闪婚"和"闪离"不是解决婚姻问题的最好办法？"试离婚"是好方法吗？
6. 你怎么看"闪婚"和"闪离"？美国有没有这种现象？

生词 New Words

#					
1	时髦	時髦	shímáo	adj.	fashionable, in vogue, stylish
2	名词	名詞	míngcí	n.	noun
3	过于	過於	guòyú	adv.	too much, excessively, unduly
4	不可思议	不可思議	bùkě-sīyì	f.e.	inconceivable, unimaginable
5	登记处	登記處	dēngjìchù	n.	registration office
6	办理	辦理	bànlǐ	v.	to handle, to conduct, to transact
7	坦然		tǎnrán	adj.	calm, unperturbed, having no misgivings
8	手机	手機	shǒujī	n.	mobile phone
9	拍照		pāi zhào	v.o.	to take (a picture), to shoot (a film)
10	协议	協議	xiéyì	n.	agreement, pact, protocol
11	规劝	規勸	guīquàn	v.	to admonish, to exhort; remonstration
12	般		bān	n.	sort, kind, way
13	涉及		shèjí	v.	to involve, to relate to, to touch upon (a topic)
14	案件		ànjiàn	n.	law suit, case
15	夫妻		fūqī	n.	husband and wife
16	独生子女	獨生子女	dúshēng zǐnǚ	n.p.	the only child
17	衣食无忧	衣食無憂	yīshí wúyōu	f.e.	need not worry about food and clothes
18	父母		fùmǔ	n.	parents, father and mother
19	祖父母		zǔfùmǔ	n.	grandparents from the father's side
20	种种	種種	zhǒngzhǒng	r.f.	all kinds of, all sorts of, various
21	疼爱	疼愛	téng'ài	v.	to love dearly, to be fond of, to dote on
22	公主		gōngzhǔ	n.	princess
23	珍惜		zhēnxī	v.	to treasure, to value, to cherish
24	感恩		gǎn'ēn	v.	to feel grateful, to be thankful
25	相比		xiāngbǐ	v.	to compared to, to contrast
26	宽容	寬容	kuānróng	v.	to forgive, to pardon, to tolerant
27	忍让	忍讓	rěnràng	v.	to exercise forbearance, to be forbearing

28	导致	導致	dǎozhì	v.	to lead to, to bring about, to result in
29	稳定性	穩定性	wěndìngxìng	n.	stability, stabilization
30	下降		xiàjiàng	v.	to descend, to drop, to fall, to decline
31	已婚		yǐhūn	adj.	married
32	雇	僱	gù	v.	to hire, to employ
33	小时工	小時工	xiǎoshígōng	n.	hourly paid workers (usually refers to houseworker)
34	家务	家務	jiāwù	n.	household duties, house work/chore
35	与此同时	與此同時	yǔ cǐ tóngshí	f.e.	at the same time, meanwhile, moreover
36	平淡		píngdàn	adj.	prosaic, ordinary, insipid
37	凑合	湊合	còuhe	adj.	not too bad, passable
38	琐事	瑣事	suǒshì	n.	trifles, trivial matters
39	引发	引發	yǐnfā	v.	to initiate, to trigger, to spark off
40	离婚率	離婚率	líhūnlǜ	n.	divorce rate
41	出于	出於	chūyú	v.p.	to be due to, to stem, to start or proceed from
42	个性	個性	gèxìng	n.	individual character, personality, individuality
43	慎重		shènzhòng	adj.	prudent, cautious, careful
44	聚		jù	v.	to assemble, to gather, to congregate
45	散		sàn	v.	to come loose, to break up, to fall apart
46	网友	網友	wǎngyǒu	n.	net friend, e-pal
47	勉强	勉強	miǎnqiǎng	v.	to force sb. to do sth., to do with difficulty, to manage with an effort
48	家长	家長	jiāzhǎng	n.	patriarch, head of a family, parent or guardian of a child
49	委屈		wěiqu	adj.	feeling wronged, nursing a grievance, be misunderstood
50	包容		bāoróng	v.	to pardon, to forgive
51	而		ér	conj.	but (rather)
52	让步	讓步	ràng bù	v.o.	to concede, to give in, to compromise

53	惜		xī	b.f.	to value, to cherish, to treasure
54	心理		xīnlǐ	n.	psychology, mentality, thoughts, emotions, etc.
55	咨询	諮詢	zīxún	v.	to seek counsel or advice from, to inquire and consult
56	闪电	閃電	shǎndiàn	n.	lightning (here is used as a figurative expression describing the fast speed of a marriage)
57	当事人	當事人	dāngshìrén	n.	litigant, client, person or party concerned
58	面对	面對	miànduì	v.	to face, to confront, to encounter
59	痛心		tòngxīn	adj.	pained, distressed, grieved
60	动机	動機	dòngjī	n.	motive, motivation, intention
61	彼此		bǐcǐ	pr.	each other, one another
62	达成	達成	dáchéng	v(c)	to arrive at, to reach (an agreement), to work out
63	共识	共識	gòngshí	n.	common understanding, consensus
64	质朴	質樸	zhìpǔ	adj.	unaffected, plain, simple and unadorned
65	引用		yǐnyòng	v.	to quote, to cite
66	诗人	詩人	shīrén	n.	poet
67	皆		jiē	adv.	all, each and every, in all cases
68	惟		wéi	adv.	only, alone, solely
69	上天		shàngtiān	n.	Heaven, Providence, God
70	恩赐	恩賜	ēncì	v.	to bestow, to favor; charity
71	复婚	復婚	fù hūn	v.o.	to marry each other again, to resume matrimonial relation
72	冲动	衝動	chōngdòng	adj./n.	getting excited, be impetuous; impulsion, impulsiveness

专有名词 Proper noun

蒲柏	Púbǎi	Alexander Pope

第2课 职场上的"90后"

主课文 Main Text

2012年是90后毕业生进入职场最集中的一年。这些上世纪90年代出生的人,以独生子女居多,被认为是掉进"蜜罐子"的幸福一代。那么,这些职场新人们有什么特点呢?近日,新华网记者走访了招聘会、多家职业咨询机构以及企业,了解了很多90后职场就业的情况。

兴趣为主

日前,湖北省人力资源中心举办了两场综合招聘会。包括软件、动漫、通信、机械、机电、制造、光电子等各行业在内的上千个岗位向求职者争递橄榄枝。但记者见到,有的招聘企业人满为患,有的则门庭冷落。

1990年出生的小庄学的是酒店管理专业。在招聘会开始前,她告诉记者，想找一份自己喜欢的工作，除此之外没什么想法。"我爱看电影、热衷于品牌服装，工作一定要和这方面挂钩。"小庄说。此前，她通过网络先后给武汉某女装服饰公司、某运动品牌公司以及某电影城发过简历。

和70后、80后选择工作要求稳定、福利齐全的择业观念不同，90后找工作时，已经时刻准备着"跳槽"换工作。对这一群体来说，两年换六七份工作很常见，极端的，有人两年内跳槽十一次。某咨询公司职业规划师洪向阳告诉记者，面试时，多数90后根本不谈薪水，也不求长远，增长见识、增加经历倒常被他们挂在嘴边。

个性超强

有关统计显示，90后小白领最看重的是工作自由度和在企业的未来发展。在工作中，他们往往个性超强，不愿妥协。二十二岁的小元，毕业后进了一家策划公司，主要工作是为客户布置会展。小元对待工作非常认真。他认为，要想长期维系良好的客户关系，就要注重细节。比如在给客户做展示时，多做一个版本作比较，既花不了多少成本，又能令客户满意。然而，在这点上，小元与老板意见相左，跟老板起了冲突。小元一气之下，辞职走人。其实这种情况完全可以通过沟通解决，但小元个性太强，不懂妥协。

手机控

90后是网络时代的优先体验者，网络对他们的生活、学习乃至求职都产生了深刻影响。工作时间发微博、玩微信、逛淘宝……手机不离手是90后的通病。他们喜欢在微博、微信上把自己生活中的点点滴滴都晒出来。小周也不例外。一次，她在微博发布了一张照片，导致公司研发的新产品资料提前曝光，损害了公司的利益。公司将小周辞退，并通过法律手段向小周索要相应赔偿。随着微博、微信等即时通信工具成为日常生活的一部分，90后职场新人们要加强保密意识，避免因一时疏忽而给公司造成损失，并给自己的职业生涯带来不利影响。

有创新意识

采访中，一家软件企业人事主管告诉记者："尽管有着不同的择业观念，但 90 后接受新兴事物能力强，具有创新意识。如果企业能够提供足够的发展空间，他们可以很快成为企业的中坚力量。" 1993 年出生的陈心怡毕业于美国普林斯顿大学数学系。读大二时她就创立了一个手机远程智能系统，因此获得了少年创业者大奖。2013 年，她加入了中关村创新企业——格灵深瞳，目前正在参与智能汽车领域中的电脑视觉运用的项目。该项目预计很快将可以实现对车速、路况、交通标志等的识别。陈心怡说，投身到一个创新项目之中，每天都能看到项目的进展和公司的进步，这让她感到既充实又有意义。

学习能力强、思路新颖、有创新能力、愿意挑战自己，这些都是 90 后职场新人最闪耀的一面。

讨论题 Discussion

根据课文内容回答下列问题
(Please answer the following questions based on the text)

1. 90 后的年轻人在职场上有哪些特点？
2. 小庄找工作注重什么？
3. 小元为什么辞职？如果你在职场中遇到这种问题，会怎样面对？
4. 小周为什么被公司辞退？
5. 陈心怡为什么能成为公司的中坚力量？
6. 美国或者你们国家的年轻人在职场上有什么特点？

生词 New Words

#					
1	职场	職場	zhíchǎng	n.	job market, workplace
2	毕业生	畢業生	bìyèshēng	n.	graduate (of a school)
3	居多		jūduō	v.p.	to be in the majority
4	蜜		mì	n./b.f.	honey, sweet
5	罐子		guànzi	n.	pot, jar, jug
6	走访	走訪	zǒufǎng	v.	to pay a visit to, to interview
7	招聘		zhāopìn	v.	to invite applications for a job, to take job applications, to advertise job offers
8	就业	就業	jiù yè	v.o.	to obtain employment, to get a job
9	为主	為主	wéizhǔ	v.p.	to rely mainly on, to give priority to
10	人力		rénlì	n.	manual labor, manpower
11	举办	舉辦	jǔbàn	v.	to conduct, to hold, to sponsor
12	软件	軟件	ruǎnjiàn	n.	computer software, software
13	动漫	動漫	dòngmàn	n.	animation, cartoon
14	通信		tōngxìn	n.	communication
15	机电	機電	jīdiàn	n.	machinery and electrical equipment
16	光电子	光電子	guāngdiànzǐ	n.	optoelectronic
17	行业	行業	hángyè	n.	industry, business, profession
18	岗位	崗位	gǎngwèi	n.	position, job, post
19	求职者	求職者	qiúzhízhě	n.	job applicant
20	橄榄枝	橄欖枝	gǎnlǎnzhī	n.	olive branch
21	人满为患	人滿為患	rénmǎn wéihuàn	f.e.	cause concerns and problems because of crowdedness or overpopulation
22	门庭	門庭	méntíng	n.	gate and courtyard
23	冷落		lěngluò	adj.	deserted, desolate, unfrequented

	简体	繁體	拼音	词性	英文
24	酒店		jiǔdiàn	n.	hotel, wine shop, public house
25	除此之外		chú cǐ zhī wài	f.e.	apart from this, in addition to this
26	热衷	熱衷	rèzhōng	v.	to be full of enthusiasm about, to crave for, to be fond of
27	品牌		pǐnpái	n.	brand name, trademark
28	服装	服裝	fúzhuāng	n.	dress, clothes, costume
29	挂钩	掛鉤	guà gōu	v.o.	to link up with, to establish contact with
30	网络	網絡	wǎngluò	n.	(computer, telecom, etc.) network
31	服饰	服飾	fúshì	n.	dress and personal adornment
32	简历	簡歷	jiǎnlì	n.	resume, curriculum vitae
33	福利		fúlì	n.	material benefits, welfare
34	齐全	齊全	qíquán	adj.	complete, all in readiness, well-stocked
35	择	擇	zé	v./b.f.	to select, to choose, to pick
36	业	業	yè	b.f.	trade, industry, occupation
37	跳槽		tiào cáo	v.o.	to abandon one occupation in favor of another, change jobs
38	群体	群體	qúntǐ	n.	group, community, colony
39	常见	常見	chángjiàn	adj.	commonly seen, common
40	极端	極端	jíduān	adj.	extreme, exceedingly
41	面试	面試	miànshì	v./n.	to interview, to audition; interview
42	薪水		xīnshuǐ	n.	salary, pay, wages
43	长远	長遠	chángyuǎn	adj.	long-term, long-range
44	见识	見識	jiànshi	n.	knowledge, experience
45	嘴边	嘴邊	zuǐbiān	n.	on one's lips
46	超强	超強	chāoqiáng	adj.p.	super strong, ultra-strong
47	统计	統計	tǒngjì	v./n.	to census, to count; statistics
48	白领	白領	báilǐng	n.	white collar, white-collar worker

	简体	繁體	Pinyin	词性	English
49	看重		kànzhòng	v.	to regard as important, to value, to think highly of
50	自由度		zìyóudù	n.	degree of freedom
51	妥协	妥協	tuǒxié	v.	to compromise
52	策划	策劃	cèhuà	v.	to plot, to scheme, to plan
53	客户		kèhù	n.	client, customer
54	会展	會展	huìzhǎn	n.	convention and exhibition
55	维系	維繫	wéixì	v.	to maintain, to hold together
56	注重		zhùzhòng	v.	to lay stress on, to pay attention to, to attach importance to
57	细节	細節	xìjié	n.	details
58	版本		bǎnběn	n.	version, edition
59	成本		chéngběn	n.	(manufacturing, production, etc.) costs
60	意见相左	意見相左	yìjiàn xiāngzuǒ	f.e.	to disagree with each other, to have difference opinions
61	一气之下	一氣之下	yíqì zhīxià	f.e.	angrily, in a pet, a fit of pique
62	辞职	辭職	cí zhí	v.o.	to resign, to quit one's job
63	走人		zǒurén	v.p.	to leave, to walk away
64	沟通	溝通	gōutōng	v.	to communicate; communication
65	控		kòng	b.f.	fanatic
66	优先	優先	yōuxiān	v.	to take precedence, to give priority
67	体验	體驗	tǐyàn	v.	to learn through personal experience; experience
68	乃至		nǎizhì	conj.	even, go so far as to, even to the extent that
69	求职	求職	qiú zhí	v.o.	to look for a job, to apply for a job
70	微博		wēibó	n.	microblog, Twitter, Tweet
71	微信		wēixìn	n.	WeChat
72	通病		tōngbìng	n.	common failing, common fault
73	点点滴滴	點點滴滴	diǎndiǎn-dīdī	n./adj.	dribs and drabs, every bit of…; bit by bit, drop by drop

74	例外		lìwài	n.	exception
75	发布	發佈	fābù	v.	to issue (orders, instructions, news etc.), to release, to announce
76	研发	研發	yánfā	v.	to research and develop
77	曝光		bào guāng	v.o.	to expose, to reveal, to disclose
78	损害	損害	sǔnhài	v.	to harm, to injure, to damage
79	辞退	辭退	cítuì	v.	to dismiss, to discharge, to politely decline
80	索要		suǒyào	v.	to ask for, to demand, to claim
81	相应	相應	xiāngyìng	adj.	corresponding, relevant, fitting
82	赔偿	賠償	péicháng	n./v.	compensation, reparations, indemnification; to compensate
83	随着	隨著	suízhe	prep.	along with, in the wake of, in pace with
84	即时	即時	jíshí	adj.	immediate
85	保密		bǎo mì	v.o.	to maintain secrecy, to keep sth. confidential
86	意识	意識	yìshí	n.	consciousness, awareness
87	疏忽		shūhu	v./n.	to neglect, to be inadvertent; negligence, oversight
88	生涯		shēngyá	n.	career, profession
89	不利		búlì	adj.	unfavorable, disadvantageous, harmful
90	创新	創新	chuàngxīn	v./n.	to innovate, to bring forth new ideas; innovation, creation
91	采访	採訪	cǎifǎng	v.	to interview, to cover (a news story), to gather material report; interview
92	人事		rénshì	n.	human resource, personnel
93	主管		zhǔguǎn	v./n.	to be responsible for, to be in charge of; person in charge
94	新兴	新興	xīnxīng	adj.	new, emerging, rising
95	足够	足夠	zúgòu	adj.	enough, ample, sufficient
96	中坚	中堅	zhōngjiān	n.	nucleus, backbone, hard core
97	数学系	數學系	shùxuéxì	n.	mathematics department

98	创立	創立	chuànglì	v.	to found, to establish, to set up
99	远程	遠程	yuǎnchéng	adj.	long-distance, remote, long-range
100	智能		zhìnéng	n.	intelligence, brain power
101	创业者	創業者	chuàngyèzhě	n.	entrepreneur
102	加入		jiārù	v.	to join, to become a member
103	领域	領域	lǐngyù	n.	field, sphere, realm
104	视觉	視覺	shìjué	n.	visual sense, vision, sense of sight
105	预计	預計	yùjì	v.	to estimate, to forecast, to predict
106	车速	車速	chēsù	n.	speed of a vehicle
107	路况	路況	lùkuàng	n.	road condition, highway condition
108	标志	標誌	biāozhì	n.	sign, mark, symbol
109	识别	識別	shíbié	v.	to distinguish, to identify; identification
110	投身		tóushēn	v.	to throw oneself into, to plunge, to join
111	进展	進展	jìnzhǎn	n.	progress, advance
112	充实	充實	chōngshí	adj.	rich, abundant, substantial
113	思路		sīlù	n.	train of thought, thinking
114	新颖	新穎	xīnyǐng	adj.	new and original, novel
115	挑战	挑戰	tiǎozhàn	v./n.	to challenge, to a contest; challenge
116	闪耀	閃耀	shǎnyào	v.	to shine, to glitter, to radiate

专有名词 Proper nouns

1	新华网	新華網	Xīnhuá Wǎng	the website of Xinhua News Agency
2	湖北		Húběi	Hubei (province)
3	小庄	小莊	Xiǎo Zhuāng	a person's name
4	武汉	武漢	Wǔhàn	Wuhan (capital of Hubei Province)

5	洪向阳	洪向陽	Hóng Xiàngyáng	a person's name
6	小元		Xiǎo Yuán	a person's name
7	淘宝(网)	淘寶(網)	Táobǎo(wǎng)	literal translation: digging treasure; used as a name for a Chinese e-shopping network
8	陈心怡	陳心怡	Chén Xīnyí	a person's name
9	普林斯顿大学	普林斯頓大學	Pǔlínsīdùn Dàxué	Princeton University
10	中关村	中關村	Zhōngguāncūn	It is a technology hub in Haidian District, Beijing, China and is often referred to as "China's Silicon Valley"
11	格灵深瞳	格靈深瞳	Gélíngshēntóng	Deep Glint, a company's name

词语注释 Vocabulary and Grammar Explanations

语素 (morphemes)

-场： 指某种活动范围。(certain activity scope or circle)

> 例 职场　官场　商场　社交场　名利场

择-/-择： 挑选。(to select)

> 例 择业　择偶　择优　择期　择交　饥不择食　选择

增-： 增加，增长。(to increase)

> 例 增长　增加　增进　增多　增高　增强

维-： 1. 连接。(to connect)

> 例 维系

2. 使存在下去，保护。(to make a situation or state continue; to protect)

> 例 维护　维持　维权　维和　维稳

注-/-注：精神、力量集中。(to pay attention to something; to gather strength to do something)

> 例 注重　注意　注视　注目　关注

-偿/偿-：归还，抵补。(to repay; to compensate)

> 例 赔偿　补偿　偿还　得不偿失

-强/强-(1)：力量大，势力大。(strong and powerful)

> 例 加强　增强　强健　强壮

-展/展-：1.张开，放开。(to select)

> 例 开展　伸展　舒展　愁眉不展　展览

2. 事物向前推进。(things or events move forward or develop)

> 例 进展　发展　展开

● 四字格和成语 (four-character expressions and idioms)

● **人满为患**

因人多容纳不了而造成了困难。(causing concerns or problems because of crowdedness or overpopulation)

> 例 (1) 有的招聘企业**人满为患**，有的则门庭冷落。
> (2) 现在很多中国的大城市都**人满为患**，带来包括交通拥挤、房价上

涨、就业难等一系列问题。
(3) 这个医院来看病的人太多，已经人满为患，需要向其他的医院疏散一些患者。
(4) 美国的"黑色星期五"是商家大降价的一天，顾客都想在这一天买到便宜的东西，所以商店里常常是人满为患。

- 门庭冷落

形容十分冷落，宾客稀少。(someone's house or business becomes desolate because of having few visitors)

(1) 有的招聘企业人满为患，有的则门庭冷落。
(2) 这个饭馆经营得不好，开业半年了，仍旧是门庭冷落，没有多少顾客。
(3) 他父亲做高官时，家中常常宾客满堂。现在他父亲失去了官职，家中渐渐门庭冷落。
(4) 北京中关村被称为中国的"硅谷"，曾经是年轻人求职创业的地方，近两年却有些门庭冷落起来。

虚词及句型 (function words and sentence patterns)

- 以……（为）…… to be considered as…

"以"是动词，意思是"用、拿"，文言词。"以……为……"是固定搭配。"为"后是形容词，表示比较起来怎么样。有时"为"可以省略（见例1和例3）。

"以" is a verb that means "to use" or "to take"; it is a written expression. "以……为……" is a fixed form. What follows "为" is an adjective, indicating a comparison. Sometimes "为" can be omitted (see examples 1 and 3).

(1) 这些上世纪90年代出生的人，<u>以</u>独生子女居多。
(2) 这部短篇小说集<u>以</u>描写军事题材的作品为多。
(3) 目前生产的电脑产品中<u>以</u>苹果公司的产品最受欢迎。
(4) 中国南方的气候、土壤和环境<u>以</u>种植水稻为宜。

- 被 *auxiliary word for passive voice*

  介词，用于被动，引进动作的施动者。前面的主语是动作的受动者。动词后面多有表示完成或结果的词语，或者动词本身包含此类成分。

  This is a preposition used in passive voice that introduces the subject of an action. The subject at the beginning of the sentence is the receiver of the action. Usually there is a word indicating the completion or the result of the action after the verb, unless the verb itself has the meaning of completion.

(1) （他们）<u>被</u>认为是掉进"蜜罐子"的幸福一代。
(2) 我的书<u>被</u>同屋小王借去了。
(3) 今天他的车<u>被</u>哥哥开走了。
(4) 你这样说很容易<u>被</u>别人误解。

- 于

  介词，用于书面语。用在动词后。表示方向、目标或追求。

  This is a preposition used in written expressions and after verbs. It indicates objective, target, or pursuit.

(1) 我爱看电影、热衷<u>于</u>品牌服装。
(2) 他立志长大后要投身<u>于</u>科学研究。
(3) 几十年来，爸爸一直致力<u>于</u>环境保护的工作。
(4) 孙中山先生一生献身<u>于</u>革命。他最有名的一句话是"革命尚未成功，同志仍须努力。"

- **根本 utterly; completely; entirely; at all**

  副词。从头到尾；始终，完全。多用于否定句，或修饰含义近于否定的动词。

  This is an adverb that means "in entirety, totally, or thoroughly". Usually it is used in a negative sentence or to modify words that have negative connotation.

  (1) 多数90后根本不谈薪水。
  (2) 王明是谁？我根本不认识他！
  (3) 她根本不同意你的看法。
  (4) 她根本没有出过国。她所知道的美国都是在电视上看到的，或者是在网上了解到的。

- **倒（倒是） but; on the contrary**

  副词。表示跟一般情理相反；反而，反倒。

  This is an adverb used to indicate situations that are contrary to common sense.

  (1) 增长见识、增加经历倒常被他们挂在嘴边。
  (2) 平时她的数学成绩最差，这次倒考了全班第一名。
  (3) 你是妹妹？怎么看上去倒比姐姐年纪大？
  (4) 真不好意思！我是主人，你这个客人倒请我吃了顿饭！

- **乃至（乃至于） and even**

  连词，表示强调。一般用在并列的词、短语或者分句的最后一项之前，表示突出最后一项所指的内容。多用于书面语，是现代汉语中经常使用的文言虚词之一。

  This is a conjunction used for emphasis. Usually it is placed before the very last item of a series of parallel words, short phrases, or sentences, emphasizing the referred item. This word is often used in written expression, and it is one of the most frequently used classical words in contemporary Chinese.

(1) "90后"是网络时代的优先体验者，网络对他们的生活、学习乃至求职都产生了深刻影响。
(2) 网络使人们的学习、工作乃至生活都发生了巨大的变化。
(3) 治理北京雾霾绝非一日之功，它需要十年、二十年乃至更长的时间。
(4) 一个城市的环境改善需要一代人乃至几代人的共同努力。

- 尽管 though; even though; in spite of; despite; not withstanding

连词。表示让步，意思相当于"虽然"。后一小句用"但（是）、可（是）、然而、还是、仍然、却"等呼应。

This is a conjunction used for a concessive clause containing "although" that is followed by a second clause with a word such as "但（是）"，"可（是）"，"然而"，"还是"，"仍然"，or "却"。

(1) 尽管有着不同的择业观念，但90后接受新兴事物能力强，具有创新意识。
(2) 尽管他还发着烧，今天还是去上班了。
(3) 尽管大家都反对，她仍然嫁给了那个比她小八岁的男人。
(4) 尽管苹果电脑贵一些，质量却很好，所以很多人都喜欢用苹果电脑。

副课文 Supplementary Text

美国大学生中国"淘金"潮

据《纽约时报》报道,近年来受金融危机影响,美国经济疲软,失业率居高不下,就业形势相当严峻。刚脱下学位服的美国大学毕业生纷纷把目光转向东方,部分毕业生开始尝试到北京、上海找工作。就连那些对汉语知之甚少,甚至一点不懂的人也跃跃欲试。中国蓬勃发展的经济、低廉的生活成本都是吸引这些年轻人的亮点。另外,还有一个因素吸引着他们:美国大学生毕业后如在当地就业需要立刻偿还所借政府贷款,而在中国就业则可以延迟还贷。更重要的是,在这里,他们有机会学到在美国学不到的东西。

约书亚·斯蒂芬斯 2007 年从美国卫斯理安大学毕业,并获得了"美国研究"专业学士学位。两年前,他到上海的一家教育旅游公司从事市场调研和项目策划工作。"我当时对中国一无所知。人们都以为我疯了,不会说汉语还到中国来。但我就是想突破自己。"现在,他已经能够说一口流利的汉语。经过在一个非盈利机构和一家公关公司的历练,目前他在北京一家网络游戏公司任经理。

萨拉贝丝·伯尔曼 2006 年毕业于美国巴纳德学院,专业是"城市研究"。她二十三岁时初到北京,就得到了一个美国同龄人难以得到的职位,担任北京一家现代舞团项目总监。"尽管我的汉语很差,而且没有在中国工作的经历,舞团还是给我机会去筹划巡回演出,进行国际交流,在北京舞蹈节上编排、导演节目……"两年的时间里,她陪同舞团游遍了中国、美国和欧洲的许多国家。许多中国公司想开拓美国市场,需要了解西方社会以及中西文化的差异,所以他们会直接聘用以英语为母语的雇员。这对于很多美国年轻人而言,意味着去中国工作可以跳过职业生涯之初的铺垫阶段,直接获得更高的职位。

其实,并非所有到中国"淘金"的外国人都有好运气。如今,在中国经济增速放缓的大背景下,就业形势的复杂和严峻仍在考验着中国数百万应届毕业生。相应地,外国人在中国的就业市场中,也似乎不再那么吃香了。正如《华尔街日报》所说,仅靠一张西方面孔就能在中国找到工作的好时候已经过去。强劲的经济增长也不意味着个人良好的就业前景。那些没有专业技能、中文较差的外国人,面对日趋激烈的竞争更不易取得成功。留学归来的中国人是外国人最大的竞争对手,他们拥有外国大学学位、多种语言技能和国际视野,是"更合格的求职者"。美国人力资源咨询公司翰威特的一项研究表明,对中国企业而言,雇用来自发达国家的员工,成本比招当地人高50%~200%。在中国的跨国公司仍需要外国人,但大多数是中高层职位,高学历和丰富的经验是最基本的要求。

讨论题 Discussion

根据课文内容回答下列问题
(Please answer the following questions based on the text)

1. 近年来部分美国大学毕业生为什么到中国去寻找就业机会?中国在哪些方面吸引了这些求职者?
2. 美国大学毕业生选择到中国就业,是否跟他们的专业和兴趣有关系?
3. 从约书亚·斯蒂芬斯的例子来看,美国年轻人到中国就业所面临的第一个挑战是什么?约书亚是怎么面对这个挑战的?
4. 从萨拉贝丝·伯尔曼的例子来看,美国年轻人会在中国得到什么样的工作机会?她为什么会得到这样的机会?
5. 文章中谈到的外国人在中国求职的困难和挑战有哪些?
6. 通过这篇文章你了解到了什么?如果你想在毕业以后去中国找工作,你会怎么做?怎样才能尽快地学好中文并了解中国的职场文化?

生词 New Words

1	淘金		táo jīn	v.o.	gold washing
2	潮		cháo	n.	tide, social upsurge, current
3	疲软	疲軟	píruǎn	adj.	fatigued and weak, weakened, sluggish
4	失业率	失業率	shīyèlǜ	n.	unemployment rate
5	居高不下		jūgāo-búxià	f.e.	to stay in a high position, without going down
6	严峻	嚴峻	yánjùn	adj.	stern, severe, grim
7	学位服	學位服	xuéwèifú	n.	academicals, academic costumes
8	目光		mùguāng	n.	sight, vision, view
9	转向	轉向	zhuǎnxiàng	v.	to change directions, to turn
10	尝试	嘗試	chángshì	v.	to attempt, to try, to have a go at
11	知之甚少		zhīzhī shènshǎo	f.e.	little is known
12	跃跃欲试	躍躍欲試	yuèyuè-yùshì	f.e.	be eager to have a try, itch to have a go
13	蓬勃		péngbó	adj.	vigorous, flourishing, full of vitality
14	低廉		dīlián	adj.	(of price) cheap, low-priced, inexpensive
15	当地	當地	dāngdì	n./attr.	at the place in question, in the locality; local
16	偿还	償還	chánghuán	v.	to repay, to reimburse
17	贷款	貸款	dàikuǎn	n.	loan, credit
18	延迟	延遲	yánchí	v.	to delay, to postpone
19	贷	貸	dài	v./b.f.	to borrow, to lend (money)
20	学士	學士	xuéshì	n.	bachelor, bachelor's degree
21	学位	學位	xuéwèi	n.	academic degree

	简体	繁體	Pinyin	词性	English
22	旅游	旅遊	lǚyóu	v./n.	to travel; trip, journey, travel
23	调研	調研	diàoyán	v./n.	to investigate and study; research, survey
24	一无所知	一無所知	yìwúsuǒzhī	f.e.	to know nothing at all
25	疯	瘋	fēng	adj.	mad, insane, crazy
26	突破		tūpò	v.	to break through, to make a break through, to surmount (difficulty)
27	盈利		yínglì	v./n.	to make a profit, to earn a profit; profit, gain
28	公关	公關	gōngguān	n.	public relations
29	历练	歷練	lìliàn	v.	to experience and toughening
30	游戏	遊戲	yóuxì	n.	recreation, game
31	任		rèn	v.	to appoint or assign to a position, to assume a post, to take up a job
32	同龄	同齡	tónglíng	v.	to be at the same age
33	难以	難以	nányǐ	adv.	hard to, difficult to
34	职位	職位	zhíwèi	n.	position, post
35	现代舞团	現代舞團	xiàndài wǔtuán	n.p.	modern dance troupe
36	总监	總監	zǒngjiān	n.	director, chief inspector
37	筹划	籌劃	chóuhuà	v.	to plan and prepare
38	巡回	巡迴	xúnhuí	v.	to tour, to make a circuit of, to go around
39	舞蹈		wǔdǎo	n.	dance
40	编排	編排	biānpái	v.	to arrange, to lay out, to write a play and rehearse
41	导演	導演	dǎoyǎn	n./v.	director; to direct a play, film, etc.
42	陪同		péitóng	v.	to accompany, to be together with guide; companion
43	游	遊	yóu	v./b.f.	to travel, to tour, to rove around
44	开拓	開拓	kāituò	v.	to open up, to enlarge or expand (territory, etc.), to pioneer

45	差异	差異	chāyì	n.	difference, discrepancy
46	聘用		pìnyòng	v.	to hire, to employ
47	母语	母語	mǔyǔ	n.	mother tongue
48	雇员	雇員	gùyuán	n.	employee
49	意味		yìwèi	v.	to mean, to indicate
50	铺垫	鋪墊	pūdiàn	v.	to foreshadow, to provide a base for
51	运气	運氣	yùnqi	n.	fortune, luck
52	缓	緩	huǎn	adj.	slow, unhurried
53	背景		bèijǐng	n.	background, backdrop, setting
54	考验	考驗	kǎoyàn	v.	to test; trial
55	应届	應屆	yīngjiè	adj.	the present graduating year, this year's (only used for graduating students or pupils)
56	相应	相應	xiāngyìng	adv.	corresponding, relevant
57	吃香		chīxiāng	adj.	be very popular, be much sought after, be well-liked
58	强劲	強勁	qiángjìng	adj.	powerful, forceful
59	前景		qiánjǐng	n.	prospect, vista
60	技能		jìnéng	n.	technical ability, skill, technique
61	日趋	日趨	rìqū	adv.	with each passing day, gradually, day by day
62	激烈		jīliè	adj.	intense, fierce
63	对手	對手	duìshǒu	n.	opponent, competitor, rival
64	拥有	擁有	yōngyǒu	v.	to possess, to have, to own
65	视野	視野	shìyě	n.	visual field, field of vision
66	合格		hégé	adj.	qualified, up to standard
67	人力资源	人力資源	rénlì zīyuán	n.p.	human resource

68	雇用		gùyòng	v.	to hire, to employ
69	成本		chéngběn	n.	prime cost
70	招		zhāo	v.	to enlist, to enroll, to recruit
71	跨国	跨國	kuàguó	adj.	transnational

专有名词 Proper nouns

1	纽约时报	紐約時報	Niǔyuē Shíbào	*The New York Times*
2	约书亚·斯蒂芬斯	約書亞·斯蒂芬斯	Yuēshūyà Sīdìfēnsī	Joshua Stephens
3	卫斯理安大学	衛斯理安大學	Wèisīlǐ'ān Dàxué	Wesleyan University
4	萨拉贝丝·伯尔曼	薩拉貝絲·伯爾曼	Sàlābèisī Bó'ěrmàn	Sarabeth Berman
5	巴纳德学院	巴納德學院	Bānàdé Xuéyuàn	Barnard College
6	欧洲	歐洲	Ōuzhōu	Europe, European
7	华尔街日报	華爾街日報	Huá'ěrjiē Rìbào	*The Wall Street Journal*
8	翰威特		Hànwēitè	Hewitt Associates Inc.

华裔虎妈教女严 中西争论起"硝烟"

主课文 Main Text

2011年1月,美国《华尔街日报》以"为什么中国母亲更胜一筹?"为题,选登了新近出版的《虎妈战歌》这部书的一些片段。书的作者耶鲁大学法学教授蔡美儿在文中讲述了自己如何对两个女儿奉行"中国式严教"助其成才的经历。此文一发表,迅速在英美媒体和网络掀起了一场中西方教育观争论。那么蔡美儿是一个什么样的母亲,她的教育方法为什么会引发如此广泛的争论呢?

蔡美儿是华裔美国人,她丈夫是犹太裔美国人,夫妻俩都是耶鲁大学法学院的教授。他们有两个女儿:大女儿索菲亚,早年学习钢琴并取得了一定的成绩;小女儿露露自幼学习小提琴,后来兴趣转向网球。两个女儿都曾参加多项音乐比赛并获得过各种奖项。大女儿申请大学,结果哈佛大学和耶鲁大学都给她发了录取通知书。

蔡美儿秉持"中国式"的教育理念，对两个女儿实行严格的家教，做了很多规定，包括：不准夜不归宿、不准随便交友、不准看电视或玩电子游戏、不准擅自选择课外活动、不准有任何科目成绩低于A、只准学练钢琴与小提琴等。她对女儿十分严厉苛刻。比方说，在一个寒冷的冬日，蔡美儿为了培养孩子的兴趣，想教她还不到三岁的小女儿露露学弹钢琴，但遭到了女儿的拒绝。她对孩子说："如果你不听妈妈的，就不能待在屋里。你说，你到底是准备做个好孩子呢还是想到外面去？"她这种强制性的管教并没有起到作用，孩子仍然不听她的。虽然孩子只穿了很少的衣服，但她还是让孩子走到了门外，冻了很长时间。

蔡美儿从自己的育儿理念出发，总结出中西方家庭教育理念的三个不同。第一，西方家长极为关注孩子的自尊心，但中国家长更关心孩子的学习，并且相信只要督促他们努力，孩子就会成功。中国家长认为只有成功，才会建立起真正的自信，而不是像西方家长那样通过不停地夸奖孩子来培养他们的自信心。第二，中国家长因为受儒家思想的影响，认为孩子应该绝对服从父母。具体表现就是孩子要听话，并让父母感到骄傲。但西方家长则认为，家长不应该越俎代庖，孩子也不必对家长唯命是从。第三，中国家长总是相信自己比孩子更知道他们需要什么，把自己的欲望和喜好强加于孩子身上，而西方家长则尊重孩子的愿望。

其实，大家的批评主要集中在一点上，即在教育孩子的过程中，家长所关注的到底应该是孩子的快乐还是成功。蔡美儿认为，孩子的学习及获得成功更为重要。孩子只对他们擅长的东西感兴趣，但要擅长，那就得努力学习。可是孩子们常常会畏惧学习的枯燥和艰苦，这就要依靠家长的监督和督促了。在她看来，西方家长总是顾及孩子一时一地的感受而任其随心所欲。她的这种观点，在西方无疑是不能接受的。因为西方的父母认为不论学习还是游戏都应该给孩子带来快乐和满足。

非常值得深思的是，对蔡美儿教育孩子的理念，很多批评和质疑之声不仅来自西方社会，也来自海外的华裔社区，甚至来自中国。有不少华裔母亲指出，在家庭教育方面没有绝对成功或失败的方法，只有是否适合自己孩子的方法。蔡美儿的教育方式根本不能代表中国妈妈，她的许多方式过于严苛，且不近人情。

这篇文章所引发的中西方家庭教育的争论和冲突一时还不会消失，而这场没有硝烟的"战争"也很难分出胜负。无论是东方还是西方，家庭教育都先于学校教育，其重要性不容忽视。家长在孩子的成长过程中扮演什么样的角色，如何助其成才，值得全社会深入思考。

讨论题 Discussion

根据课文内容回答下列问题
(Please answer the following questions based on the text)

1. 蔡美儿认为她的两个女儿成才的原因是什么？
2. 你怎么看蔡美儿做的规定？露露的例子说明了什么？
3. 说说你的父母对你的教育方式。你对那种方式有什么看法？
4. 对于蔡美儿总结的中西方教育理念，你有什么看法？
5. 如果你是家长，你会关注孩子的快乐还是成功？为什么？
6. 对蔡美儿的教育方式，批评的声音还有来自中国的，这说明了什么问题？
7. 为什么家庭教育很重要？

生词 New Words

1	华裔	華裔	Huáyì	n.	Chinese descent, ethnic Chinese, foreign citizen of Chinese origin
2	虎		hǔ	n./b.f.	tiger; brave, vigorous
3	严	嚴	yán	adj.	strict, severe, extreme
4	硝烟	硝煙	xiāoyān	n.	smoke of gunpowder
5	筹	籌	chóu	b.f.	chip, tally, counter
6	新近		xīnjìn	adv.	recently, lately
7	战	戰	zhàn	v./b.f.	to fight; battle, war
8	片段		piànduàn	n.	part, extract, fragment
9	法学	法學	fǎxué	n.	science of law, law
10	讲述	講述	jiǎngshù	v.	to tell about, to narrate, to give an account
11	奉行		fèngxíng	v.	to pursue (a course, a policy, etc.)
12	中国式	中國式	Zhōngguóshì	n.	Chinese style
13	助		zhù	v.	to help, to assist, to aid
14	成才		chéng cái	v.o.	to emerge as a talent, to become a useful person
15	媒体	媒體	méitǐ	n.	(news) media
16	犹太裔	猶太裔	Yóutàiyì	n.	Jewish descent
17	法学院	法學院	fǎxuéyuàn	n.	law school
18	早年		zǎonián	n.	many years ago, in one's early years
19	钢琴	鋼琴	gāngqín	n.	piano
20	自幼		zìyòu	ad.p.	since little, since childhood
21	小提琴		xiǎotíqín	n.	violin, fiddle
22	奖项	獎項	jiǎngxiàng	n.	award, prize

#	简体	繁體	Pinyin	词性	English
23	申请	申請	shēnqǐng	v./n.	to apply for; application
24	录取	錄取	lùqǔ	v.	to enroll, to recruit, to admit to
25	通知书	通知書	tōngzhīshū	n.	notice, notification letter
26	秉持		bǐngchí	v.	to uphold, to adhere to (principles, etc.)
27	理念		lǐniàn	n.	idea, concept, philosophy
28	家教		jiājiào	n.	family education, upbringing
29	归	歸	guī	v.	to return, to go or come back
30	宿		sù	b.f./v.	to stay overnight, to lodge for the night
31	电子	電子	diànzǐ	n./attr.	electron; electronic
32	擅自		shànzì	adv.	taking the liberty, without authorization, unauthorized
33	课外	課外	kèwài	n.	extracurricular, outside class
34	科目		kēmù	n.	school subject or course
35	低于	低於	dīyú	v.	to be lower than
36	严厉	嚴厲	yánlì	adj.	strong, severe, strict
37	苛刻		kēkè	adj.	(of condition, requirement, etc.) harsh, severe, hard
38	比方		bǐfāng	v./n.	to take for instance or example; analogy, instance
39	培养	培養	péiyǎng	v.	to foster, to develop, to cultivate
40	强制性	強制性	qiángzhìxìng	n./adj.	forcefulness; forceful, mandatory
41	管教		guǎnjiào	v.	to control and teach, to discipline
42	自尊心		zìzūnxīn	n.	self-respect, self-esteem
43	督促		dūcù	v.	to supervise and urge
44	自信(心)		zìxìn(xīn)	n.	self-confidence, self-assurance
45	夸奖	誇獎	kuājiǎng	v.	to praise, to commend, to compliment
46	儒家		rújiā	n.	Confucian School, Confucianism

	简体	繁體	Pinyin	词类	English
47	听话	聽話	tīng huà	v.o.	to heed advice, to obey, to be obedient
48	越俎代庖		yuèzǔ-dàipáo	f.e.	to take another's (sb. else's) job into one's own hands
49	唯命是从	唯命是從	wéimìng shìcóng	f.e.	to accept sb.'s instructions without a murmur, to be absolutely obedient
50	欲望	慾望	yùwàng	n.	desire, wish, lust
51	喜好		xǐhào	n./v.	like, love, be fond of
52	强加	強加	qiángjiā	v.	to impose, to force (upon)
53	身上		shēnshang	n.	on one's body, (have sth.) on one
54	尊重		zūnzhòng	v.	to respect, to value, to esteem
55	擅长	擅長	shàncháng	v.	to be good at, to be expert in, to be skilled in
56	畏惧	畏懼	wèijù	v.	to fear, to dread
57	枯燥		kūzào	adj.	dry and dull, uninteresting
58	监督	監督	jiāndū	v./n.	to supervise, to superintend, to control; supervision
59	顾及	顧及	gùjí	v.	to take into account, to give consideration to
60	感受		gǎnshòu	n./v.	feelings; to experience, to feel
61	随心所欲	隨心所欲	suíxīnsuǒyù	f.e.	to do as one pleases or wishes, to follow one's inclination, to have one's own way
62	无疑	無疑	wúyí	v.	to be beyond doubt
63	质疑	質疑	zhìyí	v.	to question, to query
64	海外		hǎiwài	n.	overseas, abroad
65	社区	社區	shèqū	n.	community
66	严苛	嚴苛	yánkē	adj.	strict and harsh
67	不近人情		bújìn-rénqíng	f.e.	unreasonable, inconsiderate, unkind
68	冲突	衝突	chōngtū	v./n.	to conflict, to clash; contradiction
69	胜负	勝負	shèngfù	n.	victory and/or defeat, success and/or failure
70	重要性		zhòngyàoxìng	n.	importance, significance

71	不容忽视	不容忽视	bùróng-hūshì	f.e.	cannot be ignored
72	扮演		bànyǎn	v.	to play the role of, to act, to impersonate
73	角色		juésè	n.	role (in a play, etc.), part
74	思考		sīkǎo	v.	to think deeply, to ponder over, to reflect on

专有名词 Proper nouns

1	耶鲁大学	耶魯大學	Yēlǔ Dàxué	Yale University
2	蔡美儿	蔡美兒	Cài Měi'ér	Amy L. Chua
3	索菲亚	索菲亞	Suǒfēiyà	Sophia
4	露露		Lùlù	Lulu
5	哈佛大学	哈佛大學	Hāfó Dàxué	Harvard University

词语注释 Vocabulary and Grammar Explanations

语素 (morphemes)

-述/述-： 陈说；叙述。(to state; to explain; to narrate; to recount)

> 例　讲述　叙述　重述　略述　述说

-行/行-： 做；办；实施。(to do; to work at; to implement)

> 例　奉行　执行　举行　实行　施行　试行　行医　行骗　行之有效

引-： 引起，使出现。(to give rise to; to lead to; to make something appear)

> 例　引发　引出　引起　引燃　抛砖引玉

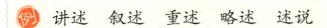

-定：决定，使确定。(to decide; to determine)

> 例 制定　指定　预定　决定　规定　商定

-自/自-：自己。(oneself)

> 例 擅自　私自　独自　亲自　自动　自爱　自卫

强-(2)：使用强力，强迫。(to use brute force; to enforce)

> 例 强制　强迫　强加　强占

关-：重视，关心。(to attach importance to; to pay attention to; to be concerned with; to care for)

> 例 关注　关心　关切　关怀　关照

-从：顺从，听从。(to be obedient to; to obey)

> 例 服从　依从　顺从　听从　力不从心　唯命是从

-督/督-：监督指挥。(to supervise; to command; to direct)

> 例 监督　督察　督促　督办　督战

● 四字格和成语 (four-character expressions and idioms)

• 越俎代庖

越：跨过；俎：古代祭祀时摆祭品的礼器；庖：厨师。比喻超出自己业务范围去处理别人所管的事。（"越" means "to bypass something or someone"; "俎" refers to utensils for sacrifices in ancient times; "庖" means "cook". This idiom means "to take another's [somebody else's] job and do it oneself".)

 (1) 西方家长认为，家长不应该越俎代庖，孩子也不必对家长唯命是从。
(2) 如果父母总是越俎代庖、替孩子解决生活和学习上的问题，那么孩子就容易事事依赖父母。这对孩子的成长没有好处。
(3) 这个问题应该由经理来决定，你不能越俎代庖。
(4) 弱小国家也应该享有独立自主的权利，大国强权不可越俎代庖。

● **唯命是从**

是命令就服从，不敢有半点违抗。(to accept somebody's instructions without a murmur; to be absolutely obedient)

 (1) 西方家长认为，家长不应该越俎代庖，孩子也不必对家长唯命是从。
(2) 一个好的领导不会喜欢唯命是从的下属，有独立见解的人更容易得到赏识。
(3) 只有奴才对主子才会唯命是从，在现代社会中，人和人的关系是平等的。
(4) 他表面上对你唯命是从，其实背后做的是另一套。

● **随心所欲**

随着自己的意思，想要干什么就干什么。(to follow one's own bent or inclinations; arbitrarily)

 (1) 在她看来，西方家长总是顾及孩子一时一地的感受而任其随心所欲。
(2) 他习惯了随心所欲、自由自在的生活，受不了别人的管制。
(3) 任何人在社会上都要遵纪守法，不能随心所欲、破坏法律去满足个人的私欲。
(4) 军队纪律严明，是最不能随心所欲的地方。

虚词及句型 (function words and sentence patterns)

● 曾（曾经） used to indicate a past action or state

副词，表示从前有过某种行为或者情况。动词后一般用"过"，也可以用"了"。否定形式可以是：1) 没有＋动词＋过；2) 不曾／未曾＋动词＋（过）。

This is an adverb indicating that a certain action or situation has happened or occurred before. The verb is followed by "过" or "了". The negative form can be: 1) 没有 + verb + 过; 2) 不曾／未曾 + verb + (过).

(1) 两人都曾参加多项音乐比赛并获得过各种奖项。
(2) 他曾经跟我在同一个公司工作过几年。
(3) 这样的情况，我未曾经历过。
(4) 除了餐馆服务员以外，他不曾做过其他工作。

● 到底 at last; in the end; after all

副词，用于疑问句，表示进一步追究；究竟。用在动词、形容词或者主语前。

This is an adverb used in question form for pursuing a matter or a case further; it means "actually or exactly". It is placed before a verb, adjective, or subject.

(1) 你到底是准备做个好孩子呢还是想到外面去？
(2) 你到底同意不同意我的建议？
(3) 你们到底什么时候去中国？
(4) 人们无法猜测他到底有多少财产。

- **仍然（仍旧、仍） still; yet; as usual; as before; notwithstanding**

  副词，表示某种情况不变；还。修饰动词、形容词。多用于书面，口语中多用"还是"。

  This is an adverb indicating that a certain situation or stage has not been changed; it means "still or yet". It modifies a verb or adjective and is often used in written expression; its spoken form is "还是".

  > (1) 她这种强制性的管教并没有起到作用，孩子仍然不听她的。
  >
  > (2) 大家都不同意她的看法，但是她仍然坚持自己的意见。
  >
  > (3) 她离开故乡三十多年了。这次回来，她发现这个地方仍然没有多大的改变。
  >
  > (4) 虽然已经是二十多岁的成人了，可是他仍旧喜欢看动画片，去游乐场，玩小孩子的游戏。

- **只有……才／还…… only if/when... sb. /sth. can...**

  "只有"是连词。表示唯一的条件，非此不可。后面多用副词"才"呼应，有时也用"还"。

  "只有" is a conjunction word. It indicates a condition that must be met, without which something cannot happen or somebody cannot do something. "只有" is usually followed by an adverb "才" and sometimes "还".

  > (1) 只有成功，才会建立起真正的自信。
  >
  > (2) 除了你以外，他谁的话都不听。只有你才能说服他。
  >
  > (3) 我们只有去向他当面解释，才有可能消除误会。
  >
  > (4) 因为空气污染，北京的夏天常有雾霾，又闷又热。只有下过雨以后才舒服一些。
  >
  > (5) 我觉得别的方案都不好，只有小李的方案还可以考虑一下。

- **不论（无论）** regardless of; irrespective of

连词。用于有表示任指的疑问代词（"哪儿""谁""谁的""哪个""什么""怎么""多少"等）或者有表示选择关系（"还是""A不A"等）的并列成分的句子里，表示在任何条件下结果或结论都不会改变。后边有"都"或者"也"呼应。

This is a conjunction used with question words (such as "哪儿"，"谁"，"谁的"，"哪个"，"什么"，"怎么"，and "多少") or followed by alternative questions (such as structures with "还是" or "A不A") and indicates the result or conclusion will be the same under any condition or circumstance. "无论" or "不论" is usually followed by "都" or "也".

(1) 西方的父母认为不论学习还是游戏都应该给孩子带来快乐和满足。
(2) 无论是东方还是西方，家庭教育都先于学校教育。
(3) 他很喜欢帮助别人，大家不论有什么事，都愿意找他。
(4) 爱是无法用金钱买来的。无论你有多少钱，也买不到真正的爱情。
(5) 生老病死是人生必有的经历。无论你喜不喜欢，都无法逃脱这些经历。

副课文 Supplementary Text

"成人青少年"——美国新一代啃老族

啃老族，在中国也叫"吃老族"或"傍老族"，是指那些衣食住行全靠父母的年轻人。他们并非找不到工作，而是主动放弃了就业的机会，赋闲在家，靠父母养活。在美国也有很多二十多岁和三十多岁的年轻人靠他们的父母生活，这样的人英文叫Adultoles，意思是"成人青少年"。

二十四岁的艾琳娜从史密斯大学毕业后只找到了一份收入不高的工作，

去年又搬回了芝加哥的家中，与同是医生的父母一起住。父母二人都感到很高兴，因为他们的理念就是要让孩子有足够的安全感。来年秋天，艾琳娜将会去上研究生；她的妹妹，来年春天于斯坦福大学毕业，也会搬回来。美国到处都有这样的父母，还在试图抚养已经二十多岁的孩子。他们或者把客厅改造成卧室给孩子住，或者付钱让他们上研究生，或者继续支付孩子的房租和保险费。结果这些青年就成了"成人青少年"。

这些已经长大的孩子们看起来非常享受父母的保护，并不认为成年以后还跟父母同住是丢脸的。根据 2000 年的统计，在二十四到三十四岁年龄段的青年人中，几乎有将近四百万人和父母同住。有迹象表明越来越多的父母会欢迎已经长大了的孩子搬回家来住。近日，工作搜寻网站 TRAK.com 做了一份调查，60% 的大学生打算毕业后和父母同住，21% 的人打算和父母同住一年以上。

和上一代人不同，"成人青少年"并不以和父母同住为耻。他们不再渴望实现传统意义上的独立，即在大学毕业几年后成家、生子、买房、在财政上完全独立。现在美国人第一次结婚的平均年龄是二十六岁，而 1970 年的平均年龄是二十二岁，第一次生孩子的年龄则推后了十年甚至更长时间。形成目前这种状况的原因是多方面的，包括就业竞争激烈，高薪工作又通常要求硕士以上学位等。另外，几十年来房价不断上涨，对于大多数三十岁以下的人来说，买房只能是个空想。

除了经济上的困难以外，还有一些心理上的原因使这些完全有能力的大学毕业生还要靠父母生活。马里兰大学心理学家杰弗里·阿恩特说："我看到现在两代人之间的关系处于二战以来的最亲密时期。这些年轻人的确非常喜欢和崇拜自己的父母。"但也有人认为，对孩子来说，这是一种危险的从属依赖关系；对父母来说，则是参与过度，而这种做法对于孩子的成长和独立没有任何好处。

讨论题 Discussion

根据课文内容回答下列问题
(Please answer the following questions based on the text)

1. 在美国"成人青少年"是指什么样的人？在中国也有这样的人吗？在中国这样的年轻人被称作什么？
2. "成人青少年"为什么在大学毕业后搬回家去跟父母住？一般来说，美国父母对这样的做法是什么态度？
3. "成人青少年"这个群体和现象的出现说明了什么？有哪些社会或者经济原因造成了这种状况？
4. 除了社会和经济的原因以外，还有什么因素促成了"成人青少年"的社会现象？
5. 你对这个社会现象怎么看？作为美国的年轻人，在你看来，面对就业难、物价高、购房贵等问题，应该怎么办？

生词 New Words

1	成人	chéngrén	n.	adult, grown man, grown-up
2	青少年	qīngshàonián	n.	young people and teenagers, youths
3	啃老族	kěnlǎozú	n.	boomerang kids, boomerang child
4	族	zú	n./b.f.	clan; race, nationality; class or group of things or people with common features
5	傍	bàng	v.	to be close to (in distance), to draw near, to have an intimate relationship with sb.
6	衣食住行	yīshízhùxíng	f.e.	clothing, food, shelter (housing) and transportation—basic necessities of life

7	并非	並非	bìngfēi	v.	to be really not
8	赋闲	賦閒	fùxián	v.	(of an official) to be unemployed
9	养活	養活	yǎnghuó	v.	to support, to provide for, to feed
10	安全感		ānquángǎn	n.	sense of security, sense of safety
11	来年	來年	láinián	n.	next year, the coming year
12	研究生		yánjiūshēng	n.	postgraduate (student), graduate student
13	试图	試圖	shìtú	v.	to attempt to (do sth.), to try to (do sth.)
14	抚养	撫養	fǔyǎng	v.	to foster, to raise, to bring up
15	客厅	客廳	kètīng	n.	sitting room, drawing room, living room
16	卧室	臥室	wòshì	n.	bedroom, bedchamber
17	支付		zhīfù	v.	to pay (money), to defray
18	房租		fángzū	n.	rent, money for renting a house
19	保险费	保險費	bǎoxiǎnfèi	n.	(insurance) premium, insurance expenses
20	看起来	看起來	kànqǐlái	v.p.	it seems (or appears), it looks as if, seemingly
21	成年		chéngnián	v.	to grow up, to come of age
22	丢脸	丟臉	diū liǎn	v.o.	to lose face, to be disgraced
23	青年人		qīngniánrén	n.	young people
24	将近	將近	jiāngjìn	adv.	close to, almost, nearly
25	迹象	跡象	jīxiàng	n.	sign, indication, mark
26	长大	長大	zhǎngdà	v(c)	to grow up, to mature
27	搜寻	搜尋	sōuxún	v.	to search for, to look for, to hunt for, to seek
28	网站	網站	wǎngzhàn	n.	website
29	耻	恥	chǐ	b.f.	shame, disgrace, humiliation
30	渴望		kěwàng	v.	to hanker after, to thirst for, to aspire to, to be anxious for
31	成家		chéng jiā	v.o.	to (of a man) get married

	简体	繁體	Pinyin	词性	English
32	财政	財政	cáizhèng	n.	finances (public), financial, fiscal administration
33	高薪		gāoxīn	n.	high pay, fat salary
34	通常		tōngcháng	adv.	generally, usually, regularly
35	硕士	碩士	shuòshì	n.	master's degree
36	房价	房價	fángjià	n.	house or apartment purchase price
37	上涨	上漲	shàngzhǎng	v.	to rise, to go up (of water level, prices, etc.)
38	空想		kōngxiǎng	n./v.	fantasy, daydream; to fantasize
39	心理学	心理學	xīnlǐxué	n.	psychology
40	处于	處於	chǔyú	v.	to be (in some state, position, or condition), to stand in
41	亲密	親密	qīnmì	adj.	close, dear, intimate
42	崇拜		chóngbài	v./n.	to admire, worship; adoration, veneration
43	从属	從屬	cóngshǔ	adj.	subordinate, dependence
44	依赖	依賴	yīlài	v.	to rely on, to be dependent on, to be interdependent
45	过度	過度	guòdù	adj.	exceeding, excessive, lavishly

专有名词 Proper nouns

	简体	繁體	Pinyin	English
1	艾琳娜		Àilínnà	Elena
2	史密斯大学	史密斯大學	Shǐmìsī Dàxué	Smith College
3	芝加哥		Zhījiāgē	Chicago
4	斯坦福大学	斯坦福大學	Sītǎnfú Dàxué	Stanford University
5	马里兰大学	馬里蘭大學	Mǎlǐlán Dàxué	University of Maryland
6	杰弗里·阿恩特	傑弗里·阿恩特	Jiéfúlǐ Ā'ēntè	Jeffrey Arnett
7	二战	二戰	Èrzhàn	World War Two

第4课 多元文化冲击"圣诞节"世俗化

主课文 Main Text

近年来，随着全球化的发展，"圣诞节"这个传统的西方节日也受到了多元文化的冲击。在欧美国家，"圣诞节"的宗教色彩越来越淡。在其他国家，随着"圣诞节"宗教色彩的淡化和节日引发的商机，越来越多的人开始庆祝这个节日。

过去，在天主教和基督教教徒占人口绝大多数的国家，圣诞节是所有人的节日。但现在，情况已发生了改变。比如，在英国、法国、加拿大等国家，随着来自亚洲等地的移民逐年增加，尽管圣诞节的传统在延续，但它的宗教意味却越来越淡。与此同时，圣诞节的内容和形式也引发了一些争议。该不该摆圣诞树，能不能祝别人"圣诞快乐"，圣诞卡上画圣诞老人还是画圣婴耶稣，已成为人们讨论的热门话题。有关圣诞节的争论，其实是欧美社会多元化之后的必然现象。中国人常常抱怨"年味"越来越淡，但那基本上是对民俗与传统消失的一种伤感，不会导致某种对抗。然而，欧美国家圣诞节的"圣味"是否变淡，则涉及各种价值观、族群、信仰者团体利益的交锋。

据报道，在加拿大这个具有多元文化的国家，很多人认为庆祝圣诞节，是对其他宗教信徒的冒犯。比如，由于公司管理人员担心庆祝圣诞会引发不平，伤害其他族裔的感情，很多公司近年来一律将"圣诞节"改称为"节日"，"圣诞树"改叫"节日树"，"圣诞快乐"改为"节日快乐"。民间尚且如此，加拿大官方机构就更小心了，有些政府部门明令禁止在办公室挂圣诞节日的装饰。在有一千多年基督教传统的英国，圣诞节一直是个隆重的大节日。可是近年来，圣诞以前，不少英国人却问："你知道圣诞节快到了吗？"因为圣诞节的气氛越来越淡了。据《约克郡邮报》的一份统计，今年有四分之三的英国公司禁止在办公室里摆放圣诞树和其他节日装饰。

在中国，"圣诞节"这个从西方"舶来"的传统宗教节日，在人们的生活中已被赋予了新的含义。在西方，平安夜的时候，人们或者在家中聚会，或者去教堂做弥撒。而中国人的圣诞体现出了中国特色：圣诞节的商机被充分利用，圣诞前夕是年度销售额最大的日子。年轻的情侣们经常把圣诞节当作一个浪漫的日子。圣诞节去滑冰场和游乐园是非常流行的庆祝方式。还有一些电影院、KTV、酒吧等娱乐场所，也纷纷打出自己的圣诞牌。美国耶鲁在线网站上还有人说："大多数庆祝这个节日的时髦人士对圣诞节的宗教含义只有模糊的认识。"对北京人进行的随机采访表明，许多人把它看作"圣诞老人日"。现在，大多数中国人只把圣诞节作为一种新奇的事物来庆祝。有人认为过圣诞节可以提前感受新年的气氛。同时，与朋友、同事聚会，也可以拉近彼此的感情。还有人认为，忙碌了一年，可以通过圣诞节放松一下。

现在的圣诞节已不再是传统的基督教节日。不论是其宗教意义在欧美的淡化，还是它在其他国家的流行，都是多元文化冲击的必然结果。

Lesson 4 多元文化冲击"圣诞节"世俗化

讨论题 Discussion

根据课文内容回答下列问题
(Please answer the following questions based on the text)

1. 圣诞节的宗教色彩为什么越来越淡？
2. 在文章中指出了哪些对圣诞节内容和形式上的争议？
3. 圣诞节的时候，加拿大公司的管理人员和官方机构会怎么做？
4. 圣诞节在英国有什么变化？
5. 中国人怎么过圣诞节？
6. 你觉得在美国或者你们国家的圣诞节有变化吗？如果有，有哪些变化？是什么原因造成的？

生词 New Words

1	多元		duōyuán	attr.	poly-, multi-, multivariate
2	冲击	衝擊	chōngjī	v.	to attack, to impact, to affect
3	世俗		shìsú	n.	social conventions
4	全球化		quánqiúhuà	n.	globalization
5	受到		shòudào	v(c)	to receive, to get, to be given
6	宗教		zōngjiào	n.	religion
7	色彩		sècǎi	n.	color, tinge
8	淡化		dànhuà	v.	(of problem, emotion, etc.) to be gradually forgotten, to fade out, to downplay

9	商机	商機	shāngjī	n.	business opportunities
10	天主教		tiānzhǔjiào	n.	Catholicism, Catholic church
11	基督教		jīdūjiào	n.	Christianity, Christian
12	教徒		jiàotú	n.	follower or believer of a religion
13	绝大多数	絕大多數	jué dàduōshù	n.p.	most, the overwhelming majority
14	移民		yímín	v.o./n.	to migrate, to emigrate or immigrate; settler
15	逐年		zhúnián	adv.	year by year, year after year
16	延续	延續	yánxù	v.	to continue, to last, to extend
17	意味		yìwèi	n.	meaning, overtone, implication
18	争议	爭議	zhēngyì	v.	to dispute, to debate
19	圣诞	聖誕	shèngdàn	n.	birthday of Jesus Christ, birthday of an emperor or empress
20	卡		kǎ	n./b.f.	card
21	热门	熱門	rèmén	n.	popular, hot
22	话题	話題	huàtí	n.	subject (of a talk or conversation), topic
23	抱怨		bàoyuàn	v.	to complain, to grumble
24	味		wèi	b.f.	taste, flavor
25	基本上		jīběnshang	adv.	basically, generally, mainly
26	民俗		mínsú	n.	folkways, folk custom
27	伤感	傷感	shānggǎn	adj.	sad, sick at heart, sentimental
28	对抗	對抗	duìkàng	v./n.	to resist, to oppose; antagonism, confrontation
29	圣	聖	shèng	b.f.	holy, sacred, saint
30	族群		zúqún	n.	ethnic group

#	简体	繁體	Pinyin	词性	English
31	信仰		xìnyǎng	v./n.	to believe in, to have faith in; faith, belief
32	团体	團體	tuántǐ	n.	group, organization, team
33	交锋	交鋒	jiāofēng	v.o./n.	to clash; confrontation
34	信徒		xìntú	n.	believer, disciple, follower
35	冒犯		màofàn	v./n.	to offend; offense
36	一律		yílǜ	adv.	all, uniformly, without exception
37	伤害	傷害	shānghài	v.	to hurt, to harm, to damage
38	民间	民間	mínjiān	n./attr.	among the people, nongovernmental, folk
39	尚且		shàngqiě	conj.	even, still, yet
40	官方		guānfāng	n./attr.	official, (by the) government
41	明令		mínglìng	n.	explicit order, formal decree, public proclamation
42	装饰	裝飾	zhuāngshì	v./n.	to decorate, to adorn; ornament, decoration
43	隆重		lóngzhòng	adj.	grand, solemn, ceremonious
44	气氛	氣氛	qìfēn	n.	atmosphere, mood, tone
45	舶来	舶來	bólái	v(c)	to import
46	赋予	賦予	fùyǔ	v.	to endow, to give, to entrust
47	含义	含義	hányì	n.	meaning, implication, sense
48	平安夜		píng'ānyè	n.	Christmas Eve
49	聚会	聚會	jùhuì	v./n.	(of people) to get together, to congregate; party, social gathering
50	教堂		jiàotáng	n.	church, temple, cathedral
51	弥撒	彌撒	mísa	n.	Mass

52	特色		tèsè	n.	characteristic, distinguishing feature or quality
53	前夕		qiánxī	n.	eve, evening of the previous day
54	年度		niándù	n./attr.	year (e.g., school year, fiscal year, etc.); annual, yearly
55	销售	銷售	xiāoshòu	v.	to sell
56	额	額	é	n./b.f.	amount, quantity, quota
57	情侣		qínglǚ	n.	sweethearts, lovers
58	当作	當作	dàngzuò	v.	to treat as, to regard as
59	浪漫		làngmàn	adj.	romantic
60	游乐	遊樂	yóulè	v.	to amuse oneself, to have fun
61	园	園	yuán	b.f.	place of recreation, park, garden
62	流行		liúxíng	adj.	popular, in vogue, prevalent
63	酒吧		jiǔbā	n.	bar, saloon, taproom
64	场所	場所	chǎngsuǒ	n.	location, place, locale
65	在线网站	在線網站	zàixiàn wǎngzhàn	n.p.	online website
66	人士		rénshì	n.	professional person, person with certain social influence
67	模糊		móhu	adj.	vague, blurred, unclear
68	随机	隨機	suíjī	adv.	randomly, probabilistic
69	看作		kànzuò	v.	to regard as, to consider, to look upon as
70	新奇		xīnqí	adj.	strange, novel, new
71	同事		tóngshì	n.	colleague, fellow-worker
72	拉近		lājìn	v(c)	to draw closer, to pull closer
73	忙碌		mánglù	adj.	busy, bustling

| 74 | 放松 | 放鬆 | fàngsōng | v. | to relax, to slacken, to loosen |

专有名词 Proper nouns

1	圣诞节	聖誕節	Shèngdàn Jié	Christmas Day
2	欧美	歐美	Ōu Měi	Europe and America
3	法国	法國	Fǎguó	France
4	加拿大		Jiānádà	Canada
5	亚洲	亞洲	Yàzhōu	Asia
6	圣诞老人	聖誕老人	Shèngdàn Lǎorén	Santa Claus
7	圣婴	聖嬰	Shèngyīng	the Holy Child
8	耶稣	耶穌	Yēsū	Jesus, Jesus Christ
9	约克郡邮报	約克郡郵報	Yuēkè Jùn Yóubào	The Yorkshire Post

词语注释 Vocabulary and Grammar Explanations

语素 (morphemes)

-化：后缀，加在名词或形容词后组成动词，相当于英文"-ize"或"-ify"。
(suffix attached to a noun or adjective to make it a verb, similar to "-ize" or "-ify" in English)

> 例 全球化　世俗化　淡化　绿化　工业化　现代化　多元化　多样化
> 扩大化　合理化　庸俗化　表面化　大众化

-额：规定的数目。(quota)

> 例　销售额　营业额　余额　金额　名额　数额　总额

商-：商业。(trade; commerce; business)

> 例　商机　商业　商人　商店　商行　商品　商界　商家

-味：味道。(taste; flavor)

> 例　年味　滋味　甜味　咸味　香味　怪味　五味俱全　风味

-裔：后代。(descendants)

> 例　族裔　华裔　亚裔　后裔　犹太裔

-予：给与。(to give)

> 例　赋予　给予　授予　赐予　赠予

同-：相同的。(in the same time or place)

> 例　同事　同学　同班　同校　同年　同窗

● **虚词及句型** (function words and sentence patterns)

• 随着　along with

　　介词，用在句首或动词前面，表示动作、行为或事件的发生所依赖的条件。常见的形式是：随着＋名词/动词短语。

This is a preposition used at the beginning of the first clause in a sentence. It indicates the condition that a certain action, behavior, or event is based on. The often seen form is: "随着" + noun/verb phrase.

(1) 近年来，随着全球化的发展，"圣诞节"这个传统的西方节日也受到了多元文化的冲击。

(2) 在其他国家，随着"圣诞节"宗教色彩的淡化和节日引发的商机，越来越多的人开始庆祝这个节日。

(3) 在中国，随着生活水平的提高，很多人都买了车。

(4) 随着时间的推移，他的工作经验越来越丰富。

(5) 随着电脑和网络的发展，我们已经进入了高科技时代。

(6) 随着年龄的增长，小张越来越成熟懂事了。

● **基本上**

1. 副词。主要地，差不多。指数量。

This is an adverb that means "generally, basically, mainly"; it mainly indicates amount or quantity.

(1) 上海的消费水平很高，我每月的工资基本上都得花完，没有什么积蓄。

(2) 这个项目的主要工作基本上他得独立完成。

(3) 这个国家的人口基本上是由外来移民组成的。

(4) 这个城市的人基本上都说方言，不说普通话。

2. 副词。大致上。指范围、程度或者水平。

This is an adverb that means "by and large, in the main, on the whole" and indicates scope, degree, or level.

(1) 中国人常常抱怨"年味"越来越淡，但那基本上是对民俗与传统消失的一种伤感，不会导致某种对抗。

(2) 我觉得他的想法基本上是正确的。

(3) 几年前四川发生了大地震，经过一段时间的重建，现在人们的生活基本上恢复了正常。

(4) 他们基本上同意我们的意见，但具体做法还要进一步商量。

- **然而**　yet; but; however; nevertheless

连词，书面语。用在句首，连接分句、句子或段落，表示转折，引出与上文相反的意思，或限制、补充上文的意思。与"虽然"配合使用时，作用相当于"但是"。

This is a conjunction and a written expression, used in the beginning of a second clause to link clauses, sentences, or paragraphs. It usually indicates a turn in meaning, introduces a contrastive meaning, or limits and complements the expression in the first clause. When it is used with "虽然" its function is the same as "但是".

 (1) 中国人常常抱怨"年味"越来越淡，但那基本上是对民俗与传统消失的一种伤感，不会导致某种对抗。然而，欧美国家圣诞节的"圣味"是否变淡，则涉及各种价值观、族群、信仰者团体利益的交锋。

(2) 这个小组在实验中失败了多次，然而他们并不灰心。

(3) 身体健康指数（BMI）是一种非常流行的衡量身体是否健康的标准。然而，许多专家指出，身体健康指数并不科学，它存在许多缺陷。

(4) 大城市就业的机会多，适合年轻人发展。然而，生活在大城市什么都贵，给年轻人的压力也很大。

- **而 (2)　but**

  连词，表示相对或相反的两件事。"而"一般用在后一分句的开头。

  This is a conjunction indicating two different or contrastive things. It usually is used at the start of the second clause.

  (1) 在西方，平安夜的时候，人们或者在家中聚会，或者去教堂做弥撒；而中国人的圣诞体现出了中国特色。
  (2) 很多人都买苹果手机，而我并不喜欢。
  (3) 沃茨尼亚克在 Facebook 上说到："乔布斯并非被排挤，而是自行选择了离开。"
  (4) WhatsApp 公司被 Facebook 收购之前，已拥有 4.5 亿用户，而公司的工程师只有 35 名。

- **由于　due to; as a result of**

  连词，表示原因，多用于书面，类似于口语里的"因为"。后一分句可以用"所以""因此"或"因而"与之呼应。

  This is a conjunction that indicates a reason (or reasons) and is similar to "因为"; however, "因为" is spoken and "由于" is a written expression. When it is used in a complex sentence, "所以", "因此", or "因而" is often used together with it.

  (1) 由于公司管理人员担心庆祝圣诞会引发不平，伤害其他族裔的感情，很多公司近年来一律将"圣诞节"改称为"节日"。
  (2) 这次试验的成功，是由于全体人员的共同努力和密切合作。
  (3) 由于老师的教导和同学们的帮助，他取得了很好的成绩。
  (4) 由于台风原因，很多航班被取消了。

- **尚且 even**

连词，用在前一小句的谓语动词前面，提出某种明显的事例做对比，后一分句对程度上有差别的同类事例做出当然的结论。

This is a conjunction used before the verb of the first clause which gives a certain obvious example to be used as the basis for comparison. The second clause is the conclusion of the comparison.

(1) 民间尚且如此，加拿大官方机构就更小心了，有些政府部门明令禁止在办公室挂圣诞节日的装饰。
(2) 她的英文很好，文学作品尚且能翻译，一般文章当然不成问题。
(3) 她是一个粗心的人，大事尚且不注意，更别说小事了！
(4) 这个地区现在尚且如此贫穷，六年以前就更是可想而知了！

- **如此 this way; such; so**

指示代词。指上文提到的某种情况。多用于书面。

This is a demonstrative pronoun that refers to a previously mentioned situation. It is usually used as a written expression.

(1) 民间尚且如此，加拿大官方机构就更小心了，有些政府部门明令禁止在办公室挂圣诞节日的装饰。
(2) 她得了癌症，但是还很乐观。不仅如此，她还经常鼓励别的病人要有勇气战胜疾病。
(3) 在国外学习有很多困难。虽然如此，还是有很多人想出国留学。
(4) 私家车的增加给北京的城市交通和环境都带来了不少问题。虽然如此，没有车的人仍旧想买车。

副课文 Supplementary Text

中国情人节　发帖租女友

　　阴历七月初七是中国传统的"七夕",又被称为"中国情人节"。正当婚恋年龄的年轻人是怎么过七夕的呢?近年来网上出现了不少"征情人""租女友"的帖子,而"租女友"这一长期被认为是单身群体用来撑场面、应付长辈的行为,如今在90后群体中风靡起来。参与"租女友"的人群也悄然发生变化:不再集中于社交途径有限、难接触到异性的人群,而是一群爱玩、爱新鲜、爱社交的新新人类。"恋爱么么哒"微信平台负责人陆伟介绍,将近八成在他们平台租女友过七夕的都是90后。绝大多数人觉得这种模式新鲜有趣,只有少数人是为了充门面或者找结婚伴侣而来的。

　　记者近日在校园论坛上发现一些"征情人"的帖子。例如:"七夕节快到了,求一名女生做一日情人!"发帖者希望"租一名男友或者女友体验一日浪漫"。在武汉某高校论坛上,一个男性网友自称大学三年从未交过女朋友,希望能在离开学校以前过一个有情人的情人节。他发帖说:"我们一起牵手看电影、吃饭、逛街,等到凌晨再宣布'分手吧'。"帖子发出后回复的人不少,可响应者却寥寥无几,有人甚至怀疑这是一场恶作剧。另一网友跟帖表示,感情是非常神圣的,不该为了应景而租"一日情人"。不过,也有女性网友称非常佩服楼主的勇气,愿意以朋友的身份一起过节。

　　除了"求租"外,还有学生发帖"出租"自己。在校大学生高同学在微博上发布了这样一条"出租"启事:"七夕当天陪吃饭五元/小时,陪看电影五元/小时,陪聊天十元/小时,但拒绝拉手哦。"高同学目前是单身,看到别人发的租"七夕恋人"的帖子后感觉很浪漫,于是效仿发了一条"出租"微博。可是她说,标价完全是为了吸引眼球,并不会真的收费。

　　他们的帖子发出后在网上引起了热议。有人对发帖者表示理解和支持,也有部分网友对此表示质疑。支持者认为这是一种新的交友方式,质疑者则认为和喜欢的人一起过七夕是温馨浪漫，和租来的临时男友或女友过节是荒唐，有何幸福可言？对此，武汉科技大学一名心理老师提醒道：在网上发帖征友是一种潮流，但为了过情人节在网上租情人则不可取。发帖者或许是真的想寻找一段恋情，但这种形式不安全，更不值得提倡。近两年来，为了降低风险，一些公司试图借七夕打造一个供年轻人交友的平台，通过微信平台，单身的年轻男女相互结识，互相了解，建立友情和恋爱关系。

讨论题 Discussion

根据课文内容回答下列问题
(Please answer the following questions based on the text)

1. "七夕节"是什么节日？你知道这个节日是怎么来的吗？这个节日跟哪个民间传说有关系？
2. 为什么有些网友要"征情人""租女友"？大家对这种做法怎么看？
3. 在美国也有个"情人节"。美国人过情人节都做些什么？
4. 你对在网上交友和网恋怎么看？
5. 在你看来，现在的年轻人社交途径怎么样？接触异性的机会多吗？你觉得理想的恋爱方式和途径是什么？

生词 New Words

1	帖（子）		tiě (zi)	n.	invitation, post
2	租		zū	v.	to rent, to hire
3	阴历	陰曆	yīnlì	n.	lunar calendar

Lesson 4 多元文化冲击"圣诞节"世俗化

4	年龄	年齡	niánlíng	n.	age
5	征	徵	zhēng	v.	to levy, to recruit, to solicit
6	情人		qíngrén	n.	lover, sweetheart
7	单身	單身	dānshēn	v./n.	to be unmarried, single; single man
8	群体	群體	qúntǐ	n.	group
9	撑		chēng	v.	to prop up, to support
10	场面	場面	chǎngmiàn	n.	appearance, front, facade
11	应付	應付	yìngfu	v.	to deal with, to cope with, to handle
12	长辈	長輩	zhǎngbèi	n.	elder member of a family, elder, senior
13	行为	行為	xíngwéi	n.	action, behavior, conduct
14	如今		rújīn	n.	nowadays, these days, at present
15	风靡	風靡	fēngmǐ	v.	to be fashionable, to sweep over
16	参与	參與	cānyù	v.	to participate; participation
17	悄然		qiǎorán	adj.	quiet, soft
18	集中		jízhōng	v.	to concentrate, to centralize, to focus
19	社交		shèjiāo	n.	social intercourse, social contact
20	途径	途徑	tújìng	n.	road, way, approach
21	有限		yǒuxiàn	adj.	limited, restricted, finite
22	接触	接觸	jiēchù	v.	to come into contact with
23	异性	異性	yìxìng	n.	the opposite sex
24	人类	人類	rénlèi	n.	human, mankind, humanity
25	恋爱	戀愛	liàn'ài	v.	to be in love, to have a love affair
26	平台	平臺	píngtái	n.	platform
27	负责	負責	fùzé	v.	to be responsible for, to be in charge of

28	成		chéng	m(n)	one tenth
29	模式		móshì	n.	model, mode, pattern
30	有趣		yǒuqù	adj.	interesting, fascinating
31	充		chōng	v.	to serve as, to act as, to pose as
32	门面	門面	ménmiàn	n.	appearance, facade
33	伴侣		bànlǚ	n.	companion, mate, partner
34	校园	校園	xiàoyuán	n.	campus, schoolyard
35	论坛	論壇	lùntán	n.	forum, tribune, place to express oneself in public
36	高校		gāoxiào	n.	colleges and universities
37	自称	自稱	zìchēng	v.	to call oneself, to style oneself, to claim to be
38	从未	從未	cóngwèi	adv.	never
39	逛街		guàng jiē	v.o.	to saunter, to stroll along the street
40	凌晨	凌晨	língchén	n.	before dawn, in the small hours, early in the morning
41	分手		fēn shǒu	v.o.	to part company, to say good-bye, to break up
42	回复	回復	huífù	v.	to reply, to restore, to recover, to return to a normal state
43	寥寥无几	寥寥無幾	liáoliáo-wújǐ	f.e.	very few left, scanty
44	神圣	神聖	shénshèng	adj.	sacred, holy
45	应景	應景	yìngjǐng	v.o./attr.	to do sth. for the occasion; seasonable, suitable to the circumstance
46	佩服		pèifú	v.	to admire, to have admiration for, to think highly of
47	楼主	樓主	lóuzhǔ	n.	cyber-word: one who posts a post
48	身份		shēnfen	n.	identity, status
49	过节	過節	guò jié	v.o.	to celebrate a festival or holiday

50	出租		chūzū	v.	to let, to rent out, to hire out
51	在校		zàixiào	attr.	attending school, in school
52	启事	啟事	qǐshì	n.	notice, announcement
53	当天	當天	dàngtiān	n.	same day, that very day
54	聊天		liáo tiān	v.o.	to chat, to hobnob
55	哦		o	intj.	expressing newly gained understanding, expressing half believing
56	恋人	戀人	liànrén	n.	lover, sweetheart, loved one
57	效仿		xiàofǎng	v.	to imitate, to follow the example of
58	标价	標價	biāo jià	v.o.	to mark a price
59	眼球		yǎnqiú	n.	eyeball
60	收费	收費	shōu fèi	v.o.	to collect fees, to charge
61	议	議	yì	v./b.f.	to discuss, to exchange views on; comment
62	理解		lǐjiě	v.	to understand; understanding
63	支持		zhīchí	v.	to support; support
64	交友		jiāo yǒu	v.o.	to make friends
65	温馨	溫馨	wēnxīn	adj.	warm and fragrant, cozy, warm
66	荒唐		huāngtáng	adj.	absurd, fantastic
67	何		hé	pr.	what, where, why, how
68	提醒		tíxǐng	v.	to remind, to warn, to call attention to
69	潮流		cháoliú	n.	tide, current, trend
70	或许	或許	huòxǔ	adv.	perhaps, maybe, probably
71	恋情	戀情	liànqíng	n.	love, love affair, romantic love
72	降低		jiàngdī	v(c)	to reduce, to cut down

73	风险	風險	fēngxiǎn	n.	risk, hazard, danger
74	打造		dǎzào	v.	to make (metal works), to forge, to create
75	供		gōng	v.	to supply, to feed
76	相互		xiānghù	adv.	mutual, reciprocal, each other
77	结识	結識	jiéshí	v.	to get acquainted with sb., to get to know sb.
78	建立		jiànlì	v.	to build, to set up, to establish
79	友情		yǒuqíng	n.	friendship

专有名词 Proper nouns

1	七夕		Qīxī	the seventh evening of the seventh month in lunar-calendar
2	情人节	情人節	Qíngrén Jié	Valentine's Day
3	恋爱么么哒	戀愛麼麼噠	Liàn'ài Mēmeda	*The name of an online platform*
4	陆伟	陸偉	Lù Wěi	*a person's name*
5	武汉科技大学	武漢科技大學	Wǔhàn Kējì Dàxué	Wuhan University of Science and Technology

第5课

你是"低头族"吗

主课文 Main Text

中国互联网信息中心最新的《中国互联网络发展状况统计报告》显示，中国的智能手机使用比例达到了人口总数的66%。截至2013年6月底，中国即时通信网民接近五亿人，手机即时通信网民接近四亿人。在中国，坐车、走路、吃饭、开会等各种场景中，你总会看到人们低头看手机或者平板电脑。微信、手机QQ、微博以及短信等即时通信工具让越来越多的人成为"低头族"。

人们用"低头族"来形容那些只顾低头看手机而冷落面前亲友的人。以前，朋友们聚在一起是为了交流感情。现在，一场聚会上，大家都在低头刷微博聊微信，过去那种热热闹闹的场面再也没有了。老人希望和家人团聚，一起吃饭聊天，享受天伦之乐，可是等来的却是低头无语。"低头族"的泛滥使越来越多的老人讨厌手机，甚至和孩子们发生矛盾。在"低头族"的反对者里,老人家是站在最前列的。

为什么人们对于微信等移动社交工具如此热衷?复旦大学社会学专家赵民认为,微信热是因为它很好地满足了人们社会交往的需要。社会交往是人类最基础的需要之一。人们从健康的社交关系中获得信息、知识,更重要的是获取归属感和亲密感,从而让人觉得更加安全和幸福。从这个意义上说,由于微信使得人们能跨越时间、空间进行沟通交流,为沟通提供了最大可能的便利性,其正面作用毋庸置疑,而"朋友圈"的照片分享则很好地满足了人们自我欣赏的需要。此外,中国人的个性比较含蓄,很多感情难以当面表达,而微信创造出了一定的时空距离感,又可以通过录音、文字、照片等多种方式交流,更容易受到中国人的欢迎。

即时通信工具极大地方便了人和人之间的沟通,然而,它也会给我们的生活带来很大的负面影响。其中最显著的就是会引起"注意力不集中""强迫症"等心理问题。据调查,39%的"低头族"表示对手机等电子设备有依赖症,并且一想到没有手机的生活就会有恐慌感,这是过度使用自媒体造成的结果。专家指出,"低头族"的日常生活受电子产品干扰后,开始漠视身边的人和事,而对网上的新鲜事物更感兴趣,因此会造成社交障碍、心理障碍、情感的冷漠化等危害。白领阿文觉得自己已经得了"微信强迫症"。他说:"我时不时就想去朋友圈,看看大家都有些什么新鲜事发生。如果是自己发了照片,就更加迫不及待地希望看到朋友们作何评论。"另外,在朋友圈里分享照片,互相攀比,也可能给人带来自卑感。

在科技高度发达的今天,有人在虚拟世界中的朋友成千上万,然而,在现实生活中却找不到一个说话的人。这不能不说是高科技带来的悲哀。手机原本只是帮助人们提高沟通效率的一个工具,如果因过于沉迷其中,让人最高效、最直接的面对面沟通能力发生退化,实在是得不偿失。所以,建议大家合理利用手机、平板电脑等电子产品,每天适当"断网",经常参加聚会、看书、进行体育锻炼,让自己有意识地从"每时每刻""无处不在"的网络中解脱出来,莫要成为信息时代的"套中人"。

讨论题 Discussion

根据课文内容回答下列问题
(Please answer the following questions based on the text)

1. 什么样的人被称为"低头族"?
2. 互联网和智能电子设备对人们的生活有什么影响?
3. 作者认为中国为什么会出现"微信热"?
4. 你常常用什么网络社交工具?为什么喜欢用那种网络工具?
5. 专家认为过度使用即时通信工具会带来什么负面影响?为什么?
6. 作者认为高科技造成的"悲哀"是什么?你有什么看法?
7. 信息时代的"套中人"是什么样的人?

生词 New Words

1	互联网	互聯網	hùliánwǎng	n.	Internet
2	截至		jiézhì	v.	by (a specified time), up to (a time)
3	网民	網民	wǎngmín	n.	net user, netizen
4	场景	場景	chǎngjǐng	n.	scene, scene in theatre, film, and TV
5	平板电脑	平板電腦	píngbǎn diànnǎo	n.p.	tablet computer
6	短信		duǎnxìn	n.	text messages
7	亲友	親友	qīnyǒu	n.	relatives and friends, kith and kin
8	热热闹闹	熱熱鬧鬧	rère-nāonāo	f.e.	bustling
9	场面	場面	chǎngmiàn	n.	scene, spectacle, occasion

10	团聚	團聚	tuánjù	v.	to reunite, to have a reunion
11	天伦之乐	天倫之樂	tiānlúnzhīlè	f.e.	family happiness
12	无语	無語	wúyǔ	adj.	speechless
13	泛滥	泛濫	fànlàn	v.	to overrun, to spread unchecked, to overflow
14	老人家		lǎorenjia	n.	(an respectful form of address for an old person) old person, parents
15	前列		qiánliè	n.	front row, leading position
16	社交		shèjiāo	n.	social contact, social life
17	交往		jiāowǎng	v.	to associate with, to be in contact with
18	获取	獲取	huòqǔ	v.	to obtain, to gain, to acquire
19	归属	歸屬	guīshǔ	v.	to belong to, to be affiliated to
20	亲密	親密	qīnmì	adj.	close, intimate
21	跨越		kuàyuè	v.	to cross, to stride across, to leap over
22	便利		biànlì	adj.	convenient
23	正面		zhèngmiàn	adj.	positive, right side
24	毋庸置疑		wúyōng-zhìyí	f.e.	unquestionably, without doubt
25	分享		fēnxiǎng	v.	to share (joy, happiness, benefit, etc.)
26	欣赏	欣賞	xīnshǎng	v.	to appreciate, to enjoy, to admire
27	含蓄		hánxù	adj.	reserved, implicate
28	当面	當面	dāngmiàn	adv.	in sb.'s present, face to face
29	时空	時空	shíkōng	n.	time and space, space-time
30	距离	距離	jùlí	n.	distance
31	负面	負面	fùmiàn	adj.	downside, negative
32	注意力		zhùyìlì	n.	attention

33	强迫	強迫	qiǎngpò	v.	to force, to compel
34	依赖		yīlài	v.	to depend on, to rely on
35	症		zhèng	b.f.	disease, malady, illness
36	恐慌		kǒnghuāng	adj.	panic, panicky, scare
37	过度	過度	guòdù	adj.	excessive, exceeding
38	自媒体		zìméitǐ	n.	self-media
39	干扰	干擾	gānrǎo	v./n.	to disturb, to interfere; interference
40	漠视	漠視	mòshì	v.	to treat with indifference, to ignore, to overlook
41	障碍	障礙	zhàng'ài	n.	obstacle, obstruction, barrier
42	情感		qínggǎn	n.	emotion, feeling
43	冷漠		lěngmò	adj.	indifferent, cold and detached
44	时不时	時不時	shíbushí	ad.p.	from time to time
45	迫不及待		pòbùjídài	f.e.	too impatient to wait, in a hurry
46	评论	評論	pínglùn	v./n.	to comment on, to discuss; comment
47	攀比		pānbǐ	v.	to compare unrealistically, to compare with the higher
48	自卑		zìbēi	adj.	low self-esteem, feeling oneself inferior
49	虚拟	虛擬	xūnǐ	adj.	virtual, invented, fictitious
50	成千上万	成千上萬	chéngqiān-shàngwàn	f.e.	by the thousands and tens of thousands, thousands
51	不能不		bùnéngbù	ad.p.	have to, cannot but
52	高科技		gāokējì	attr./n.	high tech, high-technology
53	悲哀		bēi'āi	adj.	sad, sorrow
54	原本		yuánběn	adv.	originally, formerly

55	沉迷		chénmí	v.	to addict, to wallow
56	高效		gāoxiào	n.	high efficiency
57	退化		tuìhuà	v.	to degenerate, to retrogress, to retrograde
58	得不偿失	得不償失	débùchángshī	f.e.	the loss outweighs the gain
59	每时每刻	每時每刻	měishí-měikè	f.e.	all the time, incessantly
60	无处不在	無處不在	wúchùbúzài	f.e.	everywhere
61	解脱	解脫	jiětuō	v.	to free oneself from, to extricate oneself
62	莫		mò	adv.	don't
63	套中人		tàozhōngrén	n.	people who are complacent and conservative, or people who are trapped in a certain status quo (a term originally taken from a Russian novel "The Man in a Case")

专有名词 Proper nouns

1	复旦大学	復旦大學	Fùdàn Dàxué	Fudan University
2	赵民	趙民	Zhào Mín	a person's name
3	阿文		Ā Wén	a person's name

词语注释 Vocabulary and Grammar Explanations

语素 (morphemes)

-族: 1. 指具有共同起源和共同遗传特征的人群。(race; ethnicity)

> 例 种族 汉族 满族 藏族 回族 维吾尔族 蒙古族

2. 有共同属性的一大类人或者事物。(a group of people who share common traits or characteristics)

例 低头族　工薪族　追星族　月光族

-网/网-：1. 用绳、线等结成的捕鱼捉鸟的器具。(web; net)

例 渔网　铁丝网　结网　撒网

2. 形状像网的东西。(things which looks like a net)

例 蜘蛛网　球网

3. 像网一样的纵横交错的组织或系统。(a system or organization that is like a net)

例 通信网　关系网　社交网　交通网　营销网

4. 电脑网络。(internet)

例 互联网　新闻网　腾讯网　谷歌网　网络　网通　网民　网友　网恋

-时：时间。(time)

例 即时　及时　守时　准时　按时　当时　届时　超时　定时

-微/微-：小，细小。(tiny; miniature)

例 细微　微信　微博　微电影　微小说　微型　微缩

-信/信-：1. 信件，信息。(letter; information)

例 微信　通信　短信　家信　书信　信息　信纸

2. 相信。(to believe; to trust; to have faith in)

> 例　听信　信任　信从　信托

-热/热-：1. 受很多人普遍欢迎，关注。(craze; fad; a thing that is feverishly welcomed and paid attention to by many)

> 例　微信热　出国热　留学热　淘宝热　淘金热

2. 旺、盛、情绪高涨。(zeal; with intensity)

> 例　热衷　热闹　热情　热恋　热评　热议　热卖　热销

获-/-获：得到，取得。(to obtain; to win)

> 例　获得　获取　获益　获利　收获　擒获

-感：感触，感觉。(feelings)

> 例　亲密感　归属感　成就感　失落感　认同感　距离感　恐慌感　自卑感

-面：方位，部分。(side; face)

> 例　正面　负面　对面　侧面　当面　背面

-圈/圈-：范围。(circle; scope)

> 例　势力圈　朋友圈　社交圈　生活圈　职业圈　圈子

-症：病，病状。(disease; illness)

> 例　强迫症　依赖症　综合症　多动症　抑郁症　自闭症　老年痴呆症

四字格和成语 (four-character expressions and idioms)

● **毋庸置疑**

毋庸：不必。事实明显或理由充分，不必怀疑，根本就没有怀疑的余地。（"毋庸"means "not necessary". The whole idiom means "without a doubt" or "beyond question".）

(1) 由于微信使得人们能跨越时间、空间进行沟通交流，为沟通提供了最大可能的便利性，其起到的正面作用毋庸置疑。
(2) 在发展经济的同时也要保护环境，这是毋庸置疑的。
(3) 毋庸置疑，人口的增加对经济的发展起着决定性的作用。
(4) 毋庸置疑，孩子的成长受到家庭、社会和学校三个方面的影响。

● **自我~~**

自己的意思。常用的形式：自我+名词/动词。（"自我" means "oneself" and is often used with a noun or a verb. Examples include: self-centered, self-criticism, etc.）

自我欣赏　自我中心　自我批评　自我陶醉

(1) "朋友圈"的照片分享很好地满足了人们自我欣赏的需要。
(2) 独生子女常常自我中心，不为别人考虑。
(3) 经常自我批评的人才会进步得快。
(4) 有"自恋症"的人常常会自我陶醉。

- **迫不及待**

　　迫：急迫。待：等待。及：到。急得不能再等待了，形容心情非常急切。("迫" means "urgent", "待" means "to wait", and "及" means "to reach" or "until", so the idiom means "too impatient to wait" or "unable to hold oneself back".)

(1) 自己发了照片，就迫不及待地希望看到朋友们作何评论。
(2) 考试之后，他迫不及待地想知道结果。
(3) 姐姐考上了北京大学，她迫不及待地想跟家人和朋友分享这个好消息。
(4) 这是他八年来第一次回家。一到家他就迫不及待地跟同学、好友联系，安排见面的时间。

- **得不偿失**

　　指所得的利益抵偿不了所受的损失。(This means "the loss outweighs the gain".)

(1) 手机原本只是帮助人们提高沟通效率的一个工具。如果因过于沉迷其中，让人最高效、最直接的面对面沟通能力发生退化，实在是得不偿失。
(2) 如果现代化的生活以我们的健康为代价，那就是得不偿失的。
(3) 如果人口控制造成了生产力的下降和社会老化，就有些得不偿失了。
(4) 我觉得得到了事业而失去了家庭是得不偿失的。

- **每时每刻**

　　意思是时时刻刻，无时无刻不。表示毫不间断。
(every hour and moment; all the time; without a moment's pause)

(1) 我们要经常参加聚会、看书、进行体育锻炼，让自己有意识地从"每时每刻""无处不在"的网络中解脱出来。

(2) 高考期间，学生们每时每刻都感受到考试的压力。

(3) 做了妈妈以后，她才知道父母是每时每刻都在为孩子操心的。

(4) 在国外的几年中，他无时无刻不思念家乡。

(5) 学会开车以后她无时无刻不提醒自己：安全第一。

- 无~不~

双重否定表达，就是肯定的意思："无处不在"就是"处处都在"；"无人不晓"就是"人人都知道"等。

(This is a double negative expression, indicating an affirmative: "nowhere does not have it" means "it is everywhere"; "no one does not know" means "everyone knows it", etc.)

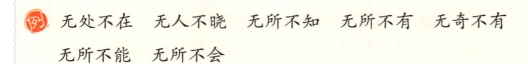
无处不在　无人不晓　无所不知　无所不有　无奇不有
无所不能　无所不会

(1) 我们要经常参加聚会、看书、进行体育锻炼，让自己有意识地从"每时每刻""无处不在"的网络中解脱出来。

(2) 安全隐患无处不在，我们得多加注意。

(3) 在中国，计划生育政策几乎无人不晓。

(4) 他非常博学，天文、地理、人文无所不知。

(5) 世界之大，无所不有，无奇不有。我们应该开阔眼界，不能做井底之蛙。

虚词及句型 (function words and sentence patterns)

• 以及 as well as; along with; and

连词，多用于书面语，表示联合关系。连接并列的名词、名词短语、动词、动词短语等。

This is a conjunction usually used in written expression that indicates joint relationship. It connects nouns, noun phrases, verbs, verb phrases, etc.

(1) 微信、手机QQ、微博以及短信等即时通信工具让越来越多的人成为"低头族"。
(2) 在北京、上海等大城市，公共交通系统很发达，有地铁、城铁、公交车，以及出租车等交通工具。
(3) 这次参加国际会议的学者主要来自欧洲、亚洲以及非洲等地。
(4) 我们学校的中国留学生大多学习经济、国际关系、数学、化学、生物以及生化等专业。
(5) 为了解决交通堵塞的问题，市政府采取的措施包括：改善公共交通系统、加宽路桥，以及限制私家车的使用等。

• 而 (3、4)

连词，多用于书面语。1) 表示因果关系（例1、例2、例3）；2) 表示意思更进一层（例4、例5、例6、例7）。

This is a conjunction usually used in written language. 1) It indicates cause-effect relationships, such as in examples 1, 2, 3; 2) It indicates a progression in meaning, such as in examples 4, 5, 6, 7.

(1) 人们用"低头族"来形容那些只顾低头看手机而冷落面前亲友的人。
(2) 小李因病而没有参加昨天的学术会议。
(3) 他们二人因性格不合而离婚。
(4) 由于微信使得人们能跨越时间、空间进行沟通交流，为沟通提供了最大可能的便利性，其正面作用毋庸置疑，而"朋友圈"的照片分享则很好地满足了人们自我欣赏的需要。
(5) 他们俩很相爱，而二人的同事朋友们也觉得他们很相配。
(6) 中国人的个性比较含蓄，很多感情难以当面表达，而微信创造出了一定的时空距离感，又可以通过录音、文字、照片等多种方式交流，更容易受到中国人的欢迎。
(7) 南方人喜欢吃米饭，而这家中式快餐店有很多米饭配炒菜的快餐，所以很受南方人欢迎。

● 再也没/不……（了）　　it is no longer…

再，表示重复或继续。"再也不/没"的意思是"没重复出现/发生"，或者 "不重复出现/发生"。

"再" indicates repetition or continuation. The phrase means "was or will be no longer or no more".

 (1) 现在，一场聚会上，大家都在低头刷微博聊微信，过去那种热热闹闹的场面再也没有了。
(2) 大学毕业以后，我们就再也没联系过。
(3) 这个饭馆的菜很难吃，服务又差，我再也不想来了。
(4) 看了这个电视节目后，他再也不想吸烟了。

- **甚至** even; (go) so far as to; so much so that

  副词，强调突出的事例。后面常用"都、也"。

  This is an adverb that emphasizes something that stands out. It is usually used with "都" or "也" in the second clause.

  (1) "低头族"的泛滥使越来越多的老人讨厌手机，甚至和孩子们发生矛盾。
  (2) 参加这次马拉松比赛的有各个年龄段的人，包括十几岁的学生、二三十岁的年轻人、四五十岁的中年人，甚至年过七十的老人。
  (3) 近两年物价涨得很快，今年甚至涨了百分之二十。
  (4) 半年没有练习中文，他把学过的汉字都忘了，甚至连"中国"都不会写了！
  (5) 这次考试没考好，她的心情坏极了！连续几天她都后悔、自责，甚至沮丧。

- **从而** thus; thereby; thereupon then; so then; as a result

  连词，用于书面语，表示结果或者进一步的行动。用于后一分句的开头，沿用前一分句的主语。

  This is a conjunction usually used in written expression that indicates a consequence or further action. It is used in the beginning of the second clause and shares the same subject with the first clause.

  (1) 人们从健康的社交关系中获得信息、知识，更重要的是获取归属感和亲密感，从而让人觉得更加安全和幸福。
  (2) 美国政府应该采取有效的控制枪支的政策，从而减少恶性枪击事件。
  (3) "全面开放二胎"的政策允许家庭生第二个孩子，从而减缓社会的老龄化等问题。

(4) 在中学和大学应该开设性教育课，从而尽量避免早孕或者未婚先孕的现象。

- **其** he, she, it, they; his, her, its, their; that, that one

代词，用于书面语。1）作领属性定语，可译为"他的""她的""它的""他们的"或者"那""那个"（例1、例2、例3和例4）；2）作兼语句中主谓短语的小主语，可译为"他""她""它""他们"（例5、例6）。

This is a pronoun and is usually used in written expression. 1) Used as a possessive pronoun; can be translated as "his", "her", "its", "their", or "that", "that one", such as in examples 1, 2, 3, and 4. 2) Used as a subject of the subject-predicate phrase in a pivotal sentence; can be translated as "he", "she", "it", "they", such as in examples 5 and 6.

例 (1) 从这个意义上说，由于微信使得人们能跨越时间、空间进行沟通交流，为沟通提供了最大可能的便利性，其正面作用毋庸置疑。

(2) 现代生活的压力很大，其原因是多方面的。

(3) 美国式的教育和中国式的教育在理念和方法上很不同，但都有其长处和问题。

(4) 现在中国不少出口企业都纷纷到越南等地去开工厂了，其目的就是要降低成本。

(5) 家长在孩子的成长过程中扮演什么样的角色，如何助其成才，值得全社会深入思考。

(6) 这位高管表现太差，公司决定劝其离职。

- **并且　besides; moreover; furthermore**

连词：1）用在两个词或两个平行结构之间，表示并列关系（例2、例3、例4）；2）表示进一层，常跟"不但"相应（例1、例5）。

This is a conjunction. 1) It is used between two words or two parallel structures, indicating coordinating relation (see examples 2-4); 2) It indicates progressive relation and often co-occurs with "不但", such as in examples 1 and 5.

(1) 据调查，39%的"低头族"表示对手机等电子设备不但有依赖症，并且一想到没有手机的生活就会有恐慌感。
(2) 我这次去纽约是去找工作，并且想看看老朋友。
(3) 智能手机有多种功能，并且携带方面，所以很受欢迎。
(4) 夏天坐地铁有空调，很凉快，并且非常准时，所以上班族都喜欢坐地铁。
(5) 他不但赞成，并且愿意帮忙。

- **进行 + 表示过程的双音节动词**

助动词，从事（某种活动）的意思；所从事的活动常常需要一个过程，并且是双音节词。

This is an auxiliary verb and means "to carry out a certain activity". It only takes disyllabic verbs as its objects, and the related activity is usually a process.

进行体育锻炼　进行研究　进行讨论　进行调查　进行思考
进行改革　进行说明

(1) 建议大家合理利用手机、平板电脑等电子产品，每天适当"断网"，经常参加聚会、看书、**进行**体育锻炼，让自己有意识地从"每时每刻""无处不在"的网络中解脱出来。

(2) 在课上大家对中国的人口政策**进行**了讨论。

(3) 警方正在对这个枪击案**进行**调查。

(4) 从上个世纪八十年代起，中国开始对经济体制**进行**全面改革。

副课文 Supplementary Text

风靡一时的"自拍奥运会"

一场极具想象力的"自拍奥运会"近期风靡国外多个社交网站，短短几天已有数十万参与者。有人将自己像衣服一样悬挂在房门之上，有人一头倒栽在浴室的盥洗池中，还有人则利用角度拍出了"人身狗脸"的效果。国外媒体调侃说，这场"自拍奥运会"的口号，应是"更高，更强，更二"。

"自拍"这个词的来源

"自拍"是"2013年最热词"。追根溯源，"自拍"其实并不算一个新词，它最早出现在2002年澳大利亚的一个互联网论坛上。当时，一名澳洲男子上传了他不慎摔下台阶导致脸部受伤的照片，并在图片说明中用了"自拍"这个词。不过，直到近几年随着智能手机、平板电脑、社交网站的发展，这个词才真正在世界范围内流行起来。

自拍与自恋

如今任何一家社交网站都会有五花八门的自拍照。无论是普通人还是公众人物都会通过自拍照来展示自己的生活和个性。知名人物还以此来扩大知名度。美国明星金·卡戴珊的自拍照曾在推特网获得一百多万网友点"赞",奥巴马在曼德拉葬礼上与丹麦首相施密特自拍引发了争议。自拍之风甚至刮到了外太空——去年年底,美国宇航员麦克·霍普金以地球为背景拍下的自拍照,也让他成为了媒体关注的焦点。

有人说如今我们已经进入一个"自恋时代",因为每个人都想把自己最好的一面展示在社交网站这个虚拟的博物馆里。社交网络时代的自拍热潮已经成为了一种网络文化。自拍流行的原因在于它激活了人本性中的自恋情结,能让人们在自我欣赏中获得满足。同时,看别人的自拍照则满足了人们的窥私欲,他们的好评和点"赞",又增加了自拍者的"创作"热情。从表面看,自拍是一种自恋而肤浅的行为,但是根据弗洛伊德理论,大多数热衷自拍的人,展现给世人的都不是真正的"自我",而是经过选择和编辑后的"自我"。自我欣赏当然没有错,但网络归根结底是一个虚拟的场所,旁人的好评很可能只是出于礼貌,甚至在绝大多数时候都是一种无意义的表达。如果将自拍当作一种自我认知和社会认同的方式,甚至失去以真实自我进行社交的能力,显然是不可取的。网络已经渐渐改变了我们的生活习惯和思维方式。但不管是通过自拍分享乐趣,还是通过自拍增加存在感,在看与被看的社交互动中,不被电子设备奴役,认清虚拟与真实的界限,才是最重要的。

讨论题 Discussion

根据课文内容回答下列问题

(Please answer the following questions based on the text)

1. 参加"自拍奥运会"的人都拍什么样的照片?"自拍"是怎么流行起来的?

2．作者认为普通人物或者公众人物为什么喜欢自拍？

3．作者认为自拍流行的原因是什么？

4．对"自拍是一种自我认知和被社会认同的方式"的观点，你有什么看法？

5．你喜欢自拍吗？为什么？

生词 New Words

1	风靡一时	風靡一時	fēngmǐ-yìshí	f.e.	to become fashionable for a time
2	自拍		zìpāi	v./n.	to take a selfie; selfie
3	想象力		xiǎngxiànglì	n.	imaginative power or imagination
4	悬挂	懸掛	xuánguà	v.	to hang, to suspend
5	倒栽		dǎozāi	v.	to fall head over heals
6	浴室		yùshì	n.	bathroom
7	盥洗		guànxǐ	v.	to wash one's hands and face
8	池		chí	b.f./n.	pond, pool
9	角度		jiǎodù	n.	point of view, angle
10	调侃	調侃	tiáokǎn	v.	to mock up
11	来源	來源	láiyuán	n./v.	origin, source; to originate, to stem from
12	追根溯源		zhuīgēn-sùyuán	f.e.	to find by hard and thorough search
13	男子		nánzǐ	n.	man, male
14	上传	上傳	shàngchuán	v.	to upload
15	不慎		búshèn	v.	to be incautious, to be careless

16	台阶	臺階	táijiē	n.	staircase
17	脸部	臉部	liǎnbù	n.	facial part
18	受伤	受傷	shòu shāng	v.o.	to sustain an injury, to be injured
19	图片	圖片	túpiàn	n.	picture, photograph, image
20	自恋	自戀	zìliàn	v./n.	to admire oneself; narcissism
21	五花八门	五花八門	wǔhuā-bāmén	f.e.	multifarious, of a wide or rich variety
22	公众	公眾	gōngzhòng	n.	public
23	知名		zhīmíng	adj.	famous, well known
24	明星		míngxīng	n.	(movie, etc.) star
25	葬礼	葬禮	zànglǐ	n.	funeral
26	首相		shǒuxiàng	n.	prime minister
27	太空		tàikōng	n.	outer space
28	宇航员	宇航員	yǔhángyuán	n.	astronaut
29	焦点	焦點	jiāodiǎn	n.	focus, focal point
30	博物馆	博物館	bówùguǎn	n.	museum
31	在于	在於	zàiyú	v.	to lie in, to consist in
32	激活		jīhuó	v.	to activate
33	本性		běnxìng	n.	natural instincts, nature
34	情结	情結	qíngjié	n.	complex
35	窥私欲	窺私慾	kuīsīyù	n.	voyeuristic interest
36	好评	好評	hǎopíng	n.	be well-judged, favorable comment
37	肤浅	膚淺	fūqiǎn	adj.	superficial, shallow
38	展现	展現	zhǎnxiàn	v.	to emerge, to show
39	世人		shìrén	n.	common people

40	编辑	編輯	biānjí	v./n.	to edit; editor
41	归根结底	歸根結底	guīgēn-jiēdǐ	f.e.	ultimately
42	旁人		pángrén	n.	someone else, other people
43	认知	認知	rènzhī	v./n.	to acknowledge; cognition
44	认同	認同	rèntóng	v./n.	to approve of; identity
45	思维	思維	sīwéi	n.	thought, thinking
46	乐趣	樂趣	lèqù	n.	delight, joy, pleasure
47	奴役		núyì	v.	to enslave
48	认清	認清	rènqīng	v(c)	to see through to, to see clearly
49	界限		jièxiàn	n.	bounds, boundaries

专有名词 Proper nouns

1	奥运会	奧運會	Àoyùnhuì	Olympic Games
2	澳大利亚	澳大利亞	Àodàlìyà	Australia
3	澳洲		Àozhōu	Australia
4	金·卡戴珊		Jīn Kǎdàishān	Kim Kardashian
5	奥巴马	奧巴馬	Àobāmǎ	Barack Obama
6	推特		Tuītè	Twitter
7	曼德拉		Màndélā	Nelson Mandela
8	丹麦	丹麥	Dānmài	Denmark
9	施密特		Shīmìtè	Helle Thorning Schmidt
10	麦克·霍普金	麥克·霍普金	Màikè Huòpǔjīn	Mike Hopkins
11	弗洛伊德		Fúluòyīdé	Sigmund Freud

第6课

女性维权非小事
社会关注人人知

"男"就业　　　　　　　　　　新华社发 蒋跃新 作

主课文 Main Text

"男女平等"的口号已经喊了很多年，如今问题真的解决了吗？当今的社会，在某些情况下性别歧视还非常严重，而这种歧视侵染了人们的语言，也反映在各种社会现象中。可喜的是现代女性的维权意识正在逐渐增强，而她们的努力向社会敲响了性别道德的警钟。

羊年"春晚"的性别歧视风波

2015年春晚，一出小品《喜乐街》让"女神与女汉子"的话题引爆网络和媒体。民间女权人士认为，这有歧视侮辱女性之嫌。但也有人觉得这是小题大做，"应该宽容乃至尊重艺术作品塑造的艺术形象，不必耿耿于怀"。

之后"网易娱乐"也就"春晚小品中出现'二手货''剩女'等是否歧视女性"进行了调查。参与的网友有三万多人，只有近四分之一的人认为"春晚有严重的大男子主义倾向"，而三分之二的人都认为"所谓歧视是过度解读"。虽然这个调查结果并不让人欣慰，但至少说明，性别歧视通过春晚事件受到了社会的广泛关注。这番争论本身已极具正面意义：因为通过民间女权人士的发声、观众的吐槽，这场讨论在社会意识层面唤起了普通大众对性别歧视的重视，强化了全社会的性别敏感性。

《中国妇女报》事后撰文说："也许，在许多人看来，'女汉子''女神''剩女'这类称谓只是生动好玩的网络用语，并不带有性别歧视色彩，甚至'女汉子'这样的词还是对独立自强、能干、有个性的女性的褒扬。他们并未深究，'女汉子'的说法本身就带有价值判断：即她们是'像男人一样的女人'，她们被人称颂的品格本该是男人所具有的，而大多数并非'汉子'的女人则柔弱无能。这其实隐含了对女性整体的歧视。'女神'的称谓虽然是褒义，但褒扬的却是女性漂亮的外貌、受男人欢迎的气质形象，仍然是从男性视角和男性对女性的价值判断来定义的。"

女大学生就业维权第一案的成功

2013年12月18日，山西籍女大学生曹菊（化名）因在应聘中遭性别限制，起诉招聘单位北京巨人环球教育科技有限公司一案，在北京市海淀区人民法院开庭审理。这是在《就业促进法》发布并生效五年后，首例以"维护女性合法权益"为由向法院提起的诉讼。此事曾被媒体广泛报道，被称为"中国就业性别歧视第一案"。

2012年6月，曹菊从北京某学院毕业。她在求职网站上看到巨人教育招聘行政助理的信息，觉得自己各方面条件都很符合要求，于是投递了求职申请。半个月后，曹菊通过电话询问巨人教育，得到一名工作人员答复："这个职位只招男性，即使你各项条件都符合，也不会予以考虑。"曹菊通过法律咨询意识到，用人单位因为性别原因拒录属于性别歧视，违反了《就业促进法》《妇女权益保障法》等相关法律法规。2012年7月，曹菊向北京市海淀区法院递上了一纸诉状，决定通过法律途径来维护自己的合法权益。

曹菊案受到了很多女性求职者的关注。法院开庭时，一位来自中华女子学院的大学生告诉记者，她一直在关注曹菊这个案件的进展，作为一名女大学生，在就业中遭遇性别歧视十分普遍，大多数人都选择沉默，而曹菊能拿起法律的武器捍卫自己的权利，值得大家为她加油、鼓劲。在庭审时，巨人教育公司董事长尹雄决定放弃辩护权，向曹菊公开道歉，并同意给曹菊人民币三万元作为赔偿。同时，巨人教育负担案件受理费。

以上的两例个案很具有代表性，反映了社会中性别歧视仍然存在的现实。把女性视为"性交对象""性感象征"，用语言给她们牢牢地钉上性别标签的大有人在。甚至有些女性自己也常常套用带有性别歧视的语言而没有意识到其对女性的不尊重。至于反映在婚恋、家庭和职场上的男女不平等现象也还是随处可见、举不胜举。我们强调的是：男女平等、维护性权、主持公正是我们需要共同努力的目标，也是社会高度文明的重要标志。希望我们的社会在这个方面不断进步、越做越好！

讨论题 Discussion

根据课文内容回答下列问题
(Please answer the following questions based on the text)

1. 中国的女权人士对"女神""女汉子""二手货""剩女"这些形容女性的词语是怎么看的？
2. 在作者看来，对春晚是否存在性别歧视的讨论有什么意义？
3. 为什么说"女神""女汉子"这样的说法本身就带有价值判断？
4. 女大学生曹菊为什么要向北京市海淀区法院起诉巨人教育？法庭审理的结果是什么？
5. 为什么很多女性求职者都很关注曹菊的案子？这个案子的意义是什么？
6. 为什么作者认为文章中的两个女性受歧视的案例很有代表性？这两个例子反映出了社会中还存在着什么样的问题？

生词 New Words

#					
1	维	維	wéi	v.	to keep, to maintain, to safeguard
2	权	權	quán	n.	right, entitlement, title
3	男女平等		nánnǚ píngděng	f.e.	men and women are equal(s), equality of men and women
4	性别		xìngbié	n.	sexual distinction, sex
5	歧视	歧視	qíshì	v.	to discriminate against, to treat with bias; discrimination (against someone)
6	侵染		qīnrǎn	v.	to infect, to pollute
7	可喜		kěxǐ	adj.	gratifying, heartening, lovely
8	增强	增強	zēngqiáng	v.	to strengthen, to heighten, to enhance
9	警钟	警鐘	jǐngzhōng	n.	alarm bell, wake-up call
10	风波	風波	fēngbō	n.	crisis, dispute, disturbance
11	小品		xiǎopǐn	n.	skit, short and simple literary or artistic creation
12	喜		xǐ	b.f.	happy, delighted, pleased
13	乐	樂	lè	n./b.f.	pleasure, enjoyment
14	女神		nǚshén	n.	goddess, nymph
15	汉子	漢子	hànzi	n.	man, fellow
16	引爆		yǐnbào	v.	to ignite, to detonate
17	侮辱		wǔrǔ	v./n.	to insult, to humiliate; humiliation
18	嫌		xián	n.	suspicion
19	小题大做	小題大做	xiǎotí-dàzuò	f.e.	to make a fuss, to make a mountain of a molehill, to intentionally exaggerate
20	塑造		sùzào	v.	to mould, to model, to shape
21	耿耿于怀	耿耿於懷	gěnggěngyúhuái	f.e.	to take sth. to heart, to brood on sth.
22	二手货	二手貨	èrshǒuhuò	n.	used goods, second-hand-goods
23	剩女		shèngnǚ	n.	leftover lady
24	大男子主义	大男子主義	dà nánzǐ zhǔyì	f.e.	male chauvinism

25	解读	解讀	jiědú	n.	reading, understanding, interpretation
26	欣慰		xīnwèi	adj.	be gratified, be delighted
27	番		fān	m(n)/m(v)	kind, sort; for times and occurrences
28	本身		běnshēn	pr.	oneself, in oneself
29	吐槽		tǔ cáo	v.o.	to comment with a sarcastic tone
30	层面	層面	céngmiàn	n.	scope, range, aspect
31	唤起	唤起	huànqǐ	v(c)	to arouse, to call, to evoke
32	大众	大眾	dàzhòng	n.	masses, populace, commonalty
33	强化	強化	qiánghuà	v.	to strengthen, to consolidate, to intensify
34	敏感		mǐngǎn	adj.	sensitive, susceptible
35	撰文		zhuàn wén	v.o.	to write articles
36	称谓	稱謂	chēngwèi	n.	appellation, term of address, title that indicates relationship, status or occupation
37	用语	用語	yòngyǔ	n.	phraseology, term
38	自强	自強	zìqiáng	v.	to strive for improvement
39	褒扬	褒揚	bāoyáng	v.	to praise, to commend
40	并未	並未	bìngwèi	ad.p.	not yet
41	深究		shēnjiū	v.	to go into (a matter) seriously, to get to the bottom of (a matter), to investigate thoroughly
42	说法	說法	shuōfa	n.	wording, way of say a thing
43	称颂	稱頌	chēngsòng	v.	to praise, to extol, to eulogize
44	品格		pǐngé	n.	one's character and morals, (of literary or artistic works') quality and style
45	柔弱		róuruò	adj.	weak, feeble, frail
46	无能	無能	wúnéng	adj.	incompetent, incapable, powerless
47	隐含	隱含	yǐnhán	v.	to imply, to denote
48	整体	整體	zhěngtǐ	n.	whole, entirety

49	褒义	褒義	bāoyì	n.	commendatory
50	外貌		wàimào	n.	looks, appearance, profile
51	气质	氣質	qìzhì	n.	temperament, disposition, demeanor
52	视角	視角	shìjiǎo	n.	visual angle, approach, perspective
53	定义	定義	dìngyì	n./v.	definition; to define
54	案		àn	n./b.f.	lawsuit, case; file
55	籍		jí	n./b.f.	native place, home town, birthplace; membership
56	化名		huàmíng	n.	alias, assumed name, pseudonym
57	应聘	應聘	yìngpìn	v.	to apply a job by responding an advertisement, to accept an offer of employment
58	遭		zāo	v.	to encounter, to meet with (disaster, misfortune, etc.), to suffer
59	起诉	起訴	qǐsù	v.	to sue, to lodge a complaint, to bring a lawsuit against
60	巨人		jùrén	n.	giant
61	有限公司		yǒuxiàn gōngsī	n.p.	limited liability company, limited company, Limited (Ltd.)
62	法院		fǎyuàn	n.	court of law, court
63	开庭	開庭	kāi tíng	v.o.	to open a court session, to call the court to order, to hold a court
64	审理	審理	shěnlǐ	v./n.	to try, to hear (a case), to bring to trial
65	生效		shēng xiào	v.o.	to go into effect, to take effect, to become effective
66	例		lì	n./b.f.	example, instance, case
67	合法		héfǎ	adj.	legal, lawful, legitimate
68	权益	權益	quányì	n.	rights and interests
69	提起		tíqǐ	v(c)	to file (a lawsuit), to raise, to arouse
70	诉讼	訴訟	sùsòng	n.	lawsuit, litigation
71	行政		xíngzhèng	n.	administrative, administration
72	助理		zhùlǐ	n.	assistant

73	投递	投遞	tóudì	v.	to deliver, to send
74	询问	詢問	xúnwèn	v.	to ask about, to enquire about, to question
75	答复	答覆	dáfù	v.	to formally reply, to answer, to respond
76	招		zhāo	v.	to enlist, to recruit
77	予以		yǔyǐ	v.	to give, to grant
78	拒		jù	v./b.f.	to refuse, to reject, to resist
79	法规	法規	fǎguī	n.	legislation, statute
80	诉状	訴狀	sùzhuàng	n.	plaint, indictment, complaint
81	途径	途徑	tújìng	n.	way, road, path
82	遭遇		zāoyù	v.	to meet with, to encounter, to run up against (an enemy, misfortune, difficulties, etc.)
83	捍卫	捍衛	hànwèi	v.	to defend, to protect, to safeguard
84	权利	權利	quánlì	n.	right, privilege
85	加油		jiā yóu	v.o./f.e.	to refuel, to make an extra effort; Go! Step on it!
86	鼓劲	鼓勁	gǔ jìn	v.o.	to give encouragement
87	庭审	庭審	tíngshěn	n.	court trial, court hearing
88	董事长	董事長	dǒngshìzhǎng	n.	chairman of the board
89	辩护	辯護	biànhù	v.	to defend, to plead, to argue in favor of
90	负担	負擔	fùdān	v./n.	to bear, to shoulder (a responsibility, work, to expense,etc); burden, load
91	受理		shòulǐ	v.	to accept and handle, (of the court) to accept and hear (a case)
92	个案	個案	gè'àn	n.	individual case
93	代表性		dàibiǎoxìng	n.	representativeness, characteristics
94	视为	視為	shìwéi	v.p.	to regard as, to consider as
95	性交		xìngjiāo	v.	to have a sexual intercourse, to make love, to have sex
96	性感		xìnggǎn	adj.	sex appeal, sexy

97	象征	象徵	xiàngzhēng	n.	symbol, token, icon
98	牢牢		láoláo	r.f.	firmly, safely
99	钉	釘	dìng	v.	to nail, to tack, to hammer a nail into sth.
100	标签	標簽	biāoqiān	n.	label, tag
101	大有人在		dàyǒurénzài	f.e.	there are plenty of people who ...
102	套用		tàoyòng	v.	to apply mechanically, to copy a set pattern mechanically, to use indiscriminately
103	随处可见	隨處可見	suíchùkějiàn	f.e.	be seen everywhere
104	举不胜举	舉不勝舉	jǔbúshèngjǔ	f.e.	too numerous to mention
105	主持		zhǔchí	v.	to uphold, to stand for
106	公正		gōngzhèng	adj.	just, impartial

专有名词 Proper nouns

1	春晚		Chūnwǎn	the abbreviation for "Spring Festival Gala" held on TV in every Spring Festival Eve
2	网易	網易	Wǎngyì	Netease (A Chinese internet company)
3	中国妇女报	中國婦女報	Zhōngguó Fùnǚ Bào	China Women's News
4	山西		Shānxī	Shanxi (province)
5	曹菊		Cáo Jú	a person's name
6	海淀区	海淀區	Hǎidiàn Qū	Haidian District (of Beijing City)
7	就业促进法	就業促進法	Jiùyè Cùjìn Fǎ	The Bill of Employment Promotion
8	妇女权益保障法	婦女權益保障法	Fùnǚ Quányì Bǎozhàng Fǎ	The Bill of Women's Rights' Protection
9	中华女子学院	中華女子學院	Zhōnghuá Nǚzǐ Xuéyuàn	China Women's University
10	尹雄		Yǐn Xióng	a person's name

词语注释 Vocabulary and Grammar Explanations

语素 (morphemes)

严–: 程度深，厉害。(high degree; severe)

> 例 严重　严苛　严厉　严冬　严寒　严刑

逐–: 挨着次序。(to follow a certain order or sequence)

> 例 逐渐　逐步　逐字　逐句　逐个　逐年　逐日　逐一

–侮/侮–: 欺负，轻慢。(to bully; to treat sb. without proper respect)

> 例 欺侮　外侮　侮慢　侮辱　侮蔑

唤–/–唤: 发出大声，使对方觉醒、注意或者随声而来。(to call out; to shout; to summon)

> 例 唤起　唤醒　唤来　唤出　呼唤

–称/称–: 1. 叫，叫做。(to be called; to be known as)

> 例 人称　自称　称为

2. 名称。(name of a thing or organization)

> 例 名称　简称　称谓　称呼

褒–: 赞扬，夸奖。(to praise; to commend; to compliment)

> 例 褒义　褒贬　褒称　褒词　褒扬　褒奖

-护/护-：保护，保卫。(to protect; to defend; to guard)

 辩护　维护　爱护　拥护　保护　护路　护航

● 四字格和成语 (four-character expressions and idioms)

● **小题大做**

不恰当地把小事当作大事来处理，有故意夸张的意思。(to make a fuss; to make a mountain of a molehill; to intentionally exaggerate)

(1) 民间女权人士认为，这有歧视侮辱女性之嫌。但也有人觉得这是小题大做。

(2) 小明有点儿感冒发烧。妈妈让他去医院看看，可是他觉得这么点儿小病，用不着小题大做。

(3) 因为孩子的事儿，她总跟丈夫吵架，于是她就要跟丈夫离婚。可朋友们都觉得夫妻之间有不同看法很正常，不用小题大做。

(4) 请你不要把这件事情想得那么复杂，真是小题大做！

● **耿耿于怀**

对一件事一直不能释怀，总放在心上。(to take something to heart; to brood on [an injury, one's neglected duty, etc.])

 (1) （我们）应该宽容乃至尊重艺术作品塑造的艺术形象，不必耿耿于怀。

(2) 小李的男朋友上次约会时迟到了一个小时。这件事让小李一直耿耿于怀。

(3) 我们应该对别人宽容一些，不计较小事，对别人的过失也不必耿耿于怀。

(4) 上次我没有满足他的无理要求，他一直耿耿于怀。

● **大有人在**

形容某种人为数不少。(there are plenty of people who...)

(1) 把女性视为"性交对象""性感象征"，用语言给她们牢牢地钉上性别标签的大有人在。

(2) 在中国，有"重男轻女"观念的还大有人在。

(3) 虽然大家都知道抽烟对身体不好，可是抽烟的还大有人在。

(4) 虽然北京的私家车早已超过五百万辆，想买车的还大有人在。

● **随处可见**

每个地方都可以见到。指某个事物非常普通常见。(to be seen everywhere)

(1) 反映在婚恋、家庭和职场上的男女不平等现象也还是随处可见、举不胜举。

(2) 这个地方又脏又乱，垃圾随处可见。

(3) 在中国，可口可乐的广告随处可见，不但大城市有，在小城市和乡下也见得到。

(4) 上海是个国际化的大城市，英文的商店招牌和外国的商品广告随处可见。

- **举不胜举**

  怎么列举也列举不完。形容数量很多。(too numerous to mention)

  (1) 反映在婚恋、家庭和职场上的男女不平等现象也还是随处可见、举不胜举。
  (2) 他很喜欢帮助别人，做的好事举不胜举。
  (3) 这个影视女演员演过上百部电影和电视剧，扮演过的大小角色举不胜举。
  (4) 在这次战争中，为了保卫祖国、抗击侵略者而死去的人举不胜举。

虚词及句型 (function words and sentence patterns)

- **就** with regard to; concerning; on; in respect to

  介词，引进动作的对象或者范围。"就"引导介词短语作状语，可放在主语后，也可放在主谓前。

  This is a preposition that introduces the object or scope of an action. The preposition phrase introduced by "就" can occur after the subject, and can occur before the subject-predicate as well.

  (1) "网易娱乐"也就"春晚小品中出现'二手货''剩女'等是否歧视女性"进行了调查。
  (2) 大家就环境保护问题进行了热烈的讨论。
  (3) 就中文水平来说，这本书要比那本书难一些。
  (4) 就工作机会而论，像纽约这样的大城市比小地方要多得多。

- **通过　by means of; by way of; by; through**

　　介词，引进动作的媒介或者手段。"通过"引导介词短语可放在主语后，也可放在主谓前。

　　This is a preposition that introduces the medium or means of an action. The preposition phrase introduced by "通过" can appear after the subject, and can occur before the subject-predicate as well.

> (1) 性别歧视通过春晚事件受到了社会的广泛关注。
> (2) 通过民间女权人士的发声、观众的吐槽，这场讨论在社会意识层面唤起了普通大众对性别歧视的重视。
> (3) 她决定通过法律途径来维护自己的合法权益。
> (4) 通过朋友介绍，我认识了她。
> (5) 通过几年得努力，他终于写完了那本书。

- **即使（即便）　even; even if; even though**

　　介词，表示假设兼让步，相当于"就是"。后面小句可用"也"。

　　This is a preposition that indicates a supposition and a concession, and is similar to "就是" (even if). The second clause following the "即使" sentence can use "也".

> (1) 这个职位只招男性，即使你各项条件都符合，也不会予以考虑。
> (2) 即使你说错了，也没有关系。
> (3) 飞机还有半个小时就起飞，而从我们这儿到机场要四十分钟。即使你现在赶去，也来不及了。
> (4) 做事要有始有终。即使有再大的困难，也要坚持下去。

- 受到

    动词，意思是接受、得到。

    This is a verb that means "to receive, to get, to gain, to obtain".

    (1) 曹菊案受到了很多女性求职者的关注。
    (2) 他今天受到了老师的批评。
    (3) 他觉得自己受到了不公平的待遇。
    (4) 曹菊起诉招聘公司是因为她觉得自己在求职时受到了性别歧视。

- 至于　as for; as to; concerning; with regard to

    介词，引进另一个话题。用在小句或者句子开头。"至于"后面的名词、动词短语、小句等是话题。

    This is a preposition that introduces a new topic. It occurs at the beginning of a sentence, and what follows "至于" (a noun or a verb phrase or a short sentence) is the topic.

    (1) 至于反映在婚恋、家庭和职场上的男女不平等现象也还是随处可见、举不胜举。
    (2) 这是我的个人看法。至于别人怎么看，我不太清楚。
    (3) 北京现在有大量流动人口。至于每年到底有多少流动人口在北京生活和工作，以及他们怎么解决住房和孩子上学的问题，就需要做具体的调查研究了。
    (4) 我只知道她计划明年到中国去学习。至于什么时候去，到哪个大学去学习，我就不知道了。

副课文 Supplementary Text

从《爸爸去哪儿》看现代男性在家庭中的角色转换

五位明星爸爸和他们的孩子出现在中国各地，在西部沙漠骑骆驼，在东部海边钓鱼，在遥远的西南部云南卖菜。一位爸爸不会给女儿梳头，另一位爸爸必须和儿子一起在沙漠里度过三天，两人只能吃方便面果腹。这就是电视真人秀《爸爸去哪儿》节目的一些片段。这个节目主要是表现妈妈不在的七十二小时里，爸爸怎样和孩子相处。据美国《大西洋月刊》杂志网站报道，自2013年10月份开播以来，该节目已经成为中国最受欢迎的电视节目之一，每周的收视人数超过六亿。

这个节目为何如此受追捧？专家指出：创意新、明星做嘉宾、与旅游结合，还有孩子们的纯真可爱是这档节目成功的几个原因。而创意新主要指的是它反映了在现代家庭中男性和女性的角色转换，以及中国新生代父亲的育儿理念和方式。

"孩子受挫了，应该如何应对？""妈妈不在，爸爸如何跟孩子交流？"真人秀中几位明星爸爸的育儿方法引发了观众对家庭教育的关注和讨论。北京师范大学学前教育副教授李敏谊说："在中国传统文化中，父亲是严厉的，母亲是慈祥的。但在这个节目里，我们看到爸爸们对孩子更温柔，更多地参与他们的成长。这个节目提出了现代中国社会的一个重要问题——在当今中国，爸爸的角色是什么？"

《爸爸去哪儿》推动"向家庭伦理的回归"，提倡父亲腾出时间，照顾孩子的衣食住行，陪伴他们学习和游戏，与孩子共度宝贵的时光。而因为工作忙忽略了孩子的生活和成长却是当今不少父母的问题。据一家广告公司对502名中国成年人进行的调查，60%的父亲表示他们感觉自己没有足够的时间陪孩子，而女性的比例为37%。

"现代父母应该跟孩子建立一种什么样的关系，是继承传统的父子关系，还是提倡平等和互相尊重"是这档节目关注的另一个问题。传统的儒家思想以孝道为先，宣扬孩子顺从父母的意愿，在父母年老时照顾他们。现在中国父母越来越意识到应与孩子讨论并尊重他们的选择，这可能是帮助他们进入现代社会更恰当的方式。

长期以来，女性一直是中国家庭中照顾孩子的主要成员，但是随着越来越多的中国女性走入职场，一些人表示男性必须更加主动地承担家长的职责。自古以来被认为天经地义的"男主外，女主内"的传统观念如今正在慢慢被打破。这种变化也在《爸爸去哪儿》这个节目中反映了出来。中国的新生代父亲似乎更愿意扮演"主内"的角色，分担养育孩子的重任。最近南京师范大学教育科学院的一项关于中学生性别角色观念的调查研究显示：61%的学生反对"男主外，女主内"的观念。他们认为不管男女，谁容易在事业上成功就应该由谁主外，事业上稍弱的一方可以同时兼顾家庭。

讨论题 Discussion

根据课文内容回答下列问题

(Please answer the following questions based on the text)

1. 《爸爸去哪儿》是个什么样的节目？节目里的爸爸是什么样的爸爸？
2. 最近的调查显示，在中国，父亲觉得自己和孩子的关系怎么样？跟你们国家有什么不同？
3. 中国新一代父母的思想和传统的儒家思想有什么不同？
4. 观众看了这个节目后有什么反思？
5. 你对"男主外，女主内"的观念有什么看法？

生词 New Words

	Simplified	Traditional	Pinyin	POS	Definition
1	转换	轉換	zhuǎnhuàn	v.	to change, to transform, to convert
2	各地		gèdì	n.	in all parts of (a country), various regions
3	骆驼	駱駝	luòtuo	n.	camel
4	钓鱼	釣魚	diào yú	v.o.	to go fishing
5	遥远	遙遠	yáoyuǎn	adj.	distant, remote, faraway
6	西南部		xīnánbù	n.	southwest
7	梳头	梳頭	shū tóu	v.o.	to comb one's hair
8	方便面	方便麵	fāngbiànmiàn	n.	instant noodles
9	果腹		guǒfù	v.	to fill the stomach, to satisfy one's hunger
10	真人秀		zhēnrénxiù	n.	reality show
11	相处	相處	xiāngchǔ	v.	to get along (with one another)
12	杂志	雜誌	zázhì	n.	magazine, journal, periodical
13	月份		yuèfèn	n.	month
14	开播	開播	kāibō	v.	to begin to broadcast
15	收视	收視	shōushì	v.	to watch (TV programs)
16	人数	人數	rénshù	n.	number of people
17	为何	為何	wèihé	adv.	why, for what reason
18	追捧		zhuīpěng	v.	to chase after (celebrity or famous people)
19	创意	創意	chuàngyì	n.	creativity, originality, novelty
20	纯真	純真	chúnzhēn	adj.	pure and sincere, naivety, innocence
21	档	檔	dàng	b.f./m(n)	files, archives (eg., for TV programs)
22	新生代		xīnshēngdài	n.	new generation

23	受挫		shòucuò	v.	to be baffled, to be thwarted, to suffer a setback
24	应对	應對	yìngduì	v.	to reply, to answer, to response
25	学前教育	學前教育	xuéqián jiàoyù	n.p.	preschool education, early childhood education
26	副教授		fù jiàoshòu	n.p.	associate professor
27	慈祥		cíxiáng	adj.	(of an old person's bearing and expression) kind and serene
28	温柔	溫柔	wēnróu	adj.	gentle and soft, tender
29	回归	回歸	huíguī	v.	to return, to go back to (the original place)
30	腾	騰	téng	v.	to make room, to clear out, to vacate
31	陪伴		péibàn	v.	to accompany, to keep sb. company
32	时光	時光	shíguāng	n.	times, years, days
33	忽略		hūlüè	v.	to ignore, to neglect
34	继承	繼承	jìchéng	v.	to carry forward, to carry on sb.'s unfinished work, to inherit (legacy of the dead, etc.)
35	父子		fùzǐ	n.	father and son
36	孝道		xiàodào	n.	filial piety
37	宣扬	宣揚	xuānyáng	v.	to publicize, to propagate, to advocate
38	顺从	順從	shùncóng	v.	to be obedient to (sb.), to submit to, to yield to
39	意愿	意願	yìyuàn	n.	wish, desire, aspiration
40	恰当	恰當	qiàdàng	adj.	appropriate, proper, suitable
41	成员	成員	chéngyuán	n.	member
42	承担	承擔	chéngdān	v.	to undertake, to bear, to assume (responsibility, etc.)
43	职责	職責	zhízé	n.	duty, obligation, responsibility
44	自古		zìgǔ	adv.	since ancient times, since antiquity

45	天经地义	天經地義	tiānjīng-dìyì	f.e.	principles of heaven and earth-right and proper, perfectly justified
46	主		zhǔ	v.	to be in charge of
47	分担	分擔	fēndān	v.	to share responsibility for
48	养育	養育	yǎngyù	v.	to bring up, to rear, to foster
49	重任		zhòngrèn	n.	important task, great commitment, heavy responsibility
50	兼顾	兼顧	jiāngù	v.	to deal with two or more things

专有名词 Proper nouns

1	云南	雲南	Yúnnán	Yunnan (province)
2	大西洋月刊		Dàxīyáng Yuèkān	*The Atlantic*
3	北京师范大学	北京師範大學	Běijīng Shīfàn Dàxué	Beijing Normal University
4	李敏谊	李敏誼	Lǐ Mǐnyì	a person's name
5	南京师范大学	南京師範大學	Nánjīng Shīfàn Dàxué	Nanjing Normal University

第7课

北京与伦敦：
雾都治霾浅议

主课文 Main Text

　　21世纪的北京就像是19世纪的伦敦——它们都是在各自时代崛起速度最快的国都，也同样受到雾霾的严重袭击，成为世界上令人注目的"雾都"。

　　让我们先看看雾霾笼罩下的北京：灰蒙蒙的天空，混浊的空气和空中悬浮着的有毒微粒，戴口罩的市民，能见度极低的街道。这样一种令人压抑的景象为什么出现在北京呢？雾霾是多种污染源共同作用的结果。北京及周边地区人口众多、工业密集，煤炭又是主要能源，再加上丘陵环绕的地形，造成了北京空气污染在一年中的某些时期达到或超过危险水平。当污染指数超过了危险水平，就会对人体造成极大的危害。根据世界卫生组织出版的《2010年全球疾病负担研究》，在中国2010年早逝人群中，120万人的死亡与户外空气污染有关。①

---

　　① Particulate Matter (PM) is the term for particles found in the air, including "dust, dirt, soot, smoke, and liquid droplets" that generally come from fossil fuel-burning activities, such as traffic,

我们再看看 19 世纪工业时代的伦敦。令人窒息的烟雾长时间地笼罩着这个城市，直到 20 世纪 50 年代还未散去。"雾都""阴霾""昏暗"等词语常常出现在 19 世纪的英国名著中。查尔斯·狄更斯的小说《荒凉山庄》细致地描述了伦敦的雾："那是一种沁人人心深处的黑暗，是一种铺天盖地的氛围。"当时，供暖的煤炭是烟雾的主要来源。到了 20 世纪中期，工业和车辆的有毒排放物使污染问题更加严重。雾霾给伦敦带来的伤害是巨大的。1952 年的伦敦烟雾事件竟在一周里造成了 4500 人死亡，在几个月内一共夺去了 12000 人的生命。

伦敦的污染时间很长，持续了一个多世纪。如果这个悲剧在北京重演，那对北京将是一场灾难。中国政府已经认识到环境污染的危害性，采取了一系列的应对措施。在 2014 年 APEC 会议期间，北京政府对重度污染的工厂和工程实行限产、停产。同时，北京和周边 8 个城市采取了汽车单双号限行政策。这些措施大大改善了空气质量，北京又重现了蓝天，人们戏称之为"APEC 蓝"。"APEC 蓝"是超常规治理的结果，虽然难以长期持续，却使人们看到了希望。伦敦对雾霾的成功治理也提供了很多值得借鉴的经验。从 1956 年开始，伦敦出台了一系列防止和控制空气污染的法案和措施：限制工业废气排放，减少烟尘和有毒颗粒物；发展公共交通，缩减机动车数量。此外，伦敦还采用清洁能源，并大力发展低碳经济。到了 1975 年，伦敦的雾霾日已由每年几十天减少到了 15 天，1980 年则进一步降到 5 天。北京应该向伦敦学习，让"APEC 蓝"常驻北京。

目前，世界上很多城市都出现了不同程度的雾霾，雾霾已经成为一个世界性的难题。各地区、各个国家需要加强合作，互相学习，采取适当有效的措施，减少污染物的排放，发展和使用清洁能源，那样让雾霾永远散去才有希望。

---

smelting, and metal processing. "Fine" particles smaller than PM2.5 (细颗粒物—diameter of 2.5 micrometers or less, which is approximately 1/30th the average width of a human hair) "are believed to pose the greatest health risks" because of their ability to lodge deeply in the lungs. According to U.S. EPA and AQI criteria, air quality conditions are deadly when the potency of PM2.5 reaches 301-500. For details, please read "Frequent Questions | Fine Particle (PM2.5) Designations | US EPA" by going to the link: http://www3.epa.gov/pmdesignations/faq.htm#0

Lesson 7

北京与伦敦：雾都治霾浅议

讨论题 Discussion

根据课文内容回答下列问题
(Please answer the following questions based on the text)

1. 在作者看来，北京和伦敦这两个城市有哪些相似之处？
2. 北京的雾霾是怎么造成的？它的危害是什么？
3. 人们怎么描述19世纪的伦敦？伦敦的"雾"是怎么形成的？为什么说它给当时的伦敦居民带来的伤害是巨大的？
4. 在2014年APEC会议期间，北京政府已经采取了哪些措施改善北京的空气质量？这些措施有效吗？
5. 伦敦在治理空气污染方面有什么好的经验？
6. 在作者看来，空气污染只是伦敦和北京这两个城市的问题吗？他认为空气污染的问题值得重视吗？为什么？

生词 New Words

1	霾		mái	n.	smog, haze
2	各自		gèzì	pr.	each, respective, oneself
3	崛起		juéqǐ	v.	to rise (as a political force), to rise abruptly
4	袭击	襲擊	xíjī	v.	to attack, to raid
5	注目		zhùmù	v.	to gaze at, to fix one's eyes on
6	笼罩	籠罩	lǒngzhào	v.	to envelop, to shroud, to cover
7	蒙蒙	濛濛	méngméng	r.f.	drizzly, misty
8	天空		tiānkōng	n.	sky, heaven

9	混浊	混濁	hùnzhuó	adj.	muddy, turbid
10	悬浮	懸浮	xuánfú	v.	to float or hang (in the air)
11	毒		dú	n.	poison, toxin
12	微粒		wēilì	n.	particle
13	口罩		kǒuzhào	n.	mask (for breathing or antiseptic purpose)
14	市民		shìmín	n.	resident, townspeople
15	能见度	能見度	néngjiàndù	n.	visibility
16	压抑	壓抑	yāyì	v.	to depress
17	景象		jǐngxiàng	n.	scene, sight (to behold)
18	源		yuán	b.f./n.	source of a river, source, cause
19	周边	周邊	zhōubiān	n.	periphery, surrounding area
20	众多	眾多	zhòngduō	adj.	numerous, many
21	密集		mìjí	adj.	concentrated, crowded together, dense
22	煤炭		méitàn	n.	coal
23	丘陵		qiūlíng	n.	hills
24	环绕	環繞	huánrào	v.	to surround, to encircle
25	地形		dìxíng	n.	topography, landform
26	指数	指數	zhǐshù	n.	index, index number, indicator
27	人体	人體	réntǐ	n.	human body
28	疾病		jíbìng	n.	disease, sickness, ailment
29	逝		shì	b.f.	to die, to pass away
30	人群		rénqún	n.	throng, crowd, multitude
31	死亡		sǐwáng	v.	to die, to pass away
32	户外		hùwài	n.	outdoor

33	窒息		zhìxī	v.	to choke, to suffocate, to asphyxiate
34	烟雾	煙霧	yānwù	n.	smoke, mist, smog
35	阴霾	陰霾	yīnmái	n.	haze
36	昏暗		hūn'àn	adj.	dim, dusky, muddled
37	词语	詞語	cíyǔ	n.	words and expressions, word and phrase
38	名著		míngzhù	n.	masterpiece, classic, famous book
39	荒凉	荒涼	huāngliáng	adj.	bleak and desolate, barren
40	山庄	山莊	shānzhuāng	n.	mountain village, villa, lodge
41	细致	細緻	xìzhì	adj.	meticulous, precise about details, fine
42	描述		miáoshù	v.	to describe; description
43	沁		qìn	v.	to permeate, to percolate, to soak into
44	深处	深處	shēnchù	n.	depth, recess, profundity
45	铺天盖地	鋪天蓋地	pūtiān-gàidì	f.e.	to blot out the sky and cover up the earth
46	氛围	氛圍	fēnwéi	n.	atmosphere
47	中期		zhōngqī	n.	middle period, mid-, mid-term
48	车辆	車輛	chēliàng	n.	vehicle, automobile
49	排放		páifàng	v.	to discharge, to exhaust (gas, etc.); emission
50	物		wù	b.f.	thing, matter, substance
51	竟		jìng	adv.	unexpectedly, actually, to go as far as to
52	持续	持續	chíxù	v.	to last, to continue, to sustain
53	悲剧	悲劇	bēijù	n.	tragedy
54	重演		chóngyǎn	v.	to recur, to repeat
55	灾难	災難	zāinàn	n.	disaster, catastrophe, calamity
56	一系列		yíxìliè	attr.	a series of

57	限产	限產	xiànchǎn	v.	to curtail the production
58	停产	停產	tíngchǎn	v.	to shut down, to suspend production
59	限行		xiànxíng	v.	to have driving curb or vehicle restriction according to the last number of the vehicle plate. For example, the vehicles that have number 9 as the last number on their plates cannot be used on Mondays.
60	大大		dàdà	r.f.	greatly, enormously
61	重现	重現	chóngxiàn	v.	to reappear, to recur
62	蓝天	藍天	lántiān	n.	blue sky
63	称之为	稱之為	chēngzhīwéi	v.p.	to call it..., to be known as
64	常规	常規	chángguī	adj./n.	conventional, common, regular
65	治理		zhìlǐ	v.	to control, to manage
66	借鉴	借鑒	jièjiàn	v.	to draw lessons from, to borrow, to learn from
67	出台	出臺	chū tái	v.o.	to unveil (a policy, measure, etc.), to disclose, to announce
68	法案		fǎ'àn	n.	bill, act, proposed law
69	废气	廢氣	fèiqì	n.	waste (exhaust) gas
70	烟尘	煙塵	yānchén	n.	smoke and dust
71	颗粒	顆粒	kēlì	n.	anything small and roundish, particle
72	缩减	縮減	suōjiǎn	v.	to reduce, to cut
73	机动车	機動車	jīdòngchē	n.	motor or automotive vehicle
74	清洁	清潔	qīngjié	adj.	clean, unpolluted
75	大力		dàlì	adv.	vigorously, energetically, to go all out
76	碳		tàn	n.	carbon
77	驻	駐	zhù	v.	to stay, to be stationed
78	难题	難題	nántí	n.	difficult problem, tough question

第7课 北京与伦敦：雾都治霾浅议
Lesson 7

专有名词 Proper nouns

1	伦敦	倫敦	Lúndūn	London
2	世界卫生组织	世界衛生組織	Shìjiè Wèishēng Zǔzhī	World Health Organization
3	查尔斯·狄更斯	查爾斯·狄更斯	Chá'ěrsī Dígēngsī	Charles Dickens

词语注释 Vocabulary and Grammar Explanations

语素 (morphemes)

-源： 来源。(source; cause)

> 例 污染源　感染源　货源　财源　来源　水源　资源　能源　根源

-物： 事物；东西。(things; objects; matter)

> 例 排放物　颗粒物　污染物　宝物　读物　财物　动物　废物　怪物

-性： 后缀。(suffix that indicates quality, scope, or method; property; quality)

> 例 危害性　世界性　积极性　决定性　主动性　普遍性　艺术性
> 戏剧性　创造性　排他性　思想性　局限性　时间性　连续性
> 可塑性　记性　弹性　忘性

-产： 生产。(production)

> 例 停产　限产　多产　减产　增产　超产　投产　生产　破产　脱产
> 欠产

超-：超出范围。(super-; ultra-; extra-; hyper-)

 超常规　超现实　超自然　超级　超薄　超长　超饱和　超大型
超低空　超高速　超音速　超高温　超强　超声波　超小型

四字格和成语 (four-character expressions and idioms)

● **令人注目**

令：使，让。注目：视线集中在一点上。指引起别人的注意或重视。("令" means "to make, to let, to cause" while "注目" means "to focus on one point", so the whole idiom means "noticeable, eye-catching, attracting one's attention".)

 (1) 21 世纪的北京就像是 19 世纪的伦敦，成为世界上令人注目的"雾都"。
(2) 英国银行的衰落，或许是发达国家中最令人注目的变化。
(3) 马航事件中中国应对突发事件的能力令人注目。
(4) 在一个由中年男性主导的专业领域，这个年轻女孩子格外令人注目。

● **令人压抑**

使人感到压抑。(depressing; to make one feel depressed)

(1) 这样一种令人压抑的景象为什么出现在北京呢？
(2) 这是一部令人压抑到窒息的电影。
(3) 这个星期，看看窗外的天，感受吹拂的风，似乎一切都正常。可是听到的看到的，却全是一些令人压抑的事情。
(4) 我特别不喜欢城市里那些令人压抑的高楼大厦，更不喜欢那喧闹的街市。

120

- **令人窒息**

  让人喘不过气来。(to make it hard for one to breathe, to the point of suffocation; breathless)

  (1) 这组照片展示了冰岛令人窒息的美丽风光。
  (2) 工厂外环境污染非常严重，臭味令人窒息。
  (3) 我们的篮球队就输在对手那种令人窒息的防守上。
  (4) 六年的感情付诸东流，心情压抑难过得令人窒息。

- **铺天盖地**

  形容来势很猛，声势大。(literally, "to blot out the sky and cover up the earth"; overspread; to describe a situation in which a strong force comes with great momentum)

  (1) 那是一种沁入人心深处的黑暗，是一种铺天盖地的氛围。
  (2) 美国大选会带来一场铺天盖地的广告潮，特别是在电视上。
  (3) 下午先下雨，然后是冰雹铺天盖地地砸下来。
  (4) 电子商务、电子银行、电子邮件、电子税务、电子娱乐等铺天盖地，几乎整个世界都被"e"化了。

虚词及句型 (function words and sentence patterns)

- **与……有关** to have sth. to do with; to relate to; regarding; relevant

  固定搭配，表示跟人或者事物有关系，否定形式是"与……无关"。

"有关"一般用在句末作谓语，不能带宾语。

This is a fixed expression indicating various relationships between people and things. Its negative form is"与……无关"."有关" usually occurs at the end of a sentence to function as its predicate, so it cannot take an object.

(1) 根据世界卫生组织出版的《2010年全球疾病负担报告》，在中国2010年早逝人群中，120万人的死亡与户外空气污染有关。

(2) 一个人的所作所为都与他所受的教育有关。

(3) 下周我们将讨论与考试有关的全部细节。

(4) 暴力案件的上升与失业的增加有关。

- **使　to make sth. become; to cause to be or become; to enable**

动词，表示致使，"让"或"叫"的书面语形式。除了祈使句以外，它们可以同"使"互换。"使"须用在兼语句中，不能独立使用。

"使" is a verb that means "to cause", and it is the written form of "让" or "叫"."让" or "叫" can be replaced by "使" except in imperative sentences. "使" must be used in a pivotal sentence, and it cannot be used independently.

(1) 到了20世纪中期，工业和车辆的有毒排放物使污染问题更加严重。

(2) 他的一些举动经常使我们感到奇怪和不快。

(3) 这件事使我们对他失去了信任。

(4) 奥运会的胜利**使**全国人民大受鼓舞。

- **大大**　greatly; enormously; tremendously

副词，表示程度很深或数量很大。用于修饰双音节的动词和动词性词组，后边可加"地"。

This is an adverb that indicates a higher degree of depth or quantity. It is used to modify disyllabic verbs or verb phrases, and can be followed by "地".

(1) 这些措施**大大**改善了空气质量，北京又重现了蓝天，人们戏称之为"APEC蓝"。
(2) 他的所做所为**大大**超出了我们的想象。
(3) 今天考试的成功**大大**地提高了他的自信心。
(4) 在电子商务时代，人们的购物习惯已经**大大**改变了。

- **称……为……**　too call…as…

称：动词，意思是"叫、称呼"。"称……为……"意思是"把……称为"或者"把……叫作……"。用于书面语。

This is a verb that means "to call"."称……为……" means "把……称为" or "把……叫作……" (to call…as…). It is used in written language.

(1) 这些措施大大改善了空气质量，北京又重现了蓝天，人们戏**称**之**为**"APEC蓝"。
(2) 作者在书前写的话**称**之**为**"前言"或者"序言"。

(3) 3D电影，我们也称它为立体电影，越来越受人们的喜爱。

(4) 琳达和大卫结婚后买了一个小公寓，布置得漂漂亮亮的，他们称之为"爱巢"。

- **之 it; him; her**

代词，大致相当于宾语位置上的"他、它"，代替人或事物。文言词，用于书面语。

This is a pronoun that is used as an object to substitute for a person or a thing. It is a classical Chinese word, thus used in written language.

 (1) 这些措施大大改善了空气质量，北京又重现了蓝天，人们戏称之为"APEC蓝"。

(2) 事情就这样过去了，但是随之而来的安静令人窒息。

(3) 消息传来，大家都为之高兴，为之欢呼。

(4) 这种事发生很多次了，我们不能再听之任之了。

- **虽然……却 although…(but)…**

"虽然"是连词，表示让步，"却"表示转折，是副词。用在表示转折关系的复句里，表示先让一步，承认或肯定某一事，然后说出不受限制的另一事。

"虽然" is a conjunction word and indicates concession; "却" is an adverb and means "turn" or "transition". Together they are used in a transitional complex sentence in which a concession is made first, namely an event or a thing being accepted, and then other things or events will happen.

> (1) "APEC蓝"是超常规治理的结果，**虽然**难以长期持续，**却**使人们看到了希望。
> (2) 她**虽然**工作很忙，**却**很关心我的学习。
> (3) 这个菜**虽然**不好看，**却**很好吃。
> (4) 她**虽然**貌不惊人，**却**十分引人注目。

● **难以**　difficult to; hard to

副词，意思是不容易，不易于做什么，后面跟动词，多用于书面语。

This is an adverb indicating "it is not easy to do something". It is followed by a verb and often used in written language.

> (1) "APEC蓝"是超常规治理的结果，虽然**难以**长期持续，却使人们看到了希望。
> (2) 不努力学好汉字是**难以**学好中文的。
> (3) 他的有些观点非常偏激，实在令人**难以**接受。
> (4) 这个电影有一种**难以**抗拒的吸引力，我不知看了多少遍。

● **此外**　besides; in addition; as well as; aside from

连词，指除了上面说的事物或者情况之外的。"此外"后边可跟肯定形式或者否定形式。后边如果是否定形式，表示除了所说的，没有别的。主要功能是连接分句和句子，用于书面语。

This is a conjunction word that indicates there is something else in addition to what was mentioned previously. It can be followed by either an affirmative expression or a negative expression. If it is followed by a negative expression, in addition to its conjunction role, it emphasizes that there are no additional options to those previously mentioned. Its main function is connecting clauses, and it is mostly used in written language.

(1) 从1956年开始，伦敦限制工业废气排放，减少烟尘和有毒颗粒物；发展公共交通，缩减机动车数量。此外，伦敦还采用清洁能源，并大力发展低碳经济。

(2) 要让自己变得更好，此外别无他法。

(3) 该节目这次邀请了很多明星加入。此外，还从国外租用了最先进的音像设备。

(4) 业余时间他只喜欢摄影和爬山，此外没有什么兴趣爱好。

- **则 however; on the other hand**

副词，表示因果或者情理上的顺承关系，有时也有转折的语气，相当于"却"。文言词，用于书面语。

This is an adverb that indicates a cause-effect relationship or reasoning. Sometimes it means "turn" or "change" and is used in the second clause of a complex sentence to form a contrast with the first clause. It has the same meaning as "却". It is a classical Chinese word, thus used in written language.

(1) 到了1975年，伦敦的雾霾日已由每年几十天减少到了15天，1980年则进一步降到5天。

(2) 这种鸟夏天迁到这里，冬天则飞到温暖的南方过冬。

(3) 他平时对任何事都满不在乎的样子，对这件事则非常关心。

(4) 房价的上涨对于有钱的大款来说不算什么，但对于买不起房，靠租房的底层打工者来说，则是一场灾难。

副课文 Supplementary Text

太平洋里的"塑料岛"

2008年初,一份美国的调查报告指出,北太平洋出现了一个343万平方公里的"塑料岛"。它由塑料垃圾组成,面积相当于6个法国。到2030年,它的面积还要增加9倍。更可怕的是,塑料垃圾会进入动物体内,然后扩大到整个生物圈。有人甚至说:"我们吃的鱼,也许就是那些塑料垃圾的另一种形式。"据统计,2007年全世界用掉12000亿个塑料袋,一个塑料袋从生产出来到被扔掉,平均只有12－20分钟。

世界卫生组织的一份报告指出,空气、水等环境污染导致全球每年有300万5岁以下儿童死亡。当今世界由于工业化、气候变化、化学产品应用等,使儿童的健康受到了威胁。儿童缺乏自我保护的能力,成了环境污染最大的受害者。

科技的发展提高了人类的生活水平,但也给我们的地球造成了严重的破坏。环境污染已成为一个全球性问题,如果这一问题得不到解决,人类将面临毁灭的危险。在过去很长时间里,人们从没感觉到环境保护的重要性。随着现代工业的发展,环境问题越来越突出,例如温室效应、臭氧层破坏、垃圾问题、水污染以及生态危机等等。

有人说:要想发展经济,一定会污染环境;要想保护环境,就得牺牲经济发展速度。现代化必须经过传统工业化这一阶段,可以先污染后治理。只要有了钱,什么都好办。英美等发达国家随着人均GDP的增长,环境污染也在减轻。

有人则认为,西方国家"先污染后治理",这不是什么经验,而是教训。环境保护和发展经济是鸡和蛋的关系,如果以污染环境为代价来发展经济,等于杀鸡取卵。经济发展的目的是提高人们的生活水平,使人类的生存环境更加美好。如果环境破坏了,即使经济发展上去,也是没有意义的。

经济发展和环境保护应该谁先谁后?这是世界上每一个国家都不能回避的问题。很多发达国家以前付出了以环境污染换取经济发展的代价,所以现在很重视保护环境，因为他们认识到"我们只有一个地球"。

德国政府对企业进行检查，制定各项法律控制温室气体排放。在 2002－2003 年期间，德国一共调查了 3909 家企业，有效地减少了空气污染。

日本对污染严重的企业进行处罚，同时鼓励人们购买绿色产品，没有环保标志的产品在市场上已经不受欢迎了。日本的工业污染从上个世纪 60 年代到 70 年代逐渐减轻，到上世纪 80 年代就已经基本得到控制。

美国政府用了大量资金进行环境治理，并实行了排污权交易，而且数量是有严格控制的，这一措施非常有效。

新加坡则重点治理垃圾，经过 8 年的努力，440 万人口的全部垃圾每天被焚烧后运到一个小岛。令人惊讶的是，这座小岛上生长着漂亮的植物和动物，吸引了很多游客来旅游。

讨论题 Discussion

根据课文内容回答下列问题
(Please answer the following questions based on the text)

1. 北太平洋的"塑料岛"是怎么形成的？这个"塑料岛"对生物圈的危害是什么？
2. 环境污染给儿童带来了什么样的威胁？儿童为什么最容易成为污染的受害者？
3. 常见的环境污染都有哪些？这些污染是怎么造成的？其严重性是什么？
4. 大家对经济发展和环境治理的关系是怎么看的？有哪几种观点？目前的主流观点是什么？
5. 近年来哪些国家在环境保护和治理上做出了成功的努力？请举例说明。
6. 在你看来，作为一个普通公民，我们应该在保护环境和环境治理上做些什么？

Lesson 7

第 7 课　北京与伦敦：雾都治霾浅议

生词 New Words

1	平方公里		píngfāng gōnglǐ	m(n)	square kilometer
2	组成	組成	zǔchéng	v.	to form, to compose; formation
3	相当于	相當於	xiāngdāngyú	v.p.	to be equivalent to, to correspond to
4	体内	體內	tǐnèi	attr.	the interior of the body
5	生物圈		shēngwùquān	n.	biosphere, ecosphere
6	威胁	威脅	wēixié	v.	to threaten; threat
7	受害		shòu hài	v.o.	to suffer injury or damage, to fall victim
9	毁灭	毀滅	huǐmiè	v.	to destroy, to exterminate, to demolish
10	温室	溫室	wēnshì	n.	greenhouse, conservatory
11	效应	效應	xiàoyìng	n.	effect (e.g., greenhouse effect)
12	臭氧层	臭氧層	chòuyǎngcéng	n.	ozone layer, ozonosphere
13	生态	生態	shēngtài	n.	ecology
14	等等		děngděng	r.f.	and so on, etc.
15	人均		rénjūn	n.	per capita, average for individuals
16	代价	代價	dàijià	n.	price, cost
17	杀鸡取卵	殺雞取卵	shājī-qǔluǎn	f.e.	to kill the hen to get the eggs, to kill the goose that lays the golden eggs, to be after only immediate interests
18	生存		shēngcún	v.	to exist, to survive, to live
19	回避		huíbì	v.	to avoid, to evade, to dodge
20	付出		fùchū	v.	to pay, to expend
21	换取	換取	huànqǔ	v.	to exchange sth. for, to get in return
22	气体	氣體	qìtǐ	n.	gas

23	处罚	處罰	chǔfá	v.	to penalize, to punish
24	购买	購買	gòumǎi	v.	to buy, to purchase
25	环保	環保	huánbǎo	n.	environmental protection
26	污	汙	wū	b.f.	dirty, filthy
27	交易		jiāoyì	v./n.	to trade; transaction, business
28	焚烧	焚燒	fénshāo	v.	to burn, to set on fire
29	惊讶	驚訝	jīngyà	adj.	surprised, astonished
30	游客	遊客	yóukè	n.	tourist, traveler, visitors

专有名词 Proper nouns

| 1 | 太平洋 | Tàipíng Yáng | the Pacific Ocean |
| 2 | 新加坡 | Xīnjiāpō | Singapore |

第8课

美国校园为何枪击案频发

主课文 Main Text

2007年4月16日，美国弗吉尼亚理工大学发生恶性校园枪击案，造成33人死亡。2012年12月14日上午，美国康涅狄格州纽镇桑迪胡克小学发生枪击案，造成26人丧生，其中包括20名6－7岁的一年级学生，6名教师死亡。2014年1月21日，美国中西部印第安纳州普渡大学校园发生枪击事件，造成一名男学生死亡。这一连串的枪击案让人们感到震惊，同时也暴露出美国在枪支管理方面的问题。据美国司法部估计，美国人现在拥有2.35亿支枪，几乎达到人手一枪；每年美国发生枪击事件多达100多万起。美国是一个枪支泛滥的国家，美国宪法赋予公民随身携带枪支的权利和自由，加上暴力文化盛行，导致暴力犯罪和枪击案数量连年持续不下。

枪支泛滥是造成美国校园枪击案频发的"导火索"。首先，美国枪支管理的松懈为人们可以轻易获得枪支提供了条件。在美国，注册的武器销售点多达10万个，比麦当劳在全世界的分店还多。年满18岁的年轻人只要无犯罪记录，就可以买枪。其次，由于美国国会对于是否制定严格的枪支管理法案争论不休，枪支泛滥的问题始终得不到解决。美国全国步枪协会一直反对加强枪支管理，为此他们对国会议员大力游说，阻挠立法。在2004年的总统选举中，全国步枪协会向共和党捐助了140万美元，帮助布什连任。他们这样做是希望执政的共和党能继续支持他们的立场。由此看来，在美国实行严格的枪支管理政策，前景不太乐观。

暴力文化是造成枪击案层出不穷的另一个原因。美国传媒有美化暴力的倾向。在宣扬暴力的影片中，那些所谓伸张正义的杀手，被当作英雄加以歌颂。他们往往不受任何法律的制约，把暴力作为解决问题最有效的方式。这对于是非分辨力还不太强的孩子来说，会有很强的蛊惑作用。据美国《国际先驱论坛报》报道，一个美国青少年18岁之前在各种传媒上能看到4万起谋杀案和20万起其他暴力行为。传媒中反映出来的暴力文化使孩子们错误地认为，使用暴力可以解决复杂的问题，发泄愤怒的方法就是开枪杀人。影视片中的枪杀情节比比皆是，孩子们耳濡目染，就相信枪能"解决"一切。

除了枪支泛滥和暴力文化的流行，在学校和家庭中缺乏道德教育也是校园枪击案频发的原因之一。科罗拉多州校园枪击案的幸存者斯科特就认为，过去美国的学校还注重道德教育，但如今学校基本上就只有一个目标，那就是学习成绩，完全轻视了道德的培养。这就容易使孩子们缺乏是非观念，走上杀人行凶的犯罪道路。

总之，近年频频发生的校园枪击案，是与枪支泛滥和暴力文化密不可分的。如果不控制枪支、净化媒体和加强学生的道德教育，校园枪击惨剧还将在美国不断上演。奥巴马强调说，不要忘记"真正的改变并不是来自华盛顿"，而是来自美国民众，因此呼吁美国民众携手共同推动控枪立法。

Lesson 8
第 8 课
美国校园为何枪击案频发

讨论题 Discussion

根据课文内容回答下列问题
(Please answer the following questions based on the text)

1. 近年来，在美国校园出现的什么现象让人们感到震惊？
2. 在作者看来，造成美国枪支泛滥的原因有哪些？美国全国步枪协会在枪支管理这个问题上的立场是什么？
3. 为什么说美国传媒有美化暴力的倾向？暴力文化跟频频发生的枪击案有什么样的关系？
4. 作者认为学校和家庭对青少年的暴力行为和校园枪击案的频发负有责任吗？你是怎么看的？
5. 在作者看来，应该怎么做才能减少和控制校园枪击案的发生？美国总统奥巴马对这个问题怎么看？

生词 New Words

1	击	擊	jī	b.f.	to strike, to attack
2	频	頻	pín	adv./b.f.	frequently, repeatedly
3	恶性	惡性	èxìng	adj./attr.	malignant, pernicious, vicious
4	丧生	喪生	sàng shēng	v.o.	to lose one's life
5	中西部		zhōngxībù	n.	midwest
6	一连串	一連串	yīliánchuàn	attr.	a succession of (actions, issues, etc.), a series of, a chain of (events, etc.)
7	震惊	震驚	zhènjīng	v./adj.	to shock, to astonish; surprised, shocked

8	暴露		bàolù	v.	to expose, to reveal
9	枪支	槍支	qiāngzhī	n.	firearms, rifles, guns
10	拥有	擁有	yōngyǒu	v.	to possess, to have, to own
11	宪法	憲法	xiànfǎ	n.	constitution (of a country)
12	公民		gōngmín	n.	citizen
13	随身	隨身	suíshēn	adj./attr.	(take) with one (self)
14	携带	攜帶	xiédài	v.	to carry, to take along, to bring along
15	暴力		bàolì	n.	violence, force
16	盛行		shèngxíng	v.	to prevail, to be very popular
17	犯罪		fàn zuì	v.o.	to commit crime or offense
18	连年	連年	liánnián	adv.	in consecutive year
19	导火索	導火索	dǎohuǒsuǒ	n.	blasting fuse
20	松懈	鬆懈	sōngxiè	adj.	inattentive, lax; to be slack
21	轻易	輕易	qīngyì	adv.	easily, simply
22	注册	註冊	zhùcè	v.	to register, to enroll
23	分店		fēndiàn	n.	branch (of a shop)
24	国会	國會	guóhuì	n.	parliament (UK), congress (US)
25	不休		bùxiū	v.	do not end, endlessly, ceaselessly
26	议员	議員	yìyuán	n.	senator
27	游说	遊說	yóushuì	v.	to lobby, to go about selling an idea
28	阻挠	阻撓	zǔnáo	v.	to obstruct, to thwart, to stand in the way
29	立法		lì fǎ	v.o.	to make (or enact) laws, to legislate
30	捐助		juānzhù	v./n.	to donate; donation

#	简体	繁體	Pinyin	词性	English
31	连任	連任	liánrèn	v.	to renew one's term of office
32	执政	執政	zhí zhèng	v.o.	to be in power, to be in office
33	前景		qiánjǐng	n.	foreground, prospect
34	层出不穷	層出不窮	céngchū-bùqióng	f.e.	to come out one after the other
35	传媒	傳媒	chuánméi	n.	media
36	美化		měihuà	v.	to beautify, to prettify, to glorify
37	宣扬	宣揚	xuānyáng	v.	to publicize, to propagate, to advocate
38	影片		yǐngpiàn	n.	film, movie
39	伸张正义	伸張正義	shēnzhāng zhèngyì	f.e.	to uphold justice
40	杀手	殺手	shāshǒu	n.	profession killer
41	歌颂	歌頌	gēsòng	v.	to sing the praises of, to extol, to eulogize
42	制约	制約	zhìyuē	v.	to restrict, to constraint, to restrain
43	是非		shìfēi	n.	right and wrong
44	分辨		fēnbiàn	v.	to distinguish, to differentiate
45	蛊惑	蠱惑	gǔhuò	v.	to bewitch, to delude
46	谋杀	謀殺	móushā	v.	to murder
47	发泄	發洩	fāxiè	v.	to let off, to vent
48	影视	影視	yǐngshì	n.	film and television
49	枪杀	槍殺	qiāngshā	v.	to shoot dead
50	情节	情節	qíngjié	n.	plot, scenario
51	比比皆是		bǐbǐ-jiēshì	f.e.	to be found or seen everywhere
52	耳濡目染		ěrrú-mùrǎn	f.e.	to be influenced by what one constantly sees and hears
53	州		zhōu	n.	state

54	幸存	倖存	xìngcún	v.	to survive
55	轻视	輕視	qīngshì	v.	to despise, to look down on
56	行凶	行兇	xíng xiōng	v.o.	to do violence, to assault
57	总之	總之	zǒngzhī	conj.	in a word, in short, in brief
58	频频	頻頻	pínpín	adv./r.f.	repeatedly, again and again, frequently
59	密不可分		mìbùkěfēn	f.e.	inseparable
60	净化	淨化	jìnghuà	v.	to purify, to purge
61	惨剧	慘劇	cǎnjù	n.	tragedy, calamity, disaster
62	上演		shàngyǎn	v.	to stage, to perform
63	民众	民眾	mínzhòng	n.	masses, common people
64	呼吁	呼籲	hūyù	v.	to appeal, to call on
65	携手	攜手	xié shǒu	v.o.	to be jointly engaged in, to cooperate

专有名词 Proper nouns

1	弗吉尼亚理工大学	弗吉尼亞理工大學	Fújíníyà Lǐgōng Dàxué	Virginia Tech (Virginia Polytechnic Institute and State University)
2	康涅狄格州		Kāngnièdígé Zhōu	Connecticut
3	纽镇	紐鎮	Niǔzhèn	Newtown
4	桑迪胡克		Sāngdíhúkè	Sandy Hook (school name)
5	印第安纳州		Yìndì'ānnà Zhōu	Indiana
6	普渡大学	普渡大學	Pǔdù Dàxué	Purdue University
7	司法部		Sīfǎ Bù	Department of Justice
8	麦当劳	麥當勞	Màidāngláo	McDonald's

9	全国步枪协会	全國步槍協會	Quánguó Bùqiāng Xiéhuì	National Rifle Association
10	共和党	共和黨	Gònghédǎng	Republican Party
11	布什		Bùshí	George Walker Bush
12	国际先驱论坛报	國際先驅論壇報	Guójì Xiānqū Lùntán Bào	International Herald Tribune
13	科罗拉多州	科羅拉多州	Kēluólāduō Zhōu	Colorado
14	斯科特		Sīkētè	Scott
15	华盛顿	華盛頓	Huáshèngdùn	Washington, D.C.

词语注释 Vocabulary and Grammar Explanations

语素 (morphemes)

-案/案-：案子，案例。(case)

> 例 谋杀案　枪杀案　杀人案　投毒案　纵火案　重案　个案
> 　　本案　奇案　案例　案情

-满：达到。(to reach; to achieve)

> 例 年满　期满　刑满　服满　任满　人满

-力/力-：力量，能力

    1.力量。(power; strength; force)

> 例 暴力　无力　武力　体力　力气

137

2. 能力。(ability; capacity; competence)

> 例　分辨力　分析力　智力　听力　脑力　生殖力　消化力

-者：指某种人。(suffix used for the person who does sth., or who is in certain profession)

> 例　幸存者　记者　学者　长者　智者　老者　勇者　弱者　强者
> 　　发起者　肇事者　逃避者

-视：看。

1. 看，具体。(concrete usages: to look at, watch, or view things)

> 例　近视　远视　仰视　俯视　斜视　透视

2. 看待，抽象。(abstract usages: to regard; to treat)

> 例　轻视　重视　忽视　小视　短视　无视　正视　歧视

四字格和成语 (four-character expressions and idioms)

● 人手一~

　　人人都有，或者人人都拿着。数量多的意思。(everyone has something, or everyone carries something; usually means a high quantity)

> 例　人手一枪　人手一册　人手一台　人手一机　人手一球　人手一技
> 　　人手一包　人手一证

> 例　(1) 美国人现在拥有 2.35 亿支枪，几乎达到人手一枪。

138

(2) 这本书对考研很有帮助，我们班的学生几乎人手一册。

(3) 这个中学给所有的老师提供笔记本电脑，做到了人手一机。

(4) 这个中学大力开展体育运动，老师们人手一球，一下课就组织学生们打球、踢球。

- ~~不休

不停止，不罢休的意思。(to not stop; to not give up)

例 争论不休　争吵不休　喋喋不休　征战不休　连年不休

例 (1) 美国国会对于是否制定严格的枪支管理法案争论不休。

(2) 这对夫妻感情不好，时常为一点儿小事争吵不休。

(3) 她是个话痨，一说起来就喋喋不休。

(4) 阿富汗是个连年征战不休的国家。

- 层出不穷

重复，接连不断地出现，没有穷尽。(to emerge one after another; to emerge endlessly)

例 (1) 暴力文化是造成枪击案层出不穷的另一个原因。

(2) 电脑业发展得很快，近年来新技术层出不穷。

(3) 这条路长年失修，几年来交通事故层出不穷。

(4) 在明清两朝，中国的江南一带人才辈出，层出不穷。

- 比比皆是

意思是到处都是，非常常见。多用在书面表达上。("can be found everywhere"; usually used in written expression)

(1) 影视片中的枪杀情节比比皆是，孩子们耳濡目染，就相信枪能"解决"一切。
(2) 现在的年轻人结婚离婚都很草率，闪婚闪离的情况比比皆是。
(3) 战争爆发以后，逃难者比比皆是。
(4) 当今商业行为早已渗透到人们的生活中，商业广告比比皆是。

- **耳濡目染**

耳朵经常听到，眼睛经常看到，不知不觉地受到影响。(to be influenced by what one constantly sees and hears)

 (1) 影视片中的枪杀情节比比皆是，孩子们耳濡目染，就相信枪能"解决"一切。
(2) 父母对孩子的影响常常是耳濡目染的。
(3) 她从小就跟着妈妈看戏，耳濡目染几十年，自己也变成了一个戏迷。
(4) 由于家庭的耳濡目染，他热爱音乐并且琴艺过人。

- **密不可分**

意思是十分紧密，不可分割。(interwoven; inseparable)

 (1) 近年频频发生的校园枪击案，是与枪支泛滥和暴力文化密不可分的。
(2) 经济的发展与政治的稳定总是密不可分的。
(3) 一个人的学习成果与其努力的程度密不可分。
(4) 中国近年来的经济发展跟其政策的宽容开放密不可分。

虚词及句型 (function words and sentence patterns)

● **其中 among (which, them, etc.); in (which, it, etc.); inside**

方位词，意思是"那里面"，指处所、范围。这是个特殊的方位词，只能单用，不能加在名词的后头。

This is a localizer that means "among it/them" and is usually used for location and scope. It can only be used alone and is unable to follow a noun.

(1) 2012年12月14日上午，美国康涅狄格州纽镇桑迪胡克小学发生枪击案，造成26人丧生，**其中**包括20名6－7岁的一年级学生、6名教师。

(2) 这个班上有30个学生，**其中**一半是留学生。

(3) 他们结婚才半年就离婚了，**其中**的原因却无人得知。

(4) 每年夏天都有很多大学生志愿到贫穷的山区去支教，**其中**有一半是来自大城市的学生。

● **据 according to; on the grounds of**

介词，依据。常见的形式有：1) 据+动词（统计、估计、估算、报道、分析）；2) 据+小句。

This is a preposition that means "according to". The usual forms include: 1) "据" + verbs (such as "统计","估计","估算","报道","分析"); 2) "据" + short sentences.

(1) **据**美国《国际先驱论坛报》报道，一个美国青少年18岁之前在各种传媒上能看到4万起谋杀案和20万起其他暴力行为。

(2) **据**统计，这个城市的亚裔人口占人口总数的四分之一。

(3) 据分析，今年北京的房价可能会下跌。
(4) 据医生说，他的病很快就会好的。

- 加上 plus; add on

  动词，意思是：加，外加。

  This is a verb that means "add; plus; with the addition of".

(1) 美国宪法赋予公民随身携带枪支的权利和自由，加上暴力文化盛行，导致暴力犯罪和枪击案数量连年持续不下。
(2) 最近他工作太忙，常常缺觉，加上很少运动，体质越来越差。
(3) 她认为自己的成功是由于勤奋加上一点儿运气。
(4) 这两天的气温达到摄氏30多度，加上潮湿，热得让人透不过气来。

- 为 for

  介词，表示原因、目的。可加"了、着"。"为了""为着"可在主语前。

  This is a preposition used to indicate the objective and purpose of or provide the reason for the following clause. "为" can be followed by "了" or "着", and when it does so, the combination can be placed before the subject.

(1) 美国枪支管理的松懈为人们可以轻易获得枪支提供了条件。
(2) 医生应该为病人着想。
(3) 小明被哈佛大学录取了，父母都为他高兴。
(4) 为了学好中文，他到中国留学了一年。
(5) 为着完成这个月的盈利指标，全公司的职员最近都在加班。

- **为此** to this end; for this reason; for this purpose

固定搭配，"为"表示原因或者目的；"此"指代前面所指的那个原因或者目的。

This is a fixed expression. "为" indicates a certain reason or objective, and "此" refers to the reason or objective mentioned earlier or in the first clause.

（1）美国全国步枪协会一直反对加强枪支管理，为此他们对国会议员大力游说，阻挠立法。
（2）姐姐找到了一份理想的工作，我们全家都为此感到高兴。
（3）他从小就梦想成为一名钢琴演奏家。为此，他付出了巨大的努力。
（4）欧洲各国在接受叙利亚难民的问题上意见不一致。大家为此争论不休。

- **加以**

助动词，用在双音节动词前，表示如何对待或处理前面所提到的事物。

This is an auxiliary verb, usually used before disyllabic verbs, that indicates how to treat or deal with previously mentioned things.

加以论证　加以讨论　加以思考　加以说明
加以统计　加以批判　加以分析

（1）在宣扬暴力的影片中，那些所谓伸张正义的杀手，被当作英雄加以歌颂。
（2）他收集了两年的资料，对研究的课题加以论证。
（3）你的这个结论是怎么得出来的？请你加以说明。
（4）这篇论文从几个方面对北京的雾霾问题加以分析，并且提出了一些改善的建议和措施。

副课文 Supplementary Text

美国人如何看枪支管制

美国是一个有三亿多人口的国家，可是民间却拥有两亿多各种枪支，各类枪击血案频发早已成为美国社会的痼疾。法律允许美国人持有枪支，但是美国人却为此付出了惨痛的代价。对枪支问题，美国人到底是怎么想的呢？

美国经历了殖民开拓、独立战争、西部大开发、地方自治与自卫。在这个历史背景下，拥枪被普遍认为是美国人自由、人权、自卫的价值观体现。美国社会首先强调的是个人权利和个人价值，而枪，恰恰是体现个人权利的重要工具。因此，大部分的美国人还是赞成私有枪支的。全国步枪协会主席基恩、首席执行官拉皮埃尔等人一再申明，是人而不是枪造成了枪击惨案，因而仅对枪支进行管理不是治本之策。他们的逻辑是，如果人人拥有枪支，这个社会将会更加安全。科罗拉多州电影院枪击惨案发生时，如果现场观众有枪，就会当场制止凶手行凶。如果桑迪胡克小学教师有枪的话，也不会使那么多孩子丧生。因此，阻止持枪行凶的唯一办法是人人都有枪。他们还认为解决美国枪击案应从人的精神健康护理入手，而不是发生枪击案后便高喊禁枪。

在美国，关于枪支问题的辩论主要集中于如何控枪，而不是是否禁枪。皮尤研究中心跟踪调查美国人对持枪的看法已经有二十年，调查的核心是保护公民的持枪权与控制枪支的拥有权哪个更重要，而是否应该禁枪从来没有被关注过。调查数据显示，目前，拥护持枪权的人数和提倡枪支管制的人数各占一半。美国人对枪支的态度至今没有根本分歧，拥枪仍有较为深厚的民意基础。拥枪派极力宣扬宪法修正案中的拥枪权，拥枪组织有着强大的影响力，尤其是针对国会的游说能力。比如，美国全国步枪协会会员规模已突破四百五十万人。好莱坞"硬汉"布鲁斯·威利斯等明星是其代言人。里根、肯尼迪、尼克松等八位美国总统也曾是会员。2004年，这个组织对反对国会延长"攻击性武器联邦禁令"起到了重要的作用。美国的控枪之路将如何走难以预料。但无论最终哪一种观点占上风，美国的民意将会是决定性的因素。

Lesson 8
第8课 美国校园为何枪击案频发

讨论题 Discussion

根据课文内容回答下列问题
(Please answer the following questions based on the text):

1. 在历史上，美国人对私有枪支的态度是什么？为什么？
2. 全国步枪协会认为应该怎样解决枪击案频发的问题？为什么？
3. 根据调查结果，保护公民的持枪权与控制枪支的拥有权哪个更重要？为什么？
4. 对美国人拥有枪支的权利，你是支持还是反对？为什么？
5. 在你看来，解决美国持枪犯罪的问题需要从哪些方面着手？

生词 New Words

1	管制		guǎnzhì	v.	to control
2	早已		zǎoyǐ	ad.p.	long ago, for a long time, previously
3	痼疾		gùjí	n.	chronic illness
4	持有		chíyǒu	v.	to hold (passport, views, etc.)
5	惨痛	惨痛	cǎntòng	adj.	agonizing, grievous, painful
6	殖民		zhímín	v.	to establish a colony, to colonize
7	独立战争	獨立戰爭	dúlì zhànzhēng	n.p.	civil war
8	自治		zìzhì	v.	to exercise autonomy; self-government
9	自卫	自衛	zìwèi	v.	to defend oneself; self-defense
10	拥	擁	yōng	v./b.f.	to possess; to hold in one's arms, to embrace

11	人权	人權	rénquán	n.	human rights
12	恰恰		qiàqià	adv.	coincidentally, exactly
13	大部分		dàbùfen	n.	greater part, mostly
14	私有		sīyǒu	adj.	be privately owned, be private
15	首席执行官	首席執行官	shǒuxí zhíxíngguān	n.p.	CEO (chief executive officer)
16	一再		yízài	adv.	time and again, repeatedly
17	惨案	慘案	cǎn'àn	n.	massacre, murder case
18	策		cè	b.f./n.	method, plan, policy
19	逻辑	邏輯	luójí	n.	logic
20	现场	現場	xiànchǎng	n.	scene (of event or incident), spot
21	当场	當場	dāngchǎng	adv.	at the scene, on the spot
22	制止		zhìzhǐ	v.	to prevent, to stop
23	凶手	兇手	xiōngshǒu	n.	assailant, murderer
24	阻止		zǔzhǐ	v.	to prevent, to stop, to hold back
25	持		chí	v./b.f.	to hold, to grasp; to support, to keep
26	唯一		wéiyī	adj./attr.	single, only, sole
27	护理	護理	hùlǐ	v.	to nurse, to take care of
28	入手		rùshǒu	v.	to put one's hand to, to begin with
29	禁		jìn	v./b.f.	to prohibit, to forbid, to ban
30	辩论	辯論	biànlùn	v.	to debate, to argue over
31	跟踪	跟蹤	gēnzōng	v.	to track, to follow the tracks of
32	核心		héxīn	n.	core, inner circle (of a political party, government, etc.)
33	分歧		fēnqí	n.	difference (of opinion, position)

34	民意		mínyì	n.	will of the people, public opinion
35	极力	極力	jílì	adv.	doing one's utmost
36	修正案		xiūzhèng'àn	n.	amendment
37	会员	會員	huìyuán	n.	member of a mass or political organization
38	汉	漢	hàn	b.f./n.	man
39	代言人		dàiyánrén	n.	spokesperson
40	攻击	攻擊	gōngjī	v.	to attack, to assault
41	联邦	聯邦	liánbāng	n.	federation
42	禁令		jìnlìng	n.	prohibition, ban
43	预料	預料	yùliào	v./n.	to expect; prediction, anticipation
44	最终	最終	zuìzhōng	n.	final, ultimate, last
45	上风	上風	shàngfēng	n.	superior position

专有名词 Proper nouns

1	基恩		Jī'ēn	Dave Keene
2	拉皮埃尔	拉皮埃爾	Lāpí'āi'ěr	Wayne LaPierre
3	皮尤研究中心		Píyóu Yánjiū Zhōngxīn	Pew Research Center
4	好莱坞	好萊塢	Hǎoláiwù	Hollywood
5	布鲁斯·威利斯	布魯斯·威利斯	Bùlǔsī Wēilìsī	Bruce Willis
6	里根		Lǐgēn	Ronald Wilson Reagan
7	肯尼迪		Kěnnídí	Kennedy
8	尼克松		Níkèsōng	Richard Milhous Nixon

生词索引

主课文部分

A

| 案 | | àn | n./b.f. | lawsuit, case; file | 6 |

B

白领	白領	báilǐng	n.	white collar, white-collar worker	2
版本		bǎnběn	n.	version, edition	2
半数	半數	bànshù	n.	half (the number)	1
伴侣		bànlǚ	n.	mate, partner, husband or wife	1
扮演		bànyǎn	v.	to play the role of, to act, to impersonate	3
褒扬	褒揚	bāoyáng	v.	to praise, to commend	6
褒义	褒義	bāoyì	n.	commendatory	6
保密		bǎo mì	v.o.	to maintain secrecy, to keep sth. confidential	2
抱怨		bàoyuàn	v.	to complain, to grumble	4
暴力		bàolì	n.	violence, force	8
暴露		bàolù	v.	to expose, to reveal	8
曝光		bào guāng	v.o.	to expose, to reveal, to disclose	2
悲哀		bēi'āi	adj.	sad, sorrow	5
悲剧	悲劇	bēijù	n.	tragedy	7
背景		bèijǐng	n.	stage setting, backdrop, background	1
本身		běnshēn	pr.	oneself, in oneself	6
比比皆是		bǐbǐ-jiēshì	f.e.	to be found or seen everywhere	8
比方		bǐfāng	v./n.	to take for instance or example; analogy, instance	3
必		bì	adv.	certainly, necessarily; must, have to	1
毕业生	畢業生	bìyèshēng	n.	graduate (of a school)	2
便利		biànlì	adj.	convenient	5
辩护	辯護	biànhù	v.	to defend, to plead, to argue in favor of	6
标签	標簽	biāoqiān	n.	label, tag	6
标志	標誌	biāozhì	n.	sign, mark, symbol	2
秉持		bǐngchí	v.	to uphold, to adhere to (principles, etc.)	3

并未	並未	bìngwèi	ad.p.	not yet	6
播出		bōchū	v(c)	to broadcast	1
舶来	舶來	bólái	v(c)	to import	4
不近人情		bújìn-rénqíng	f.e.	unreasonable, inconsiderate, unkind	3
不利		búlì	adj.	unfavorable, disadvantageous, harmful	2
不能不		bùnéngbù	ad.p.	have to, cannot but	5
不容忽视	不容忽視	bùróng-hūshì	f.e.	cannot be ignored	3
不休		bùxiū	v.	do not end, endlessly, ceaselessly	8
不由得		bùyóude	adv.	can't help, cannot but	1

C

采访	採訪	cǎifǎng	v.	to interview, to cover (a news story), to gather material report; interview	2
参与	參與	cānyù	v.	to partake, to participate in, to have a say in	1
惨剧	慘劇	cǎnjù	n.	tragedy, calamity, disaster	8
草草		cǎocǎo	adv.	carelessly, hastily, hurriedly	1
策划	策劃	cèhuà	v.	to plot, to scheme, to plan	2
层出不穷	層出不窮	céngchū-bùqióng	f.e.	to come out one after the other	8
层面	層面	céngmiàn	n.	scope, range, aspect	6
长远	長遠	chángyuǎn	adj.	long-term, long-range	2
常规	常規	chángguī	adj./n.	conventional, common, regular	7
常见	常見	chángjiàn	adj.	commonly seen, common	2
场景	場景	chǎngjǐng	n.	scene, scene in theatre, film, and TV	5
场面	場面	chǎngmiàn	n.	scene, spectacle, occasion	5
场所	場所	chǎngsuǒ	n.	location, place, locale	4
超强	超強	chāoqiáng	adj.p.	super strong, ultra-strong	2
车辆	車輛	chēliàng	n.	vehicle, automobile	7
车速	車速	chēsù	n.	speed of a vehicle	2
沉迷		chénmí	v.	to addict, to wallow	5
称颂	稱頌	chēngsòng	v.	to praise, to extol, to eulogize	6
称谓	稱謂	chēngwèi	n.	appellation, term of address, title that indicates relationship, status or occupation	6
称之为	稱之為	chēngzhīwéi	v.p.	to call it..., to be known as	7
成本		chéngběn	n.	(manufacturing, production, etc.) costs	2
成才		chéng cái	v.o.	to emerge as a talent, to become a useful person	3
成千上万	成千上萬	chéngqiān-shàngwàn	f.e.	by the thousands and tens of thousands, thousands	5

诚	誠	chéng	adj.	honest, sincere	1
持续	持續	chíxù	v.	to last, to continue, to sustain	7
冲击	衝擊	chōngjī	v.	to attack, to impact, to affect	4
冲突	衝突	chōngtū	v./n.	to conflict, to clash; contradiction	3
充实	充實	chōngshí	adj.	rich, abundant, substantial	2
筹	籌	chóu	b.f.	chip, tally, counter	3
出台	出臺	chū tái	v.o.	to unveil (a policy, measure, etc.), to disclose, to announce	7
除此之外		chú cǐ zhī wài	f.e.	apart from this, in addition to this	2
传媒	傳媒	chuánméi	n.	media	8
创立	創立	chuànglì	v.	to found, to establish, to set up	2
创新	創新	chuàngxīn	v./n.	to innovate, to bring forth new ideas; innovation, creation	2
创业者	創業者	chuàngyèzhě	n.	entrepreneur	2
词语	詞語	cíyǔ	n.	words and expressions, word and phrase	7
辞退	辭退	cítuì	v.	to dismiss, to discharge, to politely decline	2
辞职	辭職	cí zhí	v.o.	to resign, to quit one's job	2
慈善		císhàn	adj.	benevolent, philanthropic, compassionate	1
促成		cùchéng	v(c)	to facilitate, to help to bring about, to effect	1

D

答复	答覆	dáfù	v.	to formally reply, to answer, to respond	6
大大		dàdà	r.f.	greatly, enormously	7
大力		dàlì	adv.	vigorously, energetically, to go all out	7
大男子主义	大男子主義	dà nánzǐ zhǔyì	f.e.	male chauvinism	6
大有人在		dàyǒurénzài	f.e.	there are plenty of people who ...	6
大众	大眾	dàzhòng	n.	masses, populace, commonalty	6
代表性		dàibiǎoxìng	n.	representativeness, characteristics	6
担忧	擔憂	dānyōu	v.	to worry, to be anxious; anxiety	1
单身	單身	dānshēn	attr./n.	unmarried or single person	1
淡化		dànhuà	v.	(of problem, emotion, etc.) to be gradually forgotten, to fade out, to downplay	4
当今	當今	dāngjīn	n.	current, present, nowadays	1
当面	當面	dāngmiàn	adv.	in sb.'s present, face to face	5
当作	當作	dàngzuò	v.	to treat as, to regard as	4
导火索	導火索	dǎohuǒsuǒ	n.	blasting fuse	8
到场	到場	dàochǎng	v.o.	to turn up, to show up, to be present	1
道德观	道德觀	dàodéguān	n.	morality, ethics, moral outlook	1

得不偿失	得不償失	débùchángshī	f.e.	the loss outweighs the gain	5
低于	低於	dīyú	v.	to be lower than	3
地形		dìxíng	n.	topography, landform	7
点点滴滴	點點滴滴	diǎndiǎn-dīdī	n./adj.	dribs and drabs, every bit of…; bit by bit, drop by drop	2
电子	電子	diànzǐ	n./attr.	electron; electronic	3
爹		diē	n.	father, dad	1
钉	釘	dìng	v.	to nail, to tack, to hammer a nail into sth.	6
定义	定義	dìngyì	n./v.	definition; to define	6
董事长	董事長	dǒngshìzhǎng	n.	chairman of the board	6
动漫	動漫	dòngmàn	n.	animation, cartoon	2
督促		dūcù	v.	to supervise and urge	3
毒		dú	n.	poison, toxin	7
短信		duǎnxìn	n.	text messages	5
对抗	對抗	duìkàng	v./n.	to resist, to oppose; antagonism, confrontation	4
多元		duōyuán	attr.	poly-, multi-, multivariate	4

E

额	額	é	n./b.f.	amount, quantity, quota	4
恶性	惡性	èxìng	adj./attr.	malignant, pernicious, vicious	8
而已		éryǐ	part.	That's all, nothing more, nothing but	1
耳濡目染		ěrrú-mùrǎn	f.e.	to be influenced by what one constantly sees and hears	8
二手货	二手貨	èrshǒuhuò	n.	used goods, second-hand-goods	6

F

发布	發佈	fābù	v.	to issue (orders, instructions, news etc.), to release, to announce	2
发泄	發洩	fāxiè	v.	to let off, to vent	8
法案		fǎ'àn	n.	bill, act, proposed law	7
法规	法規	fǎguī	n.	legislation, statute	6
法学	法學	fǎxué	n.	science of law, law	3
法学院	法學院	fǎxuéyuàn	n.	law school	3
法院		fǎyuàn	n.	court of law, court	6
番		fān	m(n)/m(v)	kind, sort; for times and occurrences	6
犯罪		fàn zuì	v.o.	to commit crime or offense	8
泛滥	泛濫	fànlàn	v.	to overrun, to spread unchecked, to overflow	5

放松	放鬆	fàngsōng	v.	to relax, to slacken, to loosen	4
废气	廢氣	fèiqì	n.	waste (exhaust) gas	7
分辨		fēnbiàn	v.	to distinguish, to differentiate	8
分店		fēndiàn	n.	branch (of a shop)	8
分享		fēnxiǎng	v.	to share (joy, happiness, benefit, etc.)	5
氛围	氛圍	fēnwéi	n.	atmosphere	7
风波	風波	fēngbō	n.	crisis, dispute, disturbance	6
奉行		fèngxín	v.	to pursue (a course, a policy, etc.)	3
服饰	服飾	fúshì	n.	dress and personal adornment	2
服装	服裝	fúzhuāng	n.	dress, clothes, costume	2
浮躁		fúzào	adj.	impetuous, impulsive, flighty and rash	1
福利		fúlì	n.	material benefits, welfare	2
负担	負擔	fùdān	v./n.	to bear, to shoulder (a responsibility, work, to expense, etc); burden, load	6
负面	負面	fùmiàn	adj.	downside, negative	5
赋予	賦予	fùyǔ	v.	to endow, to give, to entrust	4

G

感受		gǎnshòu	n./v.	feelings; to experience, to feel	3
橄榄枝	橄欖枝	gǎnlǎnzhī	n.	olive branch	2
干扰	干擾	gānrǎo	v./n.	to disturb, to interfere; interference	5
钢琴	鋼琴	gāngqín	n.	piano	3
岗位	崗位	gǎngwèi	n.	position, job, post	2
高才生		gāocáishēng	n.	top student, gifted student	1
高科技		gāokējì	attr./n.	high tech, high-technology	5
高效		gāoxiào	n.	high efficiency	5
歌颂	歌頌	gēsòng	v.	to sing the praises of, to extol, to eulogize	8
个案	個案	gè'àn	n.	individual case	6
各自		gèzì	pr.	each, respective, oneself	7
耿耿于怀	耿耿於懷	gěnggěng yúhuái	f.e.	to take sth. to heart, to brood on sth.	6
公民		gōngmín	n.	citizen	8
公正		gōngzhèng	adj.	just, impartial	6
沟通	溝通	gōutōng	v.	to communicate; communication	2
孤儿	孤兒	gū'ér	n.	orphan	1
蛊惑	蠱惑	gǔhuò	v.	to bewitch, to delude	8
鼓劲	鼓勁	gǔ jìn	v.o.	to give encouragement	6

顾及	顧及	gùjí	v.	to take into account, to give consideration to	3
挂钩	掛鉤	guà gōu	v.o.	to link up with, to establish contact with	2
关注	關注	guānzhù	v.	to follow (an issue) closely, to pay close attention; concern, focus	1
观	觀	guān	b.f./n.	outlook, concept, notion	1
观念	觀念	guānniàn	n.	notion, idea, concept	1
官方		guānfāng	n./attr.	official, (by the) government	4
管教		guǎnjiào	v.	to control and teach, to discipline	3
罐子		guànzi	n.	pot, jar, jug	2
光电子	光電子	guāngdiànzǐ	n.	optoelectronic	2
归	歸	guī	v.	to return, to go or come back	3
归属	歸屬	guīshǔ	v.	to belong to, to be affiliated to	5
国会	國會	guóhuì	n.	parliament (UK), congress (US)	8
过度	過度	guòdù	adj.	excessive, exceeding	5

H

海外		hǎiwài	n.	overseas, abroad	3
含蓄		hánxù	adj.	reserved, implicate	5
含义	含義	hányì	n.	meaning, implication, sense	4
汉子	漢子	hànzi	n.	man, fellow	6
捍卫	捍衛	hànwèi	v.	to defend, to protect, to safeguard	6
行业	行業	hángyè	n.	industry, business, profession	2
合法		héfǎ	adj.	legal, lawful, legitimate	6
红人	紅人	hóngrén	n.	a public personality, favorite person by sb. in power, a popular person	1
呼吁	呼籲	hūyù	v.	to appeal, to call on	8
虎		hǔ	n./b.f.	tiger; brave, vigorous	3
互动	互動	hùdòng	v./n.	to interact; interaction	1
互联网	互聯網	hùliánwǎng	n.	Internet	5
户外		hùwài	n.	outdoor	7
华裔	華裔	huáyì	n.	Chinese descent, ethnic Chinese, foreign citizen of Chinese origin	3
化名		huàmíng	n.	alias, assumed name, pseudonym	6
话题	話題	huàtí	n.	subject (of a talk or conversation), topic	4
环绕	環繞	huánrào	v.	to surround, to encircle	7
唤起	喚起	huànqǐ	v(c)	to arouse, to call, to evoke	6
荒凉	荒涼	huāngliáng	adj.	bleak and desolate, barren	7
会展	會展	huìzhǎn	n.	convention and exhibition	2

昏暗		hūn'àn	adj.	dim, dusky, muddled	7
婚		hūn	b.f.	to wed, to marry; marriage, wedding	1
混浊	混濁	hùnzhuó	adj.	muddy, turbid	7
获取	獲取	huòqǔ	v.	to obtain, to gain, to acquire	5

J

击	擊	jī	b.f.	to strike, to attack	8
机电	機電	jīdiàn	n.	machinery and electrical equipment	2
机动车	機動車	jīdòngchē	n.	motor or automotive vehicle	7
基本上		jīběnshang	adv.	basically, generally, mainly	4
基督教		jīdūjiào	n.	Christianity, Christian	4
基金		jījīn	n.	fund, endowment	1
极端	極端	jíduān	adj.	extreme, exceedingly	2
极为	極為	jíwéi	adv.	extremely, exceedingly	1
即时	即時	jíshí	adj.	immediate	2
疾病		jíbìng	n.	disease, sickness, ailment	7
籍		jí	n./b.f.	native place, home town, birthplace; membership	6
加入		jiārù	v.	to join, to become a member	2
加油		jiā yóu	v.o./f.e.	to refuel, to make an extra effort; Go! Step on it!	6
家教		jiājiào	n.	family education, upbringing	3
嘉宾	嘉賓	jiābīn	n.	honored guest, distinguished guest	1
嫁		jià	v./b.f.	(of a woman) marry (a husband)	1
监督	監督	jiāndū	v./n.	to supervise, to superintend, to control; supervision	3
简历	簡歷	jiǎnlì	n.	resume, curriculum vitae	2
见识	見識	jiànshi	n.	knowledge, experience	2
讲述	講述	jiǎngshù	v.	to tell about, to narrate, to give an account	3
奖项	獎項	jiǎngxiàng	n.	award, prize	3
交锋	交鋒	jiāofēng	v.o./n.	to clash; confrontation	4
交往		jiāowǎng	v.	to associate with, to be in contact with	5
交友		jiāoyǒu	v.	to make friends	1
角色		juésè	n.	role (in a play, etc.), part	3
教堂		jiàotáng	n.	church, temple, cathedral	4
教徒		jiàotú	n.	follower or believer of a religion	4
截至		jiézhì	v.	by (a specified time), up to (a time)	5

解读	解讀	jiědú	n.	reading, understanding, interpretation	6
解脱	解脫	jiětuō	v.	to free oneself from, to extricate oneself	5
借鉴	借鑒	jièjiàn	v.	to draw lessons from, to borrow, to learn from	7
金钱	金錢	jīnqián	n.	money	1
进展	進展	jìnzhǎn	n.	progress, advance	2
景象		jǐngxiàng	n.	scene, sight (to behold)	7
警钟	警鐘	jǐngzhōng	n.	alarm bell, wake-up call	6
净化	淨化	jìnghuà	v.	to purify, to purge	8
竟		jìng	adv.	unexpectedly, actually, to go as far as to	7
酒吧		jiǔbā	n.	bar, saloon, taproom	4
酒店		jiǔdiàn	n.	hotel, wine shop, public house	2
就业	就業	jiù yè	v.o.	to obtain employment, to get a job	2
居多		jūduō	v.p.	to be in the majority	2
举办	舉辦	jǔbàn	v.	to conduct, to hold, to sponsor	2
举不胜举	舉不勝舉	jǔbúshèngjǔ	f.e.	too numerous to mention	6
巨人		jùrén	n.	giant	6
拒		jù	v./b.f.	to refuse, to reject, to resist	6
距离	距離	jùlí	n.	distance	5
聚会	聚會	jùhuì	v./n.	(of people) to get together, to congregate; party, social gathering	4
捐助		juānzhù	v./n.	to donate; donation	8
绝大多数	絕大多數	jué dàduōshù	n.p.	most, the overwhelming majority	4
崛起		juéqǐ	v.	to rise (as a political force), to rise abruptly	7

K

卡		kǎ	n./b.f.	card	4
开庭	開庭	kāi tíng	v.o.	to open a court session, to call the court to order, to hold a court	6
看重		kànzhòng	v.	to regard as important, to value, to think highly of	2
看作		kànzuò	v.	to regard as, to consider, to look upon as	4
苛刻		kēkè	adj.	(of condition, requirement, etc.) harsh, severe, hard	3
科目		kēmù	n.	school subject or course	3
颗粒	顆粒	kēlì	n.	anything small and roundish, particle	7
可喜		kěxǐ	adj.	gratifying, heartening, lovely	6
客户		kèhù	n.	client, customer	2
课外	課外	kèwài	n.	extracurricular, outside class	3

恐慌		kǒnghuāng	adj.	panic, panicky, scare	5
控		kòng	b.f.	fanatic	2
口罩		kǒuzhào	n.	mask (for breathing or antiseptic purpose)	7
枯燥		kūzào	adj.	dry and dull, uninteresting	3
夸奖	誇獎	kuājiǎng	v.	to praise, to commend, to compliment	3
跨越		kuàyuè	v.	to cross, to stride across, to leap over	5
快餐		kuàicān	n.	quick meal, snack, fast food	1
快速		kuàisù	adj.	fast, in a high speed	1

L

拉近		lājìn	v(c)	to draw closer, to pull closer	4
蓝天	藍天	lántiān	n.	blue sky	7
浪漫		làngmàn	adj.	romantic	4
牢牢		láoláo	r.f.	firmly, safely	6
老人家		lǎorenjia	n.	(an respectful form of address for an old person) old person, parents	5
乐	樂	lè	n./b.f.	pleasure, enjoyment	6
雷人		léirén	adj.	thundering (cyber word that indicates an unexpected and shocking effect)	1
冷落		lěngluò	adj.	deserted, desolate, unfrequented	2
冷漠		lěngmò	adj.	indifferent, cold and detached	5
理念		lǐniàn	n.	idea, concept, philosophy	3
立法		lì fǎ	v.o.	to make (or enact) laws, to legislate	8
例		lì	n./b.f.	example, instance, case	6
例外		lìwài	n.	exception	2
连年	連年	liánnián	adv.	in consecutive year	8
连任	連任	liánrèn	v.	to renew one's term of office	8
脸蛋	臉蛋	liǎndàn	n.	cheeks, face	1
恋	戀	liàn	b.f.	to love, to long for, to feel attached to	1
领域	領域	lǐngyù	n.	field, sphere, realm	2
令		lìng	v.	to cause, to make	1
流行		liúxíng	adj.	popular, in vogue, prevalent	4
笼罩	籠罩	lǒngzhào	v.	to envelop, to shroud, to cover	7
隆重		lóngzhòng	adj.	grand, solemn, ceremonious	4
录取	錄取	lùqǔ	v.	to enroll, to recruit, to admit to	3
路况	路況	lùkuàng	n.	road condition, highway condition	2
伦理	倫理	lúnlǐ	n.	ethics, moral principles	1

M

霾		mái	n.	smog, haze	7
忙碌		mánglù	adj.	be busy, bustling	4
盲目		mángmù	adj.	blind, aimless, lacking insight or understanding	1
冒犯		màofàn	v./n.	to offend; offense	4
媒体	媒體	méitǐ	n.	(news) media	3
煤炭		méitàn	n.	coal	7
每时每刻	每時每刻	měishí-měikè	f.e.	all the time, incessantly	5
美化		měihuà	v.	to beautify, to prettify, to glorify	8
门庭	門庭	méntíng	n.	gate and courtyard	2
蒙蒙	濛濛	méngméng	r.f.	drizzly, misty	7
弥撒	彌撒	mísa	n.	Mass	4
密不可分		mìbùkěfēn	f.e.	inseparable	8
密集		mìjí	adj.	concentrated, crowded together, dense	7
蜜		mì	n./b.f.	honey, sweet	2
面试	面試	miànshì	v./n.	to interview, to audition; interview	2
描述		miáoshù	v.	to describe; description	7
秒钟	秒鐘	miǎozhōng	m(n)	second (of time)	1
民间	民間	mínjiān	n./attr.	among the people, nongovernmental, folk	4
民俗		mínsú	n.	folkways, folk custom	4
民众	民眾	mínzhòng	n.	masses, common people	8
敏感		mǐngǎn	adj.	sensitive, susceptible	6
名著		míngzhù	n.	masterpiece, classic, famous book	7
明令		mínglìng	n.	explicit order, formal decree, public proclamation	4
模糊		móhu	adj.	vague, blurred, unclear	4
莫		mò	adv.	don't	5
漠视	漠視	mòshì	v.	to treat with indifference, to ignore, to overlook	5
谋杀	謀殺	móushā	v.	to murder	8
某个	某個	mǒugè	attr.	certain, some	1

N

乃至		nǎizhì	conj.	even, go so far as to, even to the extent that	2
男女平等		nánnǚ píngděng	f.e.	men and women are equal(s), equality of men and women	6

男性		nánxìng	n.	male sex, man	1
难题	難題	nántí	n.	difficult problem, tough question	7
能见度	能見度	néngjiàndù	n.	visibility	7
年度		niándù	n./attr.	year (e.g., school year, fiscal year, etc.); annual, yearly	4
年轻人	年輕人	niánqīngrén	n.	young people, youth	1
宁愿	寧願	nìngyuàn	conj.	would rather, preferably, prefer	1
女方		nǚfāng	n.	(oft. used on marriage-related occasions) bride's side, wife's side	1
女神		nǚshén	n.	goddess, nymph	6
女性		nǚxìng	n.	female sex, woman	1

P

排放		páifàng	v.	to discharge, to exhaust (gas, etc.); emission	7
攀比		pānbǐ	v.	to compare unrealistically, to compare with the higher	5
培养	培養	péiyǎng	v.	to foster, to develop, to cultivate	3
赔偿	賠償	péicháng	n./v.	compensation, reparations, indemnification; to compensate	2
片段		piànduàn	n.	part, extract, fragment	3
拼		pīn	v.	to fight or compete to the bitter end	1
频	頻	pín	adv./b.f.	frequently, repeatedly	8
频频	頻頻	pínpín	adv./r.f.	repeatedly, again and again, frequently	8
品格		pǐngé	n.	one's character and morals, (of literary or artistic works') quality and style	6
品牌		pǐnpái	n.	brand name, trademark	2
平安夜		píng'ānyè	n.	Christmas Eve	4
平板电脑	平板電腦	píngbǎn diànnǎo	n.p.	tablet computer	5
评论	評論	pínglùn	v./n.	to comment on, to discuss; comment	5
凭	憑	píng	prep.	depend on, go by, base on	1
迫不及待		pòbùjídài	f.e.	too impatient to wait, in a hurry	5
铺天盖地	鋪天蓋地	pūtiān-gàidì	f.e.	to blot out the sky and cover up the earth	7

Q

齐全	齊全	qíquán	adj.	complete, all in readiness, well-stocked	2
歧视	歧視	qíshì	v.	to discriminate against, to treat with bias; discrimination (against someone)	6
启示	啟示	qǐshì	n.	inspiration, revelation, implication	1

起诉	起訴	qǐsù	v.	to sue, to lodge a complaint, to bring a lawsuit against	6
气氛	氣氛	qìfēn	n.	atmosphere, mood, tone	4
气质	氣質	qìzhì	n.	temperament, disposition, demeanor	6
前景		qiánjǐng	n.	foreground, prospect	8
前列		qiánliè	n.	front row, leading position	5
前夕		qiánxī	n.	eve, evening of the previous day	4
枪杀	槍殺	qiāngshā	v.	to shoot dead	8
枪支	槍支	qiāngzhī	n.	firearms, rifles, guns	8
强化	強化	qiánghuà	v.	to strengthen, to consolidate, to intensify	6
强加	強加	qiángjiā	v.	to impose, to force (upon)	3
强迫	強迫	qiǎngpò	v.	to force, to compel	5
强制性	強制性	qiángzhìxìng	n./adj.	forcefulness; forceful, mandatory	3
侵染		qīnrǎn	v.	to infect, to pollute	6
亲密	親密	qīnmì	adj.	close, intimate	5
亲友	親友	qīnyǒu	n.	relatives and friends, kith and kin	5
沁		qìn	v.	to permeate, to percolate, to soak into	7
轻视	輕視	qīngshì	v.	to despise, to look down on	8
轻易	輕易	qīngyì	adv.	easily, simply	8
倾向	傾向	qīngxiàng	n./v.	tendency, inclination; to prefer	1
清洁	清潔	qīngjié	adj.	clean, unpolluted	7
情感		qínggǎn	n.	emotion, feeling	5
情节	情節	qíngjié	n.	plot, scenario	8
情侣		qínglǚ	n.	sweethearts, lovers	4
丘陵		qiūlíng	n.	hills	7
求职	求職	qiú zhí	v.o.	to look for a job, to apply for a job	2
求职者	求職者	qiúzhízhě	n.	job applicant	2
权	權	quán	n.	right, entitlement, title	6
权利	權利	quánlì	n.	right, privilege	6
权益	權益	quányì	n.	rights and interests	6
全球化		quánqiúhuà	n.	globalization	4
群体	群體	qúntǐ	n.	group, community, colony	2

R

扰	擾	rǎo	v./b.f.	to harass, to disturb, to bother	1
热门	熱門	rèmén	n.	popular, hot	4
热热闹闹	熱熱鬧鬧	rère-nāonāo	f.e.	bustling	5

热衷	熱衷	rèzhōng	v.	to be full of enthusiasm about, to crave for, to be fond of	2
人力		rénlì	n.	manual labor, manpower	2
人满为患	人滿為患	rénmǎn wéihuàn	f.e.	cause concerns and problems because of crowdedness or overpopulation	2
人群		rénqún	n.	throng, crowd, multitude	7
人士		rénshì	n.	professional person, person with certain social influence	4
人事		rénshì	n.	human resource, personnel	2
人体	人體	réntǐ	n.	human body	7
认可	認可	rènkě	v.	to accept, to approve; approval, acceptance, recognition	1
柔弱		róuruò	adj.	weak, feeble, frail	6
儒家		rújiā	n.	Confucian School, Confucianism	3
软件	軟件	ruǎnjiàn	n.	computer software, software	2

S

丧生	喪生	sàng shēng	v.o.	to lose one's life	8
色彩		sècǎi	n.	color, tinge	4
杀手	殺手	shāshǒu	n.	profession killer	8
山庄	山莊	shānzhuāng	n.	mountain village, villa, lodge	7
闪耀	閃耀	shǎnyào	v.	to shine, to glitter, to radiate	2
擅长	擅長	shàncháng	v.	to be good at, to be expert in, to be skilled in	3
擅自		shànzì	adv.	taking the liberty, without authorization, unauthorized	3
伤感	傷感	shānggǎn	adj.	sad, sick at heart, sentimental	4
伤害	傷害	shānghài	v.	to hurt, to harm, to damage	4
商机	商機	shāngjī	n.	business opportunities	4
上场	上場	shàng chǎng	v.o.	to enter, to appear onstage	1
上演		shàngyǎn	v.	to stage, to perform	8
尚且		shàngqiě	conj.	even, still, yet	4
社交		shèjiāo	n.	social contact, social life	5
社区	社區	shèqū	n.	community	3
申请	申請	shēnqǐng	v./n.	to apply for; application	3
伸张正义	伸張正義	shēnzhāng zhèngyì	f.e.	to uphold justice	8
身上		shēnshang	n.	on one's body, (have sth.) on one	3
深处	深處	shēnchù	n.	depth, recess, profundity	7

深究		shēnjiū	v.	to go into (a matter) seriously, to get to the bottom of (a matter), to investigate thoroughly	6
深思		shēnsī	v.	to think deeply about, to ponder deeply over	1
审理	審理	shěnlǐ	v./n.	to try, to hear (a case), to bring to trial	6
生效		shēng xiào	v.o.	to go into effect, to take effect, to become effective	6
生涯		shēngyá	n.	career, profession	2
圣	聖	shèng	b.f.	holy, sacred, saint	4
圣诞	聖誕	shèngdàn	n.	birthday of Jesus Christ, birthday of an emperor or empress	4
胜负	勝負	shèngfù	n.	victory and/or defeat, success and/or failure	3
盛行		shèngxíng	v.	to prevail, to be very popular	8
剩女		shèngnǚ	n.	leftover lady	6
时不时	時不時	shíbushí	ad.p.	from time to time	5
时空	時空	shíkōng	n.	time and space, space-time	5
识别	識別	shíbié	v.	to distinguish, to identify; identification	2
使得		shǐde	v.	to make, to cause	1
世俗		shìsú	n.	social conventions	4
市民		shìmín	n.	resident, townspeople	7
试婚	試婚	shì hūn	v.o.	to have a trial marriage	1
视角	視角	shìjiǎo	n.	visual angle, approach, perspective	6
视觉	視覺	shìjué	n.	visual sense, vision, sense of sight	2
视为	視為	shìwéi	v.p.	to regard as, to consider as	6
是非		shìfēi	n.	right and wrong	8
逝		shì	b.f.	to die, to pass away	7
收视率	收視率	shōushìlǜ	n.	audience rating	1
受到		shòudào	v(c)	to receive, to get, to be given	4
受理		shòulǐ	v.	to accept and handle, (of the court) to accept and hear (a case)	6
疏忽		shūhu	v./n.	to neglect, to be inadvertent; negligence, oversight	2
数学系	數學系	shùxuéxì	n.	mathematics department	2
说法	說法	shuōfa	n.	wording, way of say a thing	6
思考		sīkǎo	v.	to think deeply, to ponder over, to reflect on	3
思路		sīlù	n.	train of thought, thinking	2
死亡		sǐwáng	v.	to die, to pass away	7
松懈	鬆懈	sōngxiè	adj.	inattentive, lax; to be slack	8
诉讼	訴訟	sùsòng	n.	lawsuit, litigation	6

诉状	訴狀	sùzhuàng	n.	plaint, indictment, complaint	6
宿		sù	b.f./v.	to stay overnight, to lodge for the night	3
塑造		sùzào	v.	to mould, to model, to shape	6
算		suàn	v.	to consider, to regard as, to count as	1
随处可见	隨處可見	suíchùkějiàn	f.e.	be seen everywhere	6
随机	隨機	suíjī	adv.	randomly, probabilistic	4
随身	隨身	suíshēn	adj./attr.	(take) with one (self)	8
随心所欲	隨心所欲	suíxīnsuǒyù	f.e.	to do as one pleases or wishes, to follow one's inclination, to have one's own way	3
随着	隨著	suízhe	prep.	along with, in the wake of, in pace with	2
损害	損害	sǔnhài	v.	to harm, to injure, to damage	2
缩减	縮減	suōjiǎn	v.	to reduce, to cut	7
索要		suǒyào	v.	to ask for, to demand, to claim	2

T

谈婚论嫁	談婚論嫁	tán hūn lùn jià	f.e.	to talk about getting married	1
谈恋爱	談戀愛	tán liàn'ài	v.o.	to be in a love relationship, to court	1
碳		tàn	n.	carbon	7
套用		tàoyòng	v.	to apply mechanically, to copy a set pattern mechanically, to use indiscriminately	6
套中人		tàozhōngrén	n.	people who are complacent and conservative, or people who are trapped in a certain status quo (a term originally taken from a Russian novel "The Man in a Case")	5
特色		tèsè	n.	characteristic, distinguishing feature or quality	4
特邀		tèyāo	v.	to be specially invited	1
提起		tíqǐ	v(c)	to file (a lawsuit), to raise, to arouse	6
体现	體現	tǐxiàn	v.	to embody, to reflect; realization	1
体验	體驗	tǐyàn	v.	to learn through personal experience; experience	2
天空		tiānkōng	n.	sky, heaven	7
天伦之乐	天倫之樂	tiānlúnzhīlè	f.e.	family happiness	5
天主教		tiānzhǔjiào	n.	Catholicism, Catholic church	4
挑战	挑戰	tiǎozhàn	v./n.	to challenge, to a contest; challenge	2
跳槽		tiàocáo	v.o.	to abandon one occupation in favor of another, change jobs	2
听话	聽話	tīng huà	v.o.	to heed advice, to obey, to be obedient	3

庭审	庭審	tíngshěn	n.	court trial, court hearing	6
停产	停產	tíngchǎn	v.	to shut down, to suspend production	7
通病		tōngbìng	n.	common failing, common fault	2
通信		tōngxìn	n.	communication	2
通知书	通知書	tōngzhīshū	n.	notice, notification letter	3
同事		tóngshì	n.	colleague, fellow-worker	4
统计	統計	tǒngjì	v./n.	to census, to count; statistics	2
投递	投遞	tóudì	v.	to deliver, to send	6
投身		tóushēn	v.	to throw oneself into, to plunge, to join	2
途径	途徑	tújìng	n.	way, road, path	6
吐槽		tǔ cáo	v.o.	to comment with a sarcastic tone	6
团聚	團聚	tuánjù	v.	to reunite, to have a reunion	5
团体	團體	tuántǐ	n.	group, organization, team	4
退化		tuìhuà	v.	to degenerate, to retrogress, to retrograde	5
妥协	妥協	tuǒxié	v.	to compromise	2

W

外表		wàibiǎo	n.	outward appearance, surface	1
外貌		wàimào	n.	looks, appearance, profile	6
网络	網絡	wǎngluò	n.	(computer, telecom, etc.) network	2
网民	網民	wǎngmín	n.	net user, netizen	5
微博		wēibó	n.	microblog, Twitter, Tweet	2
微粒		wēilì	n.	particle	7
微信		wēixìn	n.	WeChat	2
为主	為主	wéizhǔ	v.p.	to rely mainly on, to give priority to	2
唯命是从	唯命是從	wéimìng shìcóng	f.e.	to accept sb.'s instructions without a murmur, to be absolutely obedient	3
维	維	wéi	v.	to keep, to maintain, to safeguard	6
维系	維繫	wéixì	v.	to maintain, to hold together	2
卫视	衛視	wèishì	n.	satellite television	1
味		wèi	b.f.	taste, flavor	4
畏惧	畏懼	wèijù	v.	to fear, to dread	3
无处不在	無處不在	wúchùbúzài	f.e.	everywhere	5
无能	無能	wúnéng	adj.	incompetent, incapable, powerless	6
无疑	無疑	wúyí	v.	to be beyond doubt	3
无语	無語	wúyǔ	adj.	speechless	5

毋庸置疑		wúyōngèzhìyí	f.e.	unquestionably, without doubt	5
侮辱		wǔrǔ	v./n.	to insult, to humiliate; humiliation	6
舞台	舞臺	wǔtái	n.	stage, arena, footlights	1
勿		wù	adv.	do not, never	1
物		wù	b.f.	thing, matter, substance	7
物质	物質	wùzhì	n.	materials	1

X

席		xí	m (n)	used for speech or talk	1
袭击	襲擊	xíjī	v.	to attack, to raid	7
喜		xǐ	b.f.	happy, delighted, pleased	6
喜好		xǐhào	n./v.	like, love, be fond of	3
细节	細節	xìjié	n.	details	2
细致	細緻	xìzhì	adj.	meticulous, precise about details, fine	7
嫌		xián	n.	suspicion	6
现代人	現代人	xiàndàirén	n.	modernist, modern people, neoteric	1
限产	限產	xiànchǎn	v.	to curtail the production	7
限行		xiànxíng	v.	to have driving curb or vehicle restriction according to the last number of the vehicle plate. For example, the vehicles that have number 9 as the last number on their plates cannot be used on Mondays.	7
宪法	憲法	xiànfǎ	n.	constitution (of a country)	8
相亲	相親	xiāng qīn	v.o.	to have a blind date	1
相应	相應	xiāngyìng	adj.	corresponding, relevant, fitting	2
象征	象徵	xiàngzhēng	n.	symbol, token, icon	6
硝烟	硝煙	xiāoyān	n.	smoke of gunpowder	3
销售	銷售	xiāoshòu	v.	to sell	4
小品		xiǎopǐn	n.	skit, short and simple literary or artistic creation	6
小提琴		xiǎotíqín	n.	violin, fiddle	3
小题大做	小題大做	xiǎotídàzuò	f.e.	to make a fuss, to make a mountain of a molehill, to intentionally exaggerate	6
携带	攜帶	xiédài	v.	to carry, to take along, to bring along	8
携手	攜手	xié shǒu	v.o.	to be jointly engaged in, to cooperate	8
心动	心動	xīndòng	adj.	heart-touching, heart-tempting	1
欣赏	欣賞	xīnshǎng	v.	to appreciate, to enjoy, to admire	5

欣慰		xīnwèi	adj.	be gratified, be delighted	6
新近		xīnjìn	adv.	recently, lately	3
新奇		xīnqí	adj.	strange, novel, new	4
新兴	新興	xīnxīng	adj.	new, emerging, rising	2
新颖	新穎	xīnyǐng	adj.	new and original, novel	2
薪水		xīnshuǐ	n.	salary, pay, wages	2
信徒		xìntú	n.	believer, disciple, follower	4
信仰		xìnyǎng	v./n.	to believe in, to have faith in; faith, belief	4
行凶	行兇	xíng xiōng	v.o.	to do violence, to assault	8
行政		xíngzhèng	n.	administrative, administration	6
性感		xìnggǎn	adj.	sex appeal, sexy	6
性交		xìngjiāo	v.	to have a sexual intercourse, to make love, to have sex	6
虚拟	虛擬	xūnǐ	adj.	virtual, invented, fictitious	5
宣扬	宣揚	xuānyáng	v.	to publicize, to propagate, to advocate	8
喧哗	喧嘩	xuānhuá	v.	to make an uproar; confused noise, uproar	1
悬浮	懸浮	xuánfú	v.	to float or hang (in the air)	7
寻求	尋求	xúnqiú	v.	to seek, to pursue, to look for	1
询问	詢問	xúnwèn	v.	to ask about, to enquire about, to question	6

Y

压抑	壓抑	yāyì	v.	to depress	7
烟尘	煙塵	yānchén	n.	smoke and dust	7
烟雾	煙霧	yānwù	n.	smoke, mist, smog	7
延续	延續	yánxù	v.	to continue, to last, to extend	4
严	嚴	yán	adj.	strict, severe, extreme	3
严苛	嚴苛	yánkē	adj.	strict and harsh	3
严厉	嚴厲	yánlì	adj.	strong, severe, strict	3
研发	研發	yánfā	v.	to research and develop	2
业	業	yè	b.f.	trade, industry, occupation	2
一连串	一連串	yìliánchuàn	attr.	a succession of (actions, issues, etc.), a series of, a chain of (events, etc.)	8
一律		yílǜ	adv.	all, uniformly, without exception	4
一面		yímiàn	n.	one aspect, one side (of an object)	1
一气之下	一氣之下	yíqì zhīxià	f.e.	angrily, in a pet, a fit of pique	2
一系列		yíxìliè	attr.	a series of	7

依赖		yīlài	v.	to depend on, to rely on	5
移民		yímín	v.o./n.	to migrate, to emigrate or immigrate; settler	4
以貌取人		yǐ mào qǔ rén	f.e.	to judge people by outward appearance	1
议员	議員	yìyuán	n.	senator	8
意见相左	意見相左	yìjiàn xiāngzuǒ	f.e.	to disagree with each other, to have difference opinions	2
意识	意識	yìshí	n.	consciousness, awareness	2
意味		yìwèi	n.	meaning, overtone, implication	4
阴霾	陰霾	yīnmái	n.	haze	7
引爆		yǐnbào	v.	to ignite, to detonate	6
引导	引導	yǐndǎo	v./n.	to guide, to lead, to instruct; guidance, instruction	1
隐含	隱含	yǐnhán	v.	to imply, to denote	6
影片		yǐngpiàn	n.	film, movie	8
影视	影視	yǐngshì	n.	film and television	8
应聘	應聘	yìngpìn	v.	to apply a job by responding an advertisement, to accept an offer of employment	6
拥有	擁有	yōngyǒu	v.	to possess, to have, to own	8
用语	用語	yòngyǔ	n.	phraseology, term	6
优先	優先	yōuxiān	v.	to take precedence, to give priority	2
由此		yóucǐ	conj.	from this, thus, therefrom	1
犹太裔	猶太裔	yóutàiyì	n.	Jewish descent	3
游乐	遊樂	yóulè	v.	to amuse oneself, to have fun	4
游说	遊說	yóushuì	v.	to lobby, to go about selling an idea	8
有限公司		yǒuxiàn gōngsī	n.p.	limited liability company, limited company, Limited (Ltd.)	6
娱乐	娛樂	yúlè	v./n.	to give pleasure to, to amuse; entertainment, recreation	1
予以		yǔyǐ	v.	to give, to grant	6
语惊四座	語驚四座	yǔ jīng sì zuò	f.e.	one's words electrify his listeners	1
语录	語錄	yǔlù	n.	recorded utterance, quotation	1
预计	預計	yùjì	v.	to estimate, to forecast, to predict	2
欲望	慾望	yùwàng	n.	desire, wish, lust	3
园	園	yuán	b.f.	place of recreation, park, garden	4
原本		yuánběn	adv.	originally, formerly	5
源		yuán	b.f./n.	source of a river, source, cause	7
远程	遠程	yuǎnchéng	adj.	long-distance, remote, long-range	2
越俎代庖		yuèzǔdàipáo	f.e.	to take another's (sb. else's) job into one's own hands	3

Z

灾难	災難	zāinàn	n.	disaster, catastrophe, calamity	7
在乎		zàihu	v.	(oft. used in the negative) to care about, to mind, to take to heart	1
在线网站	在線網站	zàixiàn wǎngzhàn	n.p.	online website	4
遭		zāo	v.	to encounter, to meet with (disaster, misfortune, etc.), to suffer	6
遭遇		zāoyù	v.	to meet with, to encounter, to run up against (an enemy, misfortune, difficulties, etc.)	6
早年		zǎonián	n.	many years ago, in one's early years	3
择	擇	zé	v./b.f.	to select, to choose, to pick	2
择偶	擇偶	zé ǒu	v.o.	to choose a mate	1
增强	增強	zēngqiáng	v.	to strengthen, to heighten, to enhance	6
展示		zhǎnshì	v.	to reveal, to show, to demonstrate	1
战	戰	zhàn	v./b.f.	to fight; battle, war	3
障碍	障礙	zhàng'ài	n.	obstacle, obstruction, barrier	5
招		zhāo	v.	to enlist, to recruit	6
招聘		zhāopìn	v.	to invite applications for a job, to take job applications, to advertise job offers	2
震惊	震驚	zhènjīng	v./adj.	to shock, to astonish; surprised, shocked	8
争议	爭議	zhēngyì	v.	to dispute, to debate	4
整体	整體	zhěngtǐ	n.	whole, entirety	6
正面		zhèngmiàn	adj.	positive, right side	5
症		zhèng	b.f.	disease, malady, illness	5
知		zhī	b.f./v.	to know, to realize, to be aware of	1
执政	執政	zhí zhèng	v.o.	to be in power, to be in office	8
职场	職場	zhíchǎng	n.	job market, workplace	2
指数	指數	zhǐshù	n.	index, index number, indicator	7
制约	制約	zhìyuē	v.	to restrict, to constraint, to restrain	8
质疑	質疑	zhìyí	v.	to question, to query	3
治理		zhìlǐ	v.	to control, to manage	7
窒息		zhìxī	v.	to choke, to suffocate, to asphyxiate	7
智能		zhìnéng	n.	intelligence, brain power	2
中国式	中國式	zhōngguóshì	n.	Chinese style	3
中坚	中堅	zhōngjiān	n.	nucleus, backbone, hard core	2
中期		zhōngqī	n.	middle period, mid-, mid-term	7
中西部		zhōngxībù	n.	midwest	8

中意		zhòng yì	v.o.	to be to one's liking, to catch the fancy of	1
众多	眾多	zhòngduō	adj.	numerous, many	7
重现	重現	chóngxiàn	v.	to reappear, to recur	7
重演		chóngyǎn	v.	to recur, to repeat	7
重要性		zhòngyàoxìng	n.	importance, significance	3
州		zhōu	n.	state	8
周边	周邊	zhōubiān	n.	periphery, surrounding area	7
逐年		zhúnián	adv.	year by year, year after year	4
主持		zhǔchí	v.	to uphold, to stand for	6
主持人		zhǔchírén	n.	host, anchor, emcee	1
主管		zhǔguǎn	v./n.	to be responsible for, to be in charge of; person in charge	2
助		zhù	v.	to help, to assist, to aid	3
助理		zhùlǐ	n.	assistant	6
注册	註冊	zhùcè	v.	to register, to enroll	8
注目		zhùmù	v.	to gaze at, to fix one's eyes on	7
注意力		zhùyìlì	n.	attention	5
注重		zhùzhòng	v.	to lay stress on, to pay attention to, to attach importance to	2
驻	駐	zhù	v.	to stay, to be stationed	7
撰文		zhuàn wén	v.o.	to write articles	6
装饰	裝飾	zhuāngshì	v./n.	to decorate, to adorn; ornament, decoration	4
自卑		zìbēi	adj.	low self-esteem, feeling oneself inferior	5
自媒体		zìméitǐ	n.	self-media	5
自强	自強	zìqiáng	v.	to strive for improvement	6
自信(心)		zìxìn(xīn)	n.	self-confidence, self-assurance	3
自由度		zìyóudù	n.	degree of freedom	2
自幼		zìyòu	ad.p.	since little, since childhood	3
自尊心		zìzūnxīn	n.	self-respect, self-esteem	3
宗教		zōngjiào	n.	religion	4
总之	總之	zǒngzhī	conj.	in a word, in short, in brief	8
走访	走訪	zǒufǎng	v.	to pay a visit to, to interview	2
走人		zǒurén	v.p.	to leave, to walk away	2
足够	足夠	zúgòu	adj.	enough, ample, sufficient	2
族群		zúqún	n.	ethnic group	4
阻挠	阻撓	zǔnáo	v.	to obstruct, to thwart, to stand in the way	8
嘴边	嘴邊	zuǐbiān	n.	on one's lips	2
尊重		zūnzhòng	v.	to respect, to value, to esteem	3

| 做人 | | zuò rén | v.o. | to conduct oneself, to behave | 1 |

副课文部分

A

| 安全感 | | ānquángǎn | n. | sense of security, sense of safety | 3 |
| 案件 | | ànjiàn | n. | law suit, case | 1 |

B

般		bān	n.	sort, kind, way	1
办理	辦理	bànlǐ	v.	to handle, to conduct, to transact	1
伴侣		bànlǚ	n.	companion, mate, partner	4
傍		bàng	v.	to be close to (in distance), to draw near, to have an intimate relationship with sb.	3
包容		bāoróng	v.	to pardon, to forgive	1
保险费	保險費	bǎoxiǎnfèi	n.	(insurance) premium, insurance expenses	3
背景		bèijǐng	n.	background, backdrop, setting	2
本性		běnxìng	n.	natural instincts, nature	5
彼此		bǐcǐ	pr.	each other, one another	1
编辑	編輯	biānjí	v./n.	to edit; editor	5
编排	編排	biānpái	v.	to arrange, to lay out, to write a play and rehearse	2
辩论	辯論	biànlùn	v.	to debate, to argue over	8
标价	標價	biāo jià	v.o.	to mark a price	4
并非	並非	bìngfēi	v.	to be really not	3
博物馆	博物館	bówùguǎn	n.	museum	5
不可思议	不可思議	bùkě-sīyì	f.e.	inconceivable, unimaginable	1
不慎		búshèn	v.	to be incautious, to be careless	5

C

财政	財政	cáizhèng	n.	finances (public), financial, fiscal administration	3
参与	參與	cānyù	v.	to participate; participation	4
惨案	慘案	cǎn'àn	n.	massacre, murder case	8
惨痛	慘痛	cǎntòng	adj.	agonizing, grievous, painful	8

策		cè	b.f./n.	method, plan, policy	8
差异	差異	chāyì	n.	difference, discrepancy	2
尝试	嘗試	chángshì	v.	to attempt, to try, to have a go at	2
偿还	償還	chánghuán	v.	to repay, to reimburse	2
场面	場面	chǎngmiàn	n.	appearance, front, facade	4
潮		cháo	n.	tide, social upsurge, current	2
潮流		cháoliú	n.	tide, current, trend	4
撑		chēng	v.	to prop up, to support	4
成		chéng	m(n)	one tenth	4
成本		chéngběn	n.	prime cost	2
成家		chéng jiā	v.o.	to (of a man) get married	3
成年		chéngnián	v.	to grow up, to come of age	3
成人		chéngrén	n.	adult, grown man, grown-up	3
成员	成員	chéngyuán	n.	member	6
承担	承擔	chéngdān	v.	to undertake, to bear, to assume (responsibility, etc.)	6
吃香		chīxiāng	adj.	be very popular, be much sought after, be well-liked	2
池		chí	b.f./n.	pond, pool	5
持		chí	v./b.f.	to hold, to grasp; to support, to keep	8
持有		chíyǒu	v.	to hold (passport, views, etc.)	8
耻	恥	chǐ	b.f.	shame, disgrace, humiliation	3
冲动	衝動	chōngdòng	adj./n.	getting excited, be impetuous; impulsion, impulsiveness	1
充		chōng	v.	to serve as, to act as, to pose as	4
崇拜		chóngbài	v./n.	to admire, worship; adoration, veneration	3
筹划	籌劃	chóuhuà	v.	to plan and prepare	2
臭氧层	臭氧層	chòuyǎngcéng	n.	ozone layer, ozonosphere	7
出于	出於	chūyú	v.p.	to be due to, to stem, to start or proceed from	1
出租		chūzū	v.	to let, to rent out, to hire out	4
处罚	處罰	chǔfá	v.	to penalize, to punish	7
处于	處於	chǔyú	v.	to be (in some state, position, or condition), to stand in	3
创意	創意	chuàngyì	n.	creativity, originality, novelty	6
纯真	純真	chúnzhēn	adj.	pure and sincere, naivety, innocence	6
慈祥		cíxiáng	adj.	(of an old person's bearing and expression) kind and serene	6
从属	從屬	cóngshǔ	adj.	subordinate, dependence	3

从未	從未	cóngwèi	adv.	never	4
凑合	湊合	còuhe	adj.	not too bad, passable	1

D

达成	達成	dáchéng	v(c)	to arrive at, to reach (an agreement), to work out	1
打造		dǎzào	v.	to make (metal works), to forge, to create	4
大部分		dàbùfen	n.	greater part, mostly	8
代价	代價	dàijià	n.	price, cost	7
代言人		dàiyánrén	n.	spokesperson	8
贷	貸	dài	v./b.f.	to borrow, to lend (money)	2
贷款	貸款	dàikuǎn	n.	loan, credit	2
单身	單身	dānshēn	v./n.	to be unmarried, single; single man	4
当场	當場	dāngchǎng	adv.	at the scene, on the spot	8
当地	當地	dāngdì	n./attr.	at the place in question, in the locality; local	2
当事人	當事人	dāngshìrén	n.	litigant, client, person or party concerned	1
当天	當天	dàngtiān	n.	same day, that very day	4
档	檔	dàng	b.f./m(n)	files, archives (eg., for TV programs)	6
导演	導演	dǎoyǎn	n./v.	director; to direct a play, film, etc.	2
导致	導致	dǎozhì	v.	to lead to, to bring about, to result in	1
倒栽		dǎozāi	v.	to fall head over heals	5
登记处	登記處	dēngjìchù	n.	registration office	1
等等		děngděng	r.f.	and so on, etc.	7
低廉		dīlián	adj.	(of price) cheap, low-priced, inexpensive	2
钓鱼	釣魚	diào yú	v.o.	to go fishing	6
丢脸	丟臉	diū liǎn	v.o.	to lose face, to be disgraced	3
动机	動機	dòngjī	n.	motive, motivation, intention	1
独立战争	獨立戰爭	dúlì zhànzhēng	n.p.	civil war	8
独生子女	獨生子女	dúshēng zǐnǚ	n.p.	the only child	1
对手	對手	duìshǒu	n.	opponent, competitor, rival	2

E

恩赐	恩賜	ēncì	v.	to bestow, to favor; charity	1
而		ér	conj.	but (rather)	1

F

方便面	方便麵	fāngbiànmiàn	n.	instant noodles	6

房价	房價	fángjià	n.	house or apartment purchase price	3
房租		fángzū	n.	rent, money for renting a house	3
分担	分擔	fēndān	v.	to share responsibility for	6
分歧		fēnqí	n.	difference (of opinion, position)	8
分手		fēn shǒu	v.o.	to part company, to say good-bye, to break up	4
焚烧	焚燒	fénshāo	v.	to burn, to set on fire	7
风靡	風靡	fēngmǐ	v.	to be fashionable, to sweep over	4
风靡一时	風靡一時	fēngmǐ-yìshí	f.e.	to become fashionable for a time	5
风险	風險	fēngxiǎn	n.	risk, hazard, danger	4
疯	瘋	fēng	adj.	mad, insane, crazy	2
夫妻		fūqī	n.	husband and wife	1
肤浅	膚淺	fūqiǎn	adj.	superficial, shallow	5
抚养	撫養	fǔyǎng	v.	to foster, to raise, to bring up	3
父母		fùmǔ	n.	parents, father and mother	1
父子		fùzǐ	n.	father and son	6
付出		fùchū	v.	to pay, to expend	7
负责	負責	fùzé	v.	to be responsible for, be in charge of	4
复婚	復婚	fù hūn	v.o.	to marry each other again, to resume matrimonial relation	1
副教授		fù jiàoshòu	n.p.	associate professor	6
赋闲	賦閑	fùxián	v.	(of an official) to be unemployed	3

G

感恩		gǎn'ēn	v.	to feel grateful, to be thankful	1
高校		gāoxiào	n.	colleges and universities	4
高薪		gāoxīn	n.	high pay, fat salary	3
个性	個性	gèxìng	n.	individual character, personality, individuality	1
各地		gèdì	n.	in all parts of (a country), various regions	6
跟踪	跟蹤	gēnzōng	v.	to track, to follow the tracks of	8
公关	公關	gōngguān	n.	public relations	2
公众	公眾	gōngzhòng	n.	public	5
公主		gōngzhǔ	n.	princess	1
攻击	攻擊	gōngjī	v.	to attack, to assault	8
共识	共識	gòngshí	n.	common understanding, consensus	1
供		gōng	v.	to supply, to feed	4
购买	購買	gòumǎi	v.	to buy, to purchase	7
雇	僱	gù	v.	to hire, to employ	1

雇用		gùyòng	v.	to hire, to employ	2
雇员	雇員	gùyuán	n.	employee	2
痼疾		gùjí	n.	chronic illness	8
管制		guǎnzhì	v.	to control	8
盥洗		guànxǐ	v.	to wash one's hands and face	5
逛街		guàng jiē	v.o.	to saunter, to stroll along the street	4
归根结底	歸根結底	guīgēnjiédǐ	f.e.	ultimately	5
规劝	規勸	guīquàn	v.	to admonish, to exhort; remonstration	1
果腹		guǒfù	v.	to fill the stomach, to satisfy one's hunger	6
过度	過度	guòdù	adj.	exceeding, excessive, lavishly	3
过节	過節	guò jié	v.o.	to celebrate a festival or holiday	4
过于	過於	guòyú	adv.	too much, excessively, unduly	1

H

汉	漢	hàn	b.f./n.	man	8
好评	好評	hǎopíng	n.	be well-judged, favorable comment	5
合格		hégé	adj.	qualified, up to standard	2
何		hé	pr.	what, where, why, how	4
核心		héxīn	n.	core, inner circle (of a political party, government, etc.)	8
忽略		hūlüè	v.	to ignore, to neglect	6
护理	護理	hùlǐ	v.	to nurse, to take care of	8
环保	環保	huánbǎo	n.	environmental protection	7
缓	緩	huǎn	adj.	slow, unhurried	2
换取	換取	huànqǔ	v.	to exchange sth. for, to get in return	7
荒唐		huāngtáng	adj.	absurd, fantastic	4
回避		huíbì	v.	to avoid, to evade, to dodge	7
回复	回復	huífù	v.	to reply, to restore, to recover, to return to a normal state	4
回归	回歸	huíguī	v.	to return, to go back to (the original place)	6
毁灭	毀滅	huǐmiè	v.	to destroy, to exterminate, to demolish	7
会员	會員	huìyuán	n.	member of a mass or political organization	8
或许	或許	huòxǔ	adv.	perhaps, maybe, probably	4

J

激活		jīhuó	v.	to activate	5
激烈		jīliè	adj.	intense, fierce	2

极力	極力	jílì	adv.	doing one's utmost	8
集中		jízhōng	v.	to concentrate, to centralize, to focus	4
技能		jìnéng	n.	technical ability, skill, technique	2
迹象	跡象	jīxiàng	n.	sign, indication, mark	3
继承	繼承	jìchéng	v.	to carry forward, to carry on sb.'s unfinished work, to inherit (legacy of the dead, etc.)	6
家务	家務	jiāwù	n.	household duties, house work/chore	1
家长	家長	jiāzhǎng	n.	patriarch, head of a family, parent or guardian of a child	1
兼顾	兼顧	jiāngù	v.	to deal with two or more things	6
建立		jiànlì	v.	to build, to set up, to establish	4
将近	將近	jiāngjìn	adv.	close to, almost, nearly	3
降低		jiàngdī	v(c)	to reduce, to cut down	4
交易		jiāoyì	v./n.	to trade; transaction, business	7
交友		jiāo yǒu	v.o.	to make friends	4
焦点	焦點	jiāodiǎn	n.	focus, focal point	5
角度		jiǎodù	n.	point of view, angle	5
皆		jiē	adv.	all, each and every, in all cases	1
接触	接觸	jiēchù	v.	to come into contact with	4
结识	結識	jiéshí	v.	to get acquainted with sb., to get to know sb.	4
界限		jièxiàn	n.	bounds, boundaries	5
禁		jìn	v./b.f.	to prohibit, to forbid, to ban	8
禁令		jìnlìng	n.	prohibition, ban	8
惊讶	驚訝	jīngyà	adj.	surprised, astonished	7
居高不下		jūgāo-búxià	f.e.	to stay in a high position, without going down	2
聚		jù	v.	to assemble, to gather, to congregate	1

K

开播	開播	kāibō	v.	to begin to broadcast	6
开拓	開拓	kāituò	v.	to open up, to enlarge or expand (territory, etc.), to pioneer	2
看起来	看起来	kànqǐlái	v.p.	it seems (or appears), it looks as if, seemingly	3
考验	考驗	kǎoyàn	v.	to test; trial	2
渴望		kěwàng	v.	to hanker after, to thirst for, to aspire to, to be anxious for	3
客厅	客廳	kètīng	n.	sitting room, drawing room, living room	3
啃老族		kěnlǎozú	n.	boomerang kids, boomerang child	3

空想		kōngxiǎng	n./v.	fantasy, daydream; to fantasize	3
跨国	跨國	kuàguó	adj.	transnational	2
宽容	寬容	kuānróng	v.	to forgive, to pardon, to tolerant	1
窥私欲	窺私慾	kuīsīyù	n.	voyeuristic interest	5

L

来年	來年	láinián	n.	next year, the coming year	3
来源	來源	láiyuán	n./v.	origin, source; to originate, to stem from	5
乐趣	樂趣	lèqù	n.	delight, joy, pleasure	5
离婚率	離婚率	líhūnlǜ	n.	divorce rate	1
理解		lǐjiě	v.	to understand; understanding	4
历练	歷練	lìliàn	v.	to experience and toughening	2
联邦	聯邦	liánbāng	n.	federation	8
脸部	臉部	liǎnbù	n.	facial part	5
恋爱	戀愛	liàn'ài	v.	to be in love, to have a love affair	4
恋情	戀情	liànqíng	n.	love, love affair, romantic love	4
恋人	戀人	liànrén	n.	lover, sweetheart, loved one	4
聊天		liáo tiān	v.o.	to chat, to hobnob	4
寥寥无几	寥寥無幾	liáoliáoèwújǐ	f.e.	very few left, scanty	4
凌晨	凌晨	língchén	n.	before dawn, in the small hours, early in the morning	4
楼主	樓主	lóuzhǔ	n.	cyber-word: one who posts a post	4
论坛	論壇	lùntán	n.	forum, tribune, place to express oneself in public	4
逻辑	邏輯	luójí	n.	logic	8
骆驼	駱駝	luòtuo	n.	camel	6
旅游	旅遊	lǚyóu	v./n.	to travel; trip, journey, travel	2

M

门面	門面	ménmiàn	n.	appearance, facade	4
勉强	勉強	miǎnqiǎng	v.	to force sb. to do sth., to do with difficulty, to manage with an effort	1
面对	面對	miànduì	v.	to face, to confront, to encounter	1
民意		mínyì	n.	will of the people, public opinion	8
名词	名詞	míngcí	n.	noun	1
明星		míngxīng	n.	(movie, etc.) star	5
模式		móshì	n.	model, mode, pattern	4

母语	母語	mǔyǔ	n.	mother tongue	2
目光		mùguāng	n.	sight, vision, view	2

N

男子		nánzǐ	n.	man, male	5
难以	難以	nányǐ	adv.	hard to, difficult to	2
年龄	年齡	niánlíng	n.	age	4
奴役		núyì	v.	to enslave	5

O

哦		o	intj.	expressing newly gained understanding, expressing half believing	4

P

拍照		pāi zhào	v.o.	to take (a picture), to shoot (a film)	1
旁人		pángrén	n.	someone else, other people	5
陪伴		péibàn	v.	to accompany, to keep sb. company	6
陪同		péitóng	v.	to accompany, to be together with guide; companion	2
佩服		pèifú	v.	admire, have admiration for, think highly of	4
蓬勃		péngbó	adj.	vigorous, flourishing, full of vitality	2
疲软	疲軟	píruǎn	adj.	fatigued and weak, weakened, sluggish	2
聘用		pìnyòng	v.	to hire, to employ	2
平淡		píngdàn	adj.	prosaic, ordinary, insipid	1
平方公里		píngfāng gōnglǐ	m(n)	square kilometer	7
平台	平臺	píngtái	n.	platform	4
铺垫	鋪墊	pūdiàn	v.	to foreshadow, to provide a base for	2

Q

启事	啟事	qǐshì	n.	notice, announcement	4
气体	氣體	qìtǐ	n.	gas	7
恰当	恰當	qiàdàng	adj.	appropriate, proper, suitable	6
恰恰		qiàqià	adv.	coincidentally, exactly	8
前景		qiánjǐng	n.	prospect, vista	2
强劲	強勁	qiángjìng	adj.	powerful, forceful	2
悄然		qiǎorán	adj.	quiet, soft	4

176

亲密	親密	qīnmì	adj.	close, dear, intimate	3
青年人		qīngniánrén	n.	young people	3
青少年		qīngshàonián	n.	young people and teenagers, youths	3
情结	情結	qíngjié	n.	complex	5
情人		qíngrén	n.	lover, sweetheart	4
群体	群體	qúntǐ	n.	group	4

R

让步	讓步	ràng bù	v.o.	to concede, to give in, to compromise	1
人均		rénjūn	n.	per capita, average for individuals	7
人类	人類	rénlèi	n.	human, mankind, humanity	4
人力资源	人力資源	rénlì zīyuán	n.p.	human resource	2
人权	人權	rénquán	n.	human rights	8
人数	人數	rénshù	n.	number of people	6
忍让	忍讓	rěnràng	v.	to exercise forbearance, to be forbearing	1
认清	認清	rènqīng	v(c)	to see through to, to see clearly	5
认同	認同	rèntóng	v./n.	to approve of; identity	5
认知	認知	rènzhī	v./n.	to acknowledge; cognition	5
任		rèn	v.	to appoint or assign to a position, to assume a post, to take up a job	2
日趋	日趨	rìqū	adv.	with each passing day, gradually, day by day	2
如今		rújīn	n.	nowadays, these days, at present	4
入手		rùshǒu	v.	to put one's hand to, to begin with	8

S

散		sàn	v.	to come loose, to break up, to fall apart	1
杀鸡取卵	殺雞取卵	shājī-qǔluǎn	f.e.	to kill the hen to get the eggs, to kill the goose that lays the golden eggs, to be after only immediate interests	7
闪电	閃電	shǎndiàn	n.	lightning (here is used as a figurative expression describing the fast speed of a marriage)	1
上传	上傳	shàngchuán	v.	to upload	5
上风	上風	shàngfēng	n.	superior position	8
上天		shàngtiān	n.	Heaven, Providence, God	1
上涨	上漲	shàngzhǎng	v.	to rise, to go up (of water level, prices, etc.)	3
社交		shèjiāo	n.	social intercourse, social contact	4
涉及		shèjí	v.	to involve, to relate to, to touch upon (a topic)	1

身份		shēnfen	n.	identity, status	4
神圣	神聖	shénshèng	adj.	sacred, holy	4
慎重		shènzhòng	adj.	prudent, cautious, careful	1
生存		shēngcún	v.	to exist, to survive, to live	7
生态	生態	shēngtài	n.	ecology	7
生物圈		shēngwùquān	n.	biosphere, ecosphere	7
失业率	失業率	shīyèlǜ	n.	unemployment rate	2
诗人	詩人	shīrén	n.	poet	1
时光	時光	shíguāng	n.	times, years, days	6
时髦	時髦	shímáo	adj.	fashionable, in vogue, stylish	1
世人		shìrén	n.	common people	5
试图	試圖	shìtú	v.	to attempt to (do sth.), to try to (do sth.)	3
视野	視野	shìyě	n.	visual field, field of vision	2
收费	收費	shōu fèi	v.o.	to collect fees, to charge	4
收视	收視	shōushì	v.	to watch (TV programs)	6
手机	手機	shǒujī	n.	mobile phone	1
首席执行官	首席執行官	shǒuxí zhíxíngguān	n.p.	CEO (chief executive officer)	8
首相		shǒuxiàng	n.	prime minister	5
受挫		shòucuò	v.	to be baffled, to be thwarted, to suffer a setback	6
受害		shòu hài	v.o.	to suffer injury or damage, to fall victim	7
受伤	受傷	shòu shāng	v.o.	to sustain an injury, to be injured	5
梳头	梳頭	shū tóu	v.o.	to comb one's hair	6
顺从	順從	shùncóng	v.	to be obedient to (sb.), to submit to, to yield to	6
硕士	碩士	shuòshì	n.	master's degree	3
私有		sīyǒu	adj.	be privately owned, be private	8
思维	思維	sīwéi	n.	thought, thinking	5
搜寻	搜尋	sōuxún	v.	to search for, to look for, to hunt for, to seek	3
琐事	瑣事	suǒshì	n.	trifles, trivial matters	1

T

台阶	臺階	táijiē	n.	staircase	5
太空		tàikōng	n.	outer space	5
坦然		tǎnrán	adj.	calm, unperturbed, having no misgivings	1
淘金		táo jīn	v.o.	gold washing	2
疼爱	疼愛	téng'ài	v.	to love dearly, to be fond of, to dote on	1
腾	騰	téng	v.	to make room, to clear out, to vacate	6

提醒		tíxǐng	v.	to remind, to warn, to call attention to	4
体内	體內	tǐnèi	attr.	the interior of the body	7
天经地义	天經地義	tiānjīngèdìyì	f.e.	principles of heaven and earth-right and proper, perfectly justified	6
调侃	調侃	tiáokǎn	v.	to mock up	5
调研	調研	diàoyán	v./n.	to investigate and study; research, survey	2
帖（子）		tiě (zi)	n.	invitation, post	4
通常		tōngcháng	adv.	generally, usually, regularly	3
同龄	同齡	tónglíng	v.	to be at the same age	2
痛心		tòngxīn	adj.	pained, distressed, grieved	1
突破		tūpò	v.	to break through, to make a break through, to surmount (difficulty)	2
图片	圖片	túpiàn	n.	picture, photograph, image	5
途径	途徑	tújìng	n.	road, way, approach	4

W

网友	網友	wǎngyǒu	n.	net friend, e-pal	1
网站	網站	wǎngzhàn	n.	website	3
威胁	威脅	wēixié	v.	to threaten; threat	7
为何	為何	wèihé	adv.	why, for what reason	6
唯一		wéiyī	adj./attr.	single, only, sole	8
惟		wéi	adv.	only, alone, solely	1
委屈		wěiqu	adj.	feeling wronged, nursing a grievance, be misunderstood	1
温柔	溫柔	wēnróu	adj.	gentle and soft, tender	6
温室	溫室	wēnshì	n.	greenhouse, conservatory	7
温馨	溫馨	wēnxīn	adj.	warm and fragrant, cozy, warm	4
稳定性	穩定性	wěndìngxìng	n.	stability, stabilization	1
卧室	臥室	wòshì	n.	bedroom, bedchamber	3
污	汙	wū	b.f.	dirty, filthy	7
五花八门	五花八門	wǔhuā-bāmén	f.e.	multifarious, of a wide or rich variety	5
舞蹈		wǔdǎo	n.	dance	2

X

西南部		xīnánbù	n.	southwest	6
惜		xī	b.f.	to value, to cherish, to treasure	1
下降		xiàjiàng	v.	to descend, to drop, to fall, to decline	1

现场	現場	xiànchǎng	n.	scene (of event or incident), spot	8
现代舞团	現代舞團	xiàndài wǔtuán	n.p.	modern dance troupe	2
相比		xiāngbǐ	v.	to compared to, to contrast	1
相处	相處	xiāngchǔ	v.	to get along (with one another)	6
相当于	相當於	xiāngdāngyú	v.p.	to be equivalent to, to correspond to	7
相互		xiānghù	adv.	mutual, reciprocal, each other	4
相应	相應	xiāngyìng	adv.	corresponding, relevant	2
想象力		xiǎngxiànglì	n.	imaginative power or imagination	5
小时工	小時工	xiǎoshígōng	n.	hourly paid workers (usually refers to houseworker)	1
孝道		xiàodào	n.	filial piety	6
校园	校園	xiàoyuán	n.	campus, schoolyard	4
效仿		xiàofǎng	v.	to imitate, to follow the example of	4
效应	效應	xiàoyìng	n.	effect (e.g., greenhouse effect)	7
协议	協議	xiéyì	n.	agreement, pact, protocol	1
心理		xīnlǐ	n.	psychology, mentality, thoughts, emotions, etc.	1
心理学	心理學	xīnlǐxué	n.	psychology	3
新生代		xīnshēngdài	n.	new generation	6
行为	行為	xíngwéi	n.	action, behavior, conduct	4
凶手	兇手	xiōngshǒu	n.	assailant, murderer	8
修正案		xiūzhèng'àn	n.	amendment	8
宣扬	宣揚	xuānyáng	v.	to publicize, to propagate, to advocate	6
悬挂	懸掛	xuánguà	v.	to hang, to suspend	5
学前教育	學前教育	xuéqián jiàoyù	n.p.	preschool education, early childhood education	6
学士	學士	xuéshì	n.	bachelor, bachelor's degree	2
学位	學位	xuéwèi	n.	academic degree	2
学位服	學位服	xuéwèifú	n.	academicals, academic costumes	2
巡回	巡迴	xúnhuí	v.	to tour, to make a circuit of, to go around	2

Y

延迟	延遲	yánchí	v.	to delay, to postpone	2
严峻	嚴峻	yánjùn	adj.	stern, severe, grim	2
研究生		yánjiūshēng	n.	postgraduate (student), graduate student	3
眼球		yǎnqiú	n.	eyeball	4
养活	養活	yǎnghuó	v.	to support, to provide for, to feed	3
养育	養育	yǎngyù	v.	to bring up, to rear, to foster	6
遥远	遙遠	yáoyuǎn	adj.	distant, remote, faraway	6

一无所知	一無所知	yìwúsuǒzhī	f.e.	to know nothing at all	2
一再		yízài	adv.	time and again, repeatedly	8
衣食无忧	衣食無憂	yīshí wúyōu	f.e.	need not worry about food and clothes	1
衣食住行		yīshízhùxíng	f.e.	clothing, food, shelter (housing) and transportation—basic necessities of life	3
依赖	依賴	yīlài	v.	to rely on, to be dependent on, to be interdependent	3
已婚		yǐhūn	adj.	married	1
议	議	yì	v./b.f.	to discuss, to exchange views on; comment	4
异性	異性	yìxìng	n.	the opposite sex	4
意味		yìwèi	v.	to mean, to indicate	2
意愿	意願	yìyuàn	n.	wish, desire, aspiration	6
阴历	陰曆	yīnlì	n.	lunar calendar	4
引发	引發	yǐnfā	v.	to initiate, to trigger, to spark off	1
引用		yǐnyòng	v.	to quote, to cite	1
盈利		yínglì	v./n.	to make a profit, to earn a profit; profit, gain	2
应对	應對	yìngduì	v.	to reply, to answer, to response	6
应付	應付	yìngfu	v.	to deal with, to cope with, to handle	4
应届	應屆	yīngjiè	adj.	the present graduating year, this year's (only used for graduating students or pupils)	2
应景	應景	yìngjǐng	v.o./attr.	to do sth. for the occasion; seasonable, suitable to the circumstance	4
拥	擁	yōng	v./b.f.	to possess; to hold in one's arms, to embrace	8
拥有	擁有	yōngyǒu	v.	to possess, to have, to own	2
游	遊	yóu	v./b.f.	to travel, to tour, to rove around	2
游客	遊客	yóukè	n.	tourist, traveler, visitors	7
游戏	遊戲	yóuxì	n.	recreation, game	2
友情		yǒuqíng	n.	friendship	4
有趣		yǒuqù	adj.	interesting, fascinating	4
有限		yǒuxiàn	adj.	limited, restricted, finite	4
与此同时	與此同時	yǔ cǐ tóngshí	f.e.	at the same time, meanwhile, moreover	1
宇航员	宇航員	yǔhángyuán	n.	astronaut	5
浴室		yùshì	n.	bathroom	5
预料	預料	yùliào	v./n.	to expect; prediction, anticipation	8
月份		yuèfèn	n.	month	6
跃跃欲试	躍躍欲試	yuèyuè-yùshì	f.e.	be eager to have a try, itch to have a go	2
运气	運氣	yùnqi	n.	fortune, luck	2

Z

杂志	雜誌	zázhì	n.	magazine, journal, periodical	6
在校		zàixiào	attr.	attending school, in school	4
在于	在於	zàiyú	v.	to lie in, to consist in	5
葬礼	葬禮	zànglǐ	n.	funeral	5
早已		zǎoyǐ	ad.p.	long ago, for a long time, previously	8
展现	展現	zhǎnxiàn	v.	to emerge, to show	5
长辈	長輩	zhǎngbèi	n.	elder member of a family, elder, senior	4
长大	長大	zhǎngdà	v(c)	to grow up, to mature	3
招		zhāo	v.	to enlist, to enroll, to recruit	2
珍惜		zhēnxī	v.	to treasure, to value, to cherish	1
真人秀		zhēnrénxiù	n.	reality show	6
征	徵	zhēng	v.	to levy, to recruit, to solicit	4
支持		zhīchí	v.	to support; support	4
支付		zhīfù	v.	to pay (money), to defray	3
知名		zhīmíng	adj.	famous, well known	5
知之甚少		zhīzhī shènshǎo	f.e.	little is known	2
职位	職位	zhíwèi	n.	position, post	2
职责	職責	zhízé	n.	duty, obligation, responsibility	6
殖民		zhímín	v.	to establish a colony, to colonize	8
制止		zhìzhǐ	v.	to prevent, to stop	8
质朴	質樸	zhìpǔ	adj.	unaffected, plain, simple and unadorned	1
种种	種種	zhǒngzhǒng	r.f.	all kinds of, all sorts of, various	1
重任		zhòngrèn	n.	important task, great commitment, heavy responsibility	6
主		zhǔ	v.	to be in charge of	6
转换	轉換	zhuǎnhuàn	v.	to change, to transform, to convert	6
转向	轉向	zhuǎnxiàng	v.	to change directions, to turn	2
追根溯源		zhuīgēn-sùyuán	f.e.	to find by hard and thorough search	5
追捧		zhuīpěng	v.	to chase after (celebrity or famous people)	6
咨询	諮詢	zīxún	v.	to seek counsel or advice from, to inquire and consult	1
自称	自稱	zìchēng	v.	to call oneself, to style oneself, to claim to be	4
自古		zìgǔ	adv.	since ancient times, since antiquity	6
自恋	自戀	zìliàn	v./n.	to admire oneself; narcissism	5
自拍		zìpāi	v./n.	to take a selfie; selfie	5

自卫	自衛	zìwèi	v.	to defend oneself; self-defense	8
自治		zìzhì	v.	to exercise autonomy; self-government	8
总监	總監	zǒngjiān	n.	director, chief inspector	2
租		zū	v.	to rent, to hire	4
族		zú	n./b.f.	clan; race, nationality; class or group of things or people with common features	3
阻止		zǔzhǐ	v.	to prevent, to stop, to hold back	8
组成	組成	zǔchéng	v.	to form, to compose; formation	7
祖父母		zǔfùmǔ	n.	grandparents from the father's side	1
最终	最終	zuìzhōng	n.	final, ultimate, last	8

专名索引

主课文部分

A

| 阿文 | | Ā Wén | a person's name | 5 |

B

| 宝马 | 寶馬 | Bǎomǎ | the Chinese translation of BMW car | 1 |
| 布什 | | Bùshí | George Walker Bush | 8 |

C

蔡美儿	蔡美兒	Cài Měi'ér	Amy L. Chua	3
曹菊		Cáo Jú	a person's name	6
查尔斯·狄更斯	查爾斯·狄更斯	Chá'ěrsī Dígēngsī	Charles Dickens	7
陈心怡	陳心怡	Chén Xīnyí	a person's name	2
春晚		Chūnwǎn	the abbreviation for "Spring Festival Gala" held on TV in every Spring Festival Eve	6

F

法国	法國	Fǎguó	France	4
弗吉尼亚理工大学	弗吉尼亞理工大學	Fújíníyà lǐgōng dàxué	Virginia Tech (Virginia Polytechnic Institute and State University)	8
妇女权益保障法	婦女權益保障法	Fùnǚ quányì bǎozhàng fǎ	The Bill of Women's Rights' Protection	6
复旦大学	復旦大學	Fùdàn Dàxué	Fudan University	5

G

格灵深瞳	格靈深瞳	gélíngshēntóng	Deep Glint, a company's name	2
共和党	共和黨	Gònghédǎng	Republican Party	8
国际先驱论坛报	國際先驅論壇報	Guójì xiānqū lùntán bào	International Herald Tribune	8

H

| 哈佛 | | Hāfó | Harvard (University) | 1 |

哈佛大学	哈佛大學	Hāfó Dàxué	Harvard University	3
海淀区	海淀區	Hǎidiàn qū	Haidian District (of Beijing City)	6
洪向阳	洪向陽	Hóng Xiàngyáng	*a person's name*	2
湖北		Húběi	Hubei (province)	2
华盛顿	華盛頓	Huáshèngdùn	Washington, D.C.	8

J

加拿大		Jiānádà	Canada	4
江苏	江蘇	Jiāngsū	Jiangsu province	1
就业促进法	就業促進法	Jiùyè cùjìn fǎ	The Bill of Employment Promotion	6

K

康涅狄格州		Kāngnièdígé zhōu	Connecticut	8
科罗拉多州	科羅拉多州	Kēluólāduō zhōu	Colorado	8

L

露露		Lùlù	Lulu	3
伦敦	倫敦	Lúndūn	London	7

M

马诺	馬諾	Mǎ Nuò	*a person's name*	1
麦当劳	麥當勞	Màidāngláo	McDonald's	8

N

纽镇	紐鎮	Niǔzhèn	Newtown	8

O

欧美	歐美	Ōu Měi	Europe and America	4

P

普渡大学	普渡大學	Pǔdù dàxué	Purdue University	8
普林斯顿大学	普林斯頓大學	Pǔlínsīdùn Dàxué	Princeton University	2

Q

全国步枪协会	全國步槍協會	Quánguó bùqiāng xiéhuì	National Rifle Association	8

S

桑迪胡克		Sāngdíhúkè	Sandy Hook (school name)	8
山西		Shānxī	Shanxi (province)	6
圣诞节	聖誕節	Shèngdàn jié	Christmas Day	4
圣诞老人	聖誕老人	Shèngdàn lǎorén	Santa Claus	4
圣婴	聖嬰	shèngyīng	the Holy Child	4
世界卫生组织	世界衛生組織	shìjiè wèishēng zǔzhī	World Health Organization	7
司法部		Sīfǎ bù	Department of Justice	8
斯科特		Sīkētè	Scott	8
索菲亚	索菲亞	Suǒfēiyà	Sophia	3

T

淘宝(网)	淘寶(網)	Táobǎo(wǎng)	literal translation: digging treasure; used as a name for a Chinese e-shopping network	2

W

网易	網易	Wǎngyì	Netease (A Chinese internet company)	6
武汉	武漢	Wǔhàn	Wuhan (capital of Hubei Province)	2

X

小元		Xiǎo Yuán	a person's name	2
小庄	小莊	Xiǎo Zhuāng	a person's name	2
新华网	新華網	Xīnhuá wǎng	the website of Xinhua News Agency	2

Y

亚洲	亞洲	Yàzhōu	Asia	4
耶鲁大学	耶魯大學	Yēlǔ Dàxué	Yale University	3
耶稣	耶穌	Yēsū	Jesus, Jesus Christ	4
尹雄		Yǐn Xióng	a person's name	6
印第安纳州		Yìndì'ānnà Zhōu	Indiana	8
约克郡邮报	約克郡郵報	Yuēkè Jùn Yóubào	The Yorkshire Post	4

Z

赵民	趙民	Zhào Mín	a person's name	5
中关村	中關村	Zhōngguāncūn	It is a technology hub in Haidian District, Beijing, China and is often referred to as "China's Silicon Valley"	2
中国妇女报	中國婦女報	Zhōngguó Fùnǚ Bào	China Women's News	6
中华女子学院	中華女子學院	Zhōnghuá Nǚzǐ Xuéyuàn	China Women's University	6

副课文部分

A

艾琳娜		Àilínnà	Elena	3
奥巴马	奧巴馬	Àobāmǎ	Barack Obama	5
奥运会	奧運會	Àoyùnhuì	Olympic Games	5
澳大利亚	澳大利亞	Àodàlìyà	Australia	5
澳洲		Àozhōu	Australia	5

B

巴纳德学院	巴納德學院	Bānàdé Xuéyuàn	Barnard College	2
北京师范大学	北京師範大學	Běijīng Shīfàn Dàxué	Beijing Normal University	6
布鲁斯·威利斯	布鲁斯·威利斯	Bùlǔsī Wēilìsī	Bruce Willis	8

D

大西洋月刊		Dàxīyáng Yuèkān	The Atlantic	6
丹麦	丹麥	Dānmài	Denmark	5

E

二战	二戰	Èrzhàn	World War Two	3

F

弗洛伊德		Fúluòyīdé	Sigmund Freud	5

H

翰威特		Hànwēitè	Hewitt Associates Inc.	2
好莱坞	好萊塢	Hǎoláiwù	Hollywood	8
华尔街日报	華爾街日報	Huá'ěrjiē rìbào	*The Wall Street Journal*	2

J

基恩		Jī'ēn	Dave Keene	8
杰弗里·阿恩特	傑弗里·阿恩特	Jiéfúlǐ Ā'ēntè	Jeffrey Arnett	3
金·卡戴珊		Jīn Kǎdàishān	Kim Kardashian	5

K

肯尼迪		Kěnnídí	Kennedy	8

L

拉皮埃尔	拉皮埃爾	Lāpí'āi'ěr	Wayne LaPierre	8
李敏谊	李敏誼	Lǐ Mǐnyì	*a person's name*	6
里根		Lǐgēn	Ronald Wilson Reagan	8
恋爱么么哒	戀愛麼麼噠	Liàn'ài Mēmeda	*The name of an online platform*	4
陆伟	陸偉	Lù Wěi	*a person's name*	4

M

马里兰大学	馬里蘭大學	Mǎlǐlán Dàxué	University of Maryland	3
麦克·霍普金	麥克·霍普金	Màikè Huòpǔjīn	Mike Hopkins	5
曼德拉		Màndélā	Nelson Mandela	5

N

南京师范大学	南京師範大學	Nánjīng Shīfàn Dàxué	Nanjing Normal University	6
尼克松		níkèsōng	Richard Milhous Nixon	8
纽约时报	紐約時報	Niǔyuē Shíbào	*The New York Times*	2

O

欧洲	歐洲	Ōuzhōu	Europe, European	2

P

皮尤研究中心		Píyóu Yánjiū Zhōngxīn	Pew Research Center	8
蒲柏		Púbǎi	Alexander Pope	1

Q

七夕		Qīxī	the seventh evening of the seventh month in lunar-calendar	4
情人节	情人節	Qíngrén Jié	Valentine's Day	4

S

萨拉贝丝·伯尔曼	薩拉貝絲·伯爾曼	Sàlābèisī Bó'ěrmàn	Sarabeth Berman	2
施密特		Shīmìtè	Helle Thorning Schmidt	5
史密斯大学	史密斯大學	Shǐmìsī Dàxué	Smith College	3
斯坦福大学	斯坦福大學	Sītǎnfú Dàxué	Stanford University	3

T

太平洋		Tàipíng Yáng	the Pacific Ocean	7
推特		Tuītè	Twitter	5

W

卫斯理安大学	衛斯理安大學	Wèisīlǐ'ān Dàxué	Wesleyan University	2
武汉科技大学	武漢科技大學	Wǔhàn Kējì Dàxué	Wuhan University of Science and Technology	4

X

新加坡		Xīnjiāpō	Singapore	7

Y

约书亚·斯蒂芬斯	約書亞·斯蒂芬斯	Yuēshūyà Sīdìfēnsī	Joshua Stephens	2
云南	雲南	Yúnnán	Yunnan (province)	6

Z

芝加哥		Zhījiāgē	Chicago	3

Today's World Ⅰ
Select Readings of Chinese Spotlight News

Workbook
·练习本·

今日世界面面观
汉语焦点新闻选读

上册

王 颖　王志军　徐丽莎　◎编著

北京大学出版社
PEKING UNIVERSITY PRESS

CONTENTS

目 录

第 1 课
看《非诚勿扰》 知现代婚恋观　　　　　　　　　　/1

第 2 课
职场上的"90后"　　　　　　　　　　　　　　　/8

第 3 课
华裔虎妈教女严　中西争论起"硝烟"　　　　　　/14

第 4 课
多元文化冲击　"圣诞节"世俗化　　　　　　　　/20

第 5 课
你是"低头族"吗　　　　　　　　　　　　　　　/25

第 6 课
女性维权非小事　社会关注人人知　　　　　　　　/31

第 7 课
北京与伦敦：雾都治霾浅议　　　　　　　　　　　/37

第 8 课
美国校园为何枪击案频发　　　　　　　　　　　　/43

第1课 看《非诚勿扰》 知现代婚恋观

一、请用英文解释下列词的意思
Please give the meanings of the following words in English

价值观 _____   中式 _____   能见度 _____

离婚率 _____   闪牵 _____   试用 _____

二、词汇搭配
Match the following two groups of words or phrases

提出	伴侣
谈	认可
娶	教育意义
寻求	恋爱
具有	问题
得到	白富美
反映	基金
成立	现实

三、区分下面词汇的用法并完成填空

◆ Please note the different usages of the following words and fill in the blanks

1. 具有、有

(具有 is usually used in a more abstract sense, is a written/formal expression, and means "to possess or have something immaterial such as confidence, ability, meaning, etc." 有 is often used in a more concrete sense, is a spoken/informal expression, and means "to have something, either material or immaterial".)

① 我儿子的房间里_____一台电视机和一台游戏机。

② 这次选举对他的政治生涯_____非常重大的意义。

③ 他虽然获得了博士学位，但是不_____当领导的能力和品质。

④ 这部3D电影很_____想象力，非常精彩。

2. 近、差不多

(近 is usually used in a more abstract sense, is a written/formal expression, and means "to be close to, to be near". 差不多 is often used in a more concrete sense, is a spoken/informal expression, and means "to be not different from others in quality or quantity, to be close to, to be near".)

① 参加外语教师大会的教师_____六千人，盛况空前。

② 这本书我_____两天可以看完，看完后马上还给你。

③ 我_____有二十年没回老家了，非常想念那里的亲人。

④ 他年_____六十，还坚持来上课，学习中文。

3. 凭、根据

(Both words are prepositions that mean "based on" or "according to", but 凭 can take 着 while 根据 cannot; 凭 is a spoken word, and 根据 is a written word. The object of 凭 must be some ability or thing that the subject has; in addition, 凭 has the meaning of "to rely on", but 根据 does not.)

① _____大家的意见，我们召开了一次会议。

② 毕业那天，学生可以_____学生证进入学生餐厅免费吃饭。

③ 他一直_____着自己的努力一步一步实现理想。

④ _____天气预报，这个星期每天都下雪。

4. 由于、因为

（由于 is usually used in written/formal expression and means "owing to, due to, because, etc." 因为 is often used in both formal and spoken/informal expressions and means "because, owing to". 由于 can combine with 因此 and 因而, but 因为 cannot; 因为 can occur in the second clause in a complex sentence, but 由于 cannot.）

① 他的学习成绩一直很好，_____他是一个特别用功的学生。

② 不要_____这样的小事而烦恼，我们聊聊。

③ _____年纪大了，身体又不好，因而他决定提前退休。

④ _____老师和同学的帮助，小张的英语水平提高得非常快。

四、找出与阴影词语最接近的解释

* Choose the expression that is closest in meaning to the shaded word or phrase

_____ 1. 非常欢迎与我探讨这些严肃的问题，否则 非诚勿扰。

　a. 不要忧愁　　b. 没有诚意不要打扰　　c. 欢迎打扰

_____ 2. 她和男朋友在一起10年了，今年终于要 谈婚论嫁 了。

　a. 谈恋爱　　b. 谈论有关结婚的事情　　c. 讨论恋爱结婚的意义

_____ 3. 现代人的生活节奏很快，其中一个 令人担忧 的问题是家人很少一起吃晚饭。

　　a. 让人担心、忧虑　　b. 让人觉得没有意思　　c. 令人难过

_____ 4. 年轻人找对象的时候千万不要 以貌取人 。

　　a. 觉得外貌不重要　　b. 娶个漂亮的妻子　　c. 根据人的外貌判断一个人

_____ 5. 马云在美国演讲时 语惊四座 。

　　a. 语言令人害怕　　b. 说的话让人吃惊　　c. 惊动了在座的四位客人

_____ 6. 两人相亲，一见面就 看对眼 了。

　　a. 看上对方　　　　b. 两眼对视　　　　c. 直视对方

_____ 7. 很多人认为现在这个社会就是 拼爹 ，学得好不如有个好爸爸。

　　a. 照顾爸爸　　　　b. 比拼谁的爸爸更有钱有能力　　c. 打爸爸

五、选词填空

◆ Choose the most appropriate word and fill in the blanks

| 以……方式 | 宁愿……也不 | 即 | 不由得 |
| 只是……而已 | 仅仅 | 而 | 令 |

1. 做事的时候我喜欢听音乐，_____想让自己放松一下_____。

2. _____人惊讶的是，数学课被学生选为最喜欢的科目。

3. 他_____同样的_____再次取得成功。

4. 我 _____不吃早饭_____想让自己上课迟到。

5. MBA，_____工商管理硕士，在中国很受欢迎。

6. 看到这张照片，我_____想起了那年的暑假。

7. 爸爸给他的零花钱，＿＿＿＿＿＿＿一个月他就花光了。

8. 这是一个美丽＿＿＿＿＿＿＿安静的小村子。

六、句段分析
◆ Sentence analysis

1. 找出下列句子的主语、谓语和宾语（Please indicate the subject, predicate, and object in the following sentences）

   (1) 她们根据对上场男嘉宾的印象，以亮灯或者灭灯的方式来决定男嘉宾的去留。

   主语：　　　　　　谓语：　　　　　　宾语：

   (2) 因为《非诚勿扰》节目在中国具有相当多的观众，它展示的婚恋观必将影响很多年轻人的恋爱择偶标准、婚姻家庭观念和伦理道德观。

   主语：　　　　　　谓语：　　　　　　宾语：

2. 把下列句子翻译成英文（Translate the following sentences into English）

   (1) 这不仅仅是这些登上《非诚勿扰》节目的男女嘉宾的问题，它反映的是在浮躁喧哗的今天，"以貌取人"已成为现代很多青年男女的普遍倾向。

(2) 这反映了现代青年婚恋观中很现实的一面，即金钱等物质因素成为恋爱婚姻的基本条件，有房有车才能谈婚论嫁。

七、小作文

◆ Short essay

《非诚勿扰》这一电视征婚节目反映了什么样的恋爱婚姻观？你同意这种观点吗？在婚恋问题上，现在的美国年轻人一般有什么样的想法？

（200-300字，请在你的作文中尽量用上本课所学的生词和句型结构。200-300 characters; please do your best to use the words and grammar patterns learned in this lesson.）

Lesson 1

看《非诚勿扰》 知现代婚恋观

第 2 课　职场上的 "90后"

一、请用英文解释下列词的意思
Please give the meanings of the following words in English

官场　　　　　加强　　　　　维护

偿还　　　　　展开　　　　　择偶

增多　　　　　注意　　　　　强健

二、词汇搭配
Match the following two groups of words or phrases

采访	新产品
举办	两国的关系
维系	阿里巴巴网络公司
研发	招聘会
创立	新闻
赔偿	别人的利益
损害	损失
发布	公司的管理人员

三、区分下面词汇的用法并完成填空

Please note the different usages of the following words and fill in the blanks

1. 赔偿、赔

(赔偿 is usually used in a more abstract sense and is a written/formal expression while 赔 is often used in a more concrete sense and is a spoken/informal expression.)

① _____钱；_____经济损失

② _____款；_____精神损失

③ _____不是

2. 新颖、新

(新颖 is usually used in a more abstract sense, is a written/formal expression, and means "innovative, novel" while 新 is often used in a more concrete sense, is a spoken/informal expression, and means "new".)

① 这件衣服还没有穿过，是_____的。

② 那本_____书的内容很_____。

③ 这个音乐厅的设计时尚、_____。

④ 她刚学了一首_____歌，很好听。

3. 足够、够

(足够 is usually used in a more abstract sense, is a written/formal expression, and means "enough" or "satisfactory" while 够 is often used in a more concrete sense, is a spoken/informal expression, and means "enough", "sick of", or "reaching a certain standard or satisfying a certain condition".)

① 他对自己的错误已经有了_____的认识。

② 这点儿钱不_____。

③ 开办一个公司需要有_____的资金。

④ 天天吃快餐，我可吃_____了！

⑤ 他还不能上学，因为年龄不_____。

4. 冷落、冷

（冷落 is usually used in a more abstract sense, is a written/formal expression, and means "deserted, desolate" or "cold-shoulder" while 冷 is often used in a more concrete sense, is a spoken/informal expression, and means "cold".）

① 很多加拿大人冬天住到美国的佛罗里达州去，因为加拿大的冬天太_____了。

② 妈妈让小明赶快招待大家喝茶吃点心，不要_____了客人！

③ 大家说说笑笑的，气氛很好。只有他觉得受了_____。

④ 天气预报说，这几天有_____空气来袭，温度会下降到零下。

四、找出与阴影词语最接近的解释

◆ Choose the expression that is closest in meaning to the shaded word or phrase

_____ 1. 北京是中国人口最多的城市，现在已经 人满为患 。

　　a. 人多得成问题了　　b. 人少得可怜　　c. 人口适中，不多不少

_____ 2. 他父亲做官时家中宾客很多，辞官以后就 门庭冷落 了。

　　a. 宾客很多　　b. 宾客很少　　c. 宾客不多不少

_____ 3. 这对夫妻在教育孩子的问题上常常 意见相左 。

　　a. 意见相同　　b. 意见相近　　c. 意见不同

_____ 4. 他觉得老板给他的工资太低，一气之下 就把工作辞了。

a. 因为太生气　　b. 因为太着急　　c. 因为一时疏忽

_____ 5. 他因为一时疏忽竟造成了重大损失。

a. 经常不小心　　b. 偶然的粗心大意　　c. 过分的小心谨慎

五、选词填空

◆ Choose the most appropriate word and fill in the blanks

| 乃至 | 以 | 于 | 根本 |
| 倒(是) | 尽管 | 被 | |

1. 妈妈说了他很多次，可是他_____不听。

2. 在互联网时代，人们_____什么方式互相联系？

3. 小张工作十多年了，一直致力_____电脑软件的开发。

4. 冰箱里的水果都_____小王的同屋吃了。

5. 她都六十多岁了，可身体_____比年轻人还好！

6. _____去过北京几次，但是她都没有机会去长城看看。

7. 学好一门外语需要几年_____十几年的坚持和努力。

六、句段分析

◆ Sentence analysis

1. 找出下列句子的主语、谓语和宾语（Please indicate the subject, predicate, and object in the following sentences）

   (1) 新华网记者走访了招聘会、多家职业咨询机构以及企业。

   主语：　　　　谓语：　　　　宾语：

   (2) 她通过网络先后给武汉某女装服饰公司、某运动品牌公司以及某电影城发过简历。

主语：＿＿＿＿＿＿ 谓语：＿＿＿＿＿＿ 宾语：＿＿＿＿＿＿

2. 把下列句子翻译成英文（Translate the following sentences into English）

(1) 包括软件、动漫、通信、机械、机电、制造、光电子等各行业在内的上千个岗位向求职者争递橄榄枝。

(2) 和70后、80后选择工作要求稳定、福利齐全的择业观念不同，90后找工作时，已经时刻准备着"跳槽"换工作。

七、小作文

◆ Short essay

在美国90后的大学毕业生在就业方面有什么特点？
（200-300字，请在你的作文中尽量用上本课所学的生词和句型结构。200–300 characters; please do your best to use the words and grammar patterns learned in this lesson.）

第3课 华裔虎妈教女严 中西争论起"硝烟"

一、请用英文解释下列词的意思

Please give the meanings of the following words in English

实行 _____ 制定 _____

叙述 _____ 引出 _____ 听从 _____

私自 _____ 关心 _____

强加 _____ 督办 _____

二、词汇搭配

Match the following two groups of words or phrases

尊重	工作
扮演	同事
申请	计划生育政策
顾及	"自力更生"的理念
监督	重要的角色
奉行	孩子的学习
培养	别人的感受
秉持	年轻一代

Lesson 3

华裔虎妈教女严 中西争论起"硝烟"

三、区分下面词汇的用法并完成填空

◆ Please note the different usages of the following words and fill in the blanks

1. 畏惧、怕

(畏惧 is usually used in a more abstract sense, is a written/formal expression, and means "to fear" or "to dread" while 怕 is often used in a more concrete sense, is a spoken/informal expression, and means "to fear" or "to be unable to stand something".)

① 我很_____热。

② 我们不能_____困难和问题。

③ 他什么都不_____。

④ 严格管教孩子并不是让他们有_____心理。

2. 枯燥、枯

(枯燥 is usually used in a more abstract sense, is a written/formal expression, and means "dry and dull, uninteresting" while 枯 is often used in a more concrete sense, is a spoken/informal expression, and means "a plant or a flower withered" or "a well, river, etc. dried up".)

① 那是一个_____井,已经没有水了。

② 那个老师上课很_____,学生不太喜欢。

③ 那棵树已经_____死了。

④ 今天的讲座很_____无味,我听着听着就睡着了!

3. 扮演、演

(扮演 is usually used in a more abstract sense, is a written/formal expression, and means "to act, to disguise oneself as, to dress up as, to play the part of" while 演 is often used in a more concrete sense, is a spoken/informal expression, and means "to act and play, to develop, evolve, or deduce".)

① 他很喜欢_____戏。

② 那个女演员_____过很多电影和电视剧。

③ 俄罗斯在全球政治中_____着重要角色。

④ 像脸书、微信这样的社交媒体目前在人们生活中_____着不可缺少的角色。

四、找出与阴影词语最接近的解释

◆ Choose the expression that is closest in meaning to the shaded word or phrase

_____ 1. 家长要从小培养孩子独立生活的能力，不能事事 越俎代庖 。

    a. 家长跟孩子一起做   b. 让孩子自己做   c. 替孩子做

_____ 2. 尊重父母并不意味着对父母的话 唯命是从 。

    a. 完全听从   b. 完全不听从   c. 根据情况决定是否听从

_____ 3. 他是一个喜欢 随心所欲 的人。

    a. 想好了才做   b. 不想就做   c. 想怎么做就怎么做

_____ 4. 那个公司老板的做法实在是有些 不近人情 。

    a. 太随心所欲   b. 太苛刻   c. 太宽容

_____ 5. 环境污染直接影响到了人们的日常生活和身体健康，不容忽视 。

    a. 不能不重视   b. 可以不重视   c. 不必太重视

五、选词填空

Choose the most appropriate word and fill in the blanks

| 到底 | 不论 | 只有 | 曾 | 仍然 |

1. 我_____在北京生活过十年。

2. 你_____想怎么办？

3. 这个孩子别人的话都不听。_____老师说他，他才听。

4. _____明天的天气好不好，我们都得去一趟纽约。

5. 公司很多人都买了车，开车上班。可是他_____坐公交车上下班。

6. 附近的饭馆都很糟糕，_____这家做上海菜的饭馆还可以。

六、句段分析

Sentence analysis

1. 找出下列句子的主语、谓语和宾语（Please indicate the subject, predicate, and object in the following sentences）

(1) 美国《华尔街日报》以"为什么中国母亲更胜一筹？"为题，选登了新近出版的《虎妈战歌》这部书的一些片段。

主语：　　　　　谓语：　　　　　宾语：

(2) 蔡美儿从自己的育儿理念出发，总结出中西方家庭教育理念的三个不同。

主语：　　　　　谓语：　　　　　宾语：

2. 把下列句子翻译成英文（Translate the following sentences into English）

(1) 书的作者耶鲁大学法学教授蔡美儿在文中讲述了自己如何对两个女儿奉行"中国式严教"助其成才的经历。

(2) 这篇文章所引发的中西方家庭教育的争论和冲突一时还不会消失。

七、小作文

◆ **Short essay**

美国家长在教育和培养孩子方面秉持什么样的理念？他们更注意孩子成长过程中的哪些方面？他们的育儿方法跟蔡美儿这样的家长有什么不同？

（200-300字，请在你的作文中尽量用上本课所学的生词和句型结构。200-300 characters; please do your best to use the words and grammar patterns learned in this lesson.）

Lesson 3
第3课 华裔虎妈教女严 中西争论起"硝烟"

第4课　多元文化冲击　"圣诞节"世俗化

一、请用英文解释下列词的意思
Please give the meanings of the following words in English

美化 _____　　余额 _____

苦味 _____　　商人 _____　　亚裔 _____

授予 _____

二、词汇搭配
Match the following two groups of words or phrases

赋予	传统
引发	权利
延续	火灾
导致	中国特色
伤害	婚姻破裂
体现	少数族裔的感情
抱怨	房间
装饰	功课太多

Lesson 4 多元文化冲击"圣诞节"世俗化

三、区分下面词汇的用法并完成填空

Please note the different usages of the following words and fill in the blanks

1. 热门、热

(热门 means "hot, in great demand, popular"; it is usually used in a more abstract sense and is a written/formal expression. 热 means "hot, craze, fever"; it is often used in a more concrete sense and is a spoken/informal expression.)

① 习近平主席访问美国是当前的一个_____新闻。

② 今天天气真_____。

③ 电脑专业是一个_____专业。

④ 随着中国经济的发展，中文_____已经遍及各个国家。

2. 伤害、害

(伤害 is usually used in a more abstract sense, is a written/formal expression, and means "to hurt" or "to harm" while 害 is often used in a more concrete sense, is a spoken/informal expression, and means "to impair, to cause trouble to, to kill".)

① 夫妻常常吵架会_____俩人的感情。

② 我们不能有_____人之心。

③ 据报道，那个电影明星昨天被_____了。

④ 老师在课堂严厉地训斥学生会_____他们的自尊心。

3. 气氛、气

(气氛 is usually used in a more abstract sense, is a written/formal expression, and means "atmosphere" while 气 is often used in a more concrete sense, is a spoken/informal expression, and means "air, breath".)

① 晚会充满着友好的_____。

② 房间里太闷，请打开窗户透透_____。

③ 会议室里的_____令我透不过_____来。

④ 灯光不要太强，因为可以创造一种舒适的_____。

四、找出与阴影词语最接近的解释

◆ Choose the expression that is closest in meaning to the shaded word or phrase

_____ 1. 毕业典礼上，女学生们 一律 穿着白裙子。

a. 一个　　　　b. 全部　　　　c. 一些

_____ 2. 教皇Pope Francis于周二下午抵达了这里，他受到了 隆重 的欢迎。

a. 重要　　　　b. 冷落　　　　c. 盛大热烈

_____ 3. 她很多年没回家乡了，对那儿的人和事的记忆已经 模糊 了。

a. 不清楚　　　b. 忘了　　　　c. 很清楚

_____ 4. 在对美国进行国事访问 前夕 ，国家主席习近平接受了美国《华尔街日报》的采访。

a. 最近　　　　b. 之后　　　　c. 之前

五、选词填空

◆ Choose the most appropriate word and fill in the blanks

随着	然而	基本上	而
尚且	如此	不论	

1. _____实验多么难，我都得继续做下去。

2. 大家_____同意她的看法。

3. 项目在进行过程中遇到了很大的困难，_____他们并不灰心。

4. 今天下了大雪，特别冷，可虽然_____，还是有很多人在外面打雪仗。

5. 大家都问："Robin Williams自己_____不快乐，怎么给别人创造快乐呢？"

6. _____生活水平的提高，人们越来越注意养生。

7. 大家假期都出去玩儿了，_____我却得留在学校准备GRE考试。

六、句段分析

◆ *Sentence analysis*

1. 找出下列句子的主语、谓语和宾语（Please indicate the subject, predicate, and object in the following sentences）

(1) 圣诞节的内容和形式也引发了一些争议。

主语：　　　　　　谓语：　　　　　　宾语：

(2) 政府部门明令禁止在办公室挂圣诞节的装饰。

主语：　　　　　　谓语：　　　　　　宾语：

2. 把下列句子翻译成英文（Translate the following sentences into English）

(1) 欧美国家圣诞节的"圣味"是否变淡，则涉及各种价值观、族群、信仰者团体利益的交锋。

(2) 对北京人进行的随机采访表明,许多人把它看作"圣诞老人日"。

七、小作文

◆ Short essay

在美国或者你的国家,在多元文化的冲击下,社会和文化方面有哪些改变?你对这些改变有什么看法?

(200–300 字,请在你的作文中尽量用上本课所学的生词和句型结构。200–300 characters; please do your best to use the words and grammar patterns learned in this lesson.)

第5课 你是"低头族"吗

一、请用英文解释下列词的意思
◆ Please give the meanings of the following words in English

新华网 _____   加时 _____

微小 _____   短信 _____

获利 _____   负面 _____   危机感 _____

旅游热 _____   商业圈 _____

多动症 _____

二、词汇搭配
◆ Match the following two groups of words or phrases

分享	时空的限制
欣赏	别人的存在
干扰	成功的快乐
漠视	网络游戏
沉迷	那位钢琴家的才华
获取	室友的学习
跨越	大家的信任

三、区分下面词汇的用法并完成填空

◆ Please note the different usages of the following words and fill in the blanks

1. 跨越、跨

（跨越 is usually used in a more abstract sense and is a written/formal expression while 越 is often used in a more concrete sense and is a spoken/informal expression.）

① _____时空；_____过那座山

② _____国度；_____过那条小河

③ _____重重障碍

2. 沉迷、迷

（沉迷 is usually used in a more abstract sense and is a written/formal expression while 迷 is often used in a more concrete sense and is a spoken/informal expression.）

① _____于物质享受；_____上了京剧

② _____于赞美的言词；_____上了足球

③ _____于幻想；_____上了音乐

3. 解脱、脱

（解脱 is usually used in a more abstract sense and is a written/formal expression while 脱 is often used in a more concrete sense and is a spoken/informal expression.）

① _____思想负担；_____衣服

② _____鞋；_____负罪感

③ _____病痛；_____裙子

四、找出与阴影词语最接近的解释

Choose the expression that is closest in meaning to the shaded word or phrase

_____ 1. 毋庸置疑，北京是中国人口最多的城市。

   a. 值得怀疑　　　b. 没有疑问　　　c. 可以提问

_____ 2. 别人并没有称赞他，他只是自我欣赏而已。

   a. 人人都欣赏　　b. 无人欣赏　　　c. 自己欣赏自己

_____ 3. 小王饿死了！一下课他就迫不及待地跑到餐厅去吃饭。

   a. 急忙　　　　　b. 慢慢　　　　　c. 不急不忙

_____ 4. 因为看电影而考不好试，那不是得不偿失了吗？！

   a. 有得有失　　　b. 因小失大　　　c. 因大失小

_____ 5. 如今电脑网络每时每刻在影响着我们的生活。

   a. 无时无刻都　　b. 时时刻刻不　　c. 无时无刻不

_____ 6. 在现代中国，重男轻女的思想仍然无处不在。

   a. 没有地方存在　b. 哪儿都存在　　c. 哪儿都不存在

五、选词填空

Choose the most appropriate word and fill in the blanks

| 以及 | 而 | 甚至 | 从而 |
| 其 | 并且 | 进行 | |

1. 北京的雾霾很严重，_____对人民生活的负面影响是显而易见的。

2. 你知道他们两个是因为什么_____离婚的吗？

3. 中国政府20世纪70年代推行了计划生育的政策，_____控制了人口的增长。

4. 北京、上海，_____天津等大城市都通了高铁。

5. 高铁又快又舒服，_____不受天气的影响，大家现在都很喜欢坐高铁出行。

6. 在课上我们对美国枪击案频发的问题_____了讨论。

7. 他来了美国几年，哪儿都没去过，_____连纽约都没去过。

六、句段分析

◆ Sentence analysis

1. 找出下列句子的主语、谓语和宾语(Please indicate the subject, predicate, and object in the following sentences)

(1) 网络信息以及微信、手机QQ、微博以及短信等即时通信工具让越来越多的人成为"低头族"。

主语：　　　　　　谓语：　　　　　　宾语：

(2) 手机原本只是帮助人们提高沟通效率的一个工具。

主语：　　　　　　谓语：　　　　　　宾语：

2. 把下列句子翻译成英文(Translate the following sentences into English)

(1) 人们用"低头族"来形容那些只顾低头看手机而冷落面前亲友的人。

(2) 中国互联网信息中心最新的《中国互联网络发展状况统计报告》显示，中国的智能手机使用比例达到了人口总数的66%。

七、小作文
◆ Short essay

请你谈谈你对"低头族"现象的看法。你觉得自己是"低头族"吗？在你身边有"低头族"吗？你同意课文中对"低头族"的批评吗？

（200—300字，请在你的作文中尽量用上本课所学的生词和句型结构。200–300 characters; please do your best to use the words and grammar patterns learned in this lesson.）

第6课 女性维权非小事　社会关注人人知

一、请用英文解释下列词的意思
Please give the meanings of the following words in English

侮辱 ▢　　严重 ▢　　称谓 ▢

唤出 ▢　　褒奖 ▢

逐渐 ▢　　爱护 ▢　　自称 ▢

逐年 ▢

二、词汇搭配
Match the following two groups of words or phrases

塑造	大众的注意
唤起	电视节目
强化	一个新的人物
隐含	妇女的权益
审理	别的意思
主持	听力的训练
捍卫	全家人的生活
负担	一起杀人案

三、区分下面词汇的用法并完成填空

Please note the different usages of the following words and fill in the blanks

1. 塑造、造

（塑造 is usually used in a more abstract sense, is a written/formal expression, and means "to model, to mould, to shape, to portray" while 造 is often used in a more concrete sense, is a spoken/informal expression, and means "to make, to build, to cook up, to fabricate".）

① 这个房子是新_____的。

② 老师让学生用刚学的生词_____句子。

③ 他是演员，在银幕上_____了各式各样的人物。

④ 敦煌石窟中的壁画_____了很多佛教的人物和形象。

2. 解读、读

（解读 is usually used in a more abstract sense, is a written/formal expression, and means "to read, to explain, to interpret" while 读 is often used in a more concrete sense, is a spoken/informal expression, and means "to read".）

① 他这个星期_____了三本小说。

② 大多数人不赞同他这种对经济形势的_____。

③ 你是怎么_____中国的"全面开放二胎"政策的？

④ 这篇文章我_____了两遍还没_____懂。

3. 询问、问

（询问 is usually used in a more abstract sense, is a written/formal expression, and means "to inquire, to enquire, to question" while 问 is often used in a more concrete sense, is a spoken/informal expression, and means "to ask, to question".）

① 你有问题可以在上课的时候_____老师。

② 小明明年要上大学了，妈妈跟他一起走访了几所大学，_____了很多方面的情况。

③ 我们想暑假去法国旅游，就跟去过法国的朋友_____了许多交通、酒店方面的情况。

④ 你想出国留学吗？那得先_____(please use reduplication of the verb here) 你父母同意不同意。

四、找出与阴影词语最接近的解释

Choose the expression that is closest in meaning to the shaded word or phrase

_____ 1. 不就是一次考试没考好吗？没有必要 小题大作 。

　　a. 因小失大　　　　b. 大事化小　　　　c. 把小事说成大事

_____ 2. 小王的男朋友有一次约会迟到了，小王到现在还 耿耿于怀 。

　　a. 记不清楚了　　b. 念念不忘　　　　c. 忘得一干二净了

_____ 3. 吸烟在很多公共场合是禁止的，但是吸烟者还 大有人在 。

　　a. 为数不少　　　b. 为数甚少　　　　c. 为数不多

_____ 4. 上海是个国际化的大城市。在上海，英文的路标和商家品牌 随处可见 。

　　a. 无处可见　　　b. 何处可见　　　　c. 到处可见

_____ 5. 这个城市的服务行业非常好，包括交通、餐饮、医疗、旅游等，举不胜举 。

　　a. 可以举出的例子很多　　　b. 没有什么例子可以举出

　　c. 可以举出的例子很少

五、选词填空

◆ Choose the most appropriate word and fill in the blanks

| 就 | 通过 | 即使 | 受到 | 至于 |

1. 大家_____中国经济发展的问题展开了讨论。

2. 我不同意这种做法。_____他怎么看这件事，我也不清楚。

3. 小张的英文原来很差，但是_____几年的努力，他的英文有了很大的进步。

4. 最近空气污染的问题_____了很多人的关注。

5. 这件事太重要了！_____你不说，我也会把它办好。

六、句段分析

◆ Sentence analysis

1. 找出下列句子的主语、谓语和宾语(Please indicate the subject, predicate, and object in the following sentences)

    (1) "网易娱乐"就"春晚小品中出现'二手货''剩女'等是否歧视女性"进行了调查。

    主语：　　　　　谓语：　　　　　宾语：

    (2) 从北京某学院毕业的曹菊在求职网站上看到了巨人教育招聘行政助理的信息。

    主语：　　　　　谓语：　　　　　宾语：

2. 把下列句子翻译成英文(Translate the following sentences into English)

    (1) 山西籍女大学生曹菊（化名）因在应聘中遭性别限制，起诉招聘单位北京巨人环球教育科技有限公司一案，在北京市海淀区人民法院开庭审理。

(2) 这是在《就业促进法》发布并生效五年后，首例以"维护女性合法权益"为由向法院提起的诉讼。

七、小作文

◆ *Short essay*

美国存在哪些性别歧视的现象？请举例说明。你觉得我们应该怎样做才能维护女性的权益，进一步实现男女平等？

（200-300字，请在你的作文中尽量用上本课所学的生词和句型结构。200-300 characters; please do your best to use the words and grammar patterns learned in this lesson.）

第7课 北京与伦敦：雾都治霾浅议

一、请用英文解释下列词的意思
Please give the meanings of the following words in English

污染物 ＿＿＿＿　　能源 ＿＿＿＿＿＿＿＿＿＿

超自然 ＿＿＿＿　　超产 ＿＿＿＿＿＿＿＿

艺术性 ＿＿＿＿＿＿＿＿

二、词汇搭配
Match the following two groups of words or phrases

受到	袭击
造成	水平
达到	措施
采取	危害
治理	质量
改善	经验
借鉴	合作
防止	数量
减少	污染
加强	雾霾

37

三、区分下面词汇的用法并完成填空

Please note the different usages of the following words and fill in the blanks

1. 持续、继续

（Both 持续 and 继续 can mean "to continue", but 持续 is usually used in written/formal expression while 继续 is used in both written and spoken/informal expression. The conditions for 持续 are more objective and cannot be controlled by human beings, whereas 继续 emphasizes a subjective situation and is more volitional. In addition, 继续 can take an object, but 持续 cannot.）

① 无论这个工程多难多复杂，我们一定要把它_____做下去。

② 为了保证经济的可_____发展，我们必须大力搞好科研开发，同时加大环境保护的力度。

③ 暴风雪_____了三天三夜。

④ 新经理_____以前的做法，鼓励员工们努力工作，让公司不断成长。

2. 死亡、死

（死亡 is usually used in a more abstract sense, is a written/formal expression, and means "to die, to pass away, to cease to be" while 死 is often used in a more concrete sense, is a spoken/informal expression, and means "to die, to pass away".）

① 她的小狗_____了，她特别伤心。

② 奶奶已经_____了好多年了，至今我还时常想起她。

③ 这次地震发生在人口密集的城市，上万人_____。

④ 这次车祸造成了七人_____。

Lesson 7

四、找出与阴影词语最接近的解释
♦ Choose the expression that is closest in meaning to the shaded word or phrase

_____ 1. 她打扮时髦，走在街上非常 令人注目。

a. 引起别人注意　　b. 看了很久　　　　c. 不太好

_____ 2. 家里的气氛太 令人压抑 了，我出来走走。

a. 太热烈　　　　　b. 太沉闷　　　　　c. 太轻松

_____ 3. 我不敢直视她，她的美真是 令人窒息。

a. 让人生气　　　　b. 让人想休息　　　c. 让人喘不过气来

_____ 4. 关于选举的广告真是 铺天盖地，我不知道谁说的是真的。

a. 数量多，声势大　　b. 数量少，声势小　　c. 特别少

五、选词填空
♦ Choose the most appropriate word and fill in the blanks

与……有关	称……为	之	使
虽然……却	大大	则	

1. 这些工厂搬到郊区以后，城里的空气质量_____改善了。

2. 得肺癌的人越来越多，这一状况_____空气污染_____。

3. 这样的考试成绩_____他的父母极为失望。

4. 地震过去了，但是随_____而来的安静令人窒息。

5. 他的儿子不太喜欢学习，对玩游戏_____兴趣十足。

6. _____政府采取了很多措施保护环境，效果_____不太理想。

7. 我们把一切在网上进行的商业活动_____之____电子商务。

39

六、句段分析

◆ Sentence analysis

1. 找出下列句子的主语、谓语和宾语(Please indicate the subject, predicate, and object in the following sentences)

(1) 根据世界卫生组织出版的《2010年全球疾病负担研究》，在中国2010年早逝人群中，120万人的死亡与户外空气污染有关。

主语：　　　　　　谓语：　　　　　　宾语：

(2) 伦敦对雾霾的成功治理也提供了很多值得借鉴的经验。

主语：　　　　　　谓语：　　　　　　宾语：

(3) 在2014年APEC会议期间，北京政府对重度污染的工厂和工程实行限产、停产。

主语：　　　　　　谓语：　　　　　　宾语：

2. 把下列句子翻译成英文(Translate the following sentences into English)

(1) 北京及周边地区人口众多、工业密集，煤炭又是主要能源，再加上丘陵环绕的地形，造成了北京空气污染在一年中的某些时期达到或超过危险水平。

(2) 从1956年开始,伦敦出台了一系列防止和控制空气污染的法案和措施:限制工业废气排放,减少烟尘和有毒颗粒物;发展公共交通,缩减机动车数量。

(3) 各地区、各个国家需要加强合作,互相学习,采取适当有效的措施,减少污染物的排放,发展和使用清洁能源,那样让雾霾永远散去才有希望。

七、小作文

Short essay

北京和伦敦的雾霾是什么原因造成的？两地各自采取了什么样的措施治理雾霾？你对治理雾霾有什么看法？

（200-300字，请在你的作文中尽量用上本课所学的生词和句型结构。200-300 characters; please do your best to use the words and grammar patterns learned in this lesson.）

第8课 美国校园为何枪击案频发

一、请用英文解释下列词的意思
◆ Please give the meanings of the following words in English

自杀案 _____   电脑化 _____

再生性 _____   仇视 _____

参赛者 _____   文学性 _____

理解力 _____

自发式 _____   寄予 _____

任满 _____

二、完成构词
◆ Complete the following word constructions

低头族	_____族	_____族	_____族
微信热	_____热	_____热	_____热
亲密感	_____感	_____感	_____感
社交圈	_____圈	_____圈	_____圈
强迫症	_____症	_____症	_____症
污染源	_____源	_____源	_____源
危害性	_____性	_____性	_____性
枪击案	_____案	_____案	_____案

三、区分下面词汇的用法并完成填空

Please note the different usages of the following words and fill in the blanks

1. 缺乏、缺

（缺乏 is usually used in a more abstract sense and is a written/formal expression while 缺 is often used in a more concrete sense and is a spoken/informal expression.）

① _____资源；_____水；_____人

② _____钱；_____资金；_____成就感

③ _____研究；_____电；_____经验

④ _____老师

2. 暴露、露

（暴露 is usually used in a more abstract sense and is a written/formal expression while 露 is often used in a more concrete sense and is a spoken/informal expression.）

① 中国的经济发展太快，近几年_____出了不少问题。

② 她打开手包，_____出了里边的化妆品。

③ 鲁迅的作品_____了中国社会的黑暗。

④ 这件衣服很透明，_____出了内衣的颜色。

3. 上演、演

（上演 is usually used in a more abstract sense and is a written/formal expression while 演 is often used in a more concrete sense and is a spoken/informal expression.）

① 这个政府最近_____了一幕政治丑剧。

② 他戏_____得很好。

③ 这部新电影六月会在北京和上海等大城市_____。

Lesson 8
美国校园为何枪击案频发

④ 学校今天晚上_____什么电影？

4. 携手、拉着手

（携手 is usually used in a more abstract sense and is a written/formal expression while 拉着手 is often used in a more concrete sense and is a spoken/informal expression.）

① 我们要_____合作，共同建立一个和谐公平的社会。

② 他们_____一起去散步。

③ 世界和平需要各个国家_____共同维护。

④ 让我们_____并肩，创造一个美好的未来。

⑤ 这两个年轻人在公园里_____又唱又跳。

5. 松懈、松

（松懈 is usually used in a more abstract sense and is a written/formal expression while 松 is often used in a more concrete sense and is a spoken/informal expression.）

① 那个孩子的鞋带_____了，妈妈帮他系了一下。

② 由于纪律_____，这个学校的学生出了不少问题。

③ 枪支管理_____使得枪击案频发。

④ 面对困难不能意志_____。

⑤ 她最近瘦了不少，裤子都_____了。

四、找出与阴影词语最接近的解释

Choose the expression that is closest in meaning to the shaded word or phrase

_____ 1. 这个中学推行 人手 一球的体育运动计划，希望提高孩子们的身体素质。

  a. 人人都有 b. 随身携带 c. 手中拿着

_____ 2. 这个会已经开了四个小时了，大家对明年的工作计划一直争论不休。

    a. 不明白   b. 不休息   c. 不停

_____ 3. 网上关于这个演员的花边新闻层出不穷。

    a. 不断出现   b. 越来越少   c. 到处都是

_____ 4. 政治动乱带来的社会问题比比皆是。

    a. 一年比一年多 b. 不时常有   c. 到处都是

_____ 5. 朋友之间互相影响，而这种影响常常是耳濡目染的。

    a. 密不可分   b. 不知不觉   c. 慢慢发生

_____ 6. 孩子的成长跟家庭教育密不可分。

    a. 关系十分紧密 b. 关系非常亲密 c. 无法分辨

五、选词填空

◆ Choose the most appropriate word and fill in the blanks

其中	加上	加以	据
为此	为		

1. _____天气预报说，明天会有大雨。

2. 经验丰富_____勤奋努力，他在公司提升得很快。

3. 她考上了清华大学，我们都_____她高兴。

4. 加州新移民很多，_____不少是讲西班牙语的。

5. 她决定移民加拿大，_____她放弃了稳定的工作。

6. _____统计，中国现在的男女比例是严重失衡。

7. 病人死亡的原因不清楚，还要_____分析。

8. 美国枪击案频发的原因很多，_____一个主要的原因是枪支管理太松懈。

9. 车多_____人多，北京上下班的时间常常堵车。

10. 这个电脑软件带有中英文的说明书，对使用方法_____说明。

六、句段分析

◆ *Sentence analysis*

1. 找出下列句子的主语、谓语和宾语(Please indicate the subject, predicate, and object in the following sentences)

   (1) 美国枪支管理的松懈为人们可以轻易获得枪支提供了条件。

   主语：　　　　　谓语：　　　　　宾语：

   (2) 一个美国青少年18岁之前在各种传媒上能看到4万起谋杀案和20万起其他暴力行为。

   主语：　　　　　谓语：　　　　　宾语：

2. 把下列句子翻译成英文(Translate the following sentences into English)

   (1) 由于美国国会对于是否制定严格的枪支管理法案争论不休，枪支泛滥的问题始终得不到解决。

(2) 这对于是非分辨力还不太强的孩子来说，会有很强的蛊惑作用。

七、小作文

◆ Short essay

作为一名学生，你对美国校园枪击案频发的现象怎么看？在你看来，怎么做才可以尽量避免枪击惨剧的发生？

（200–300 字，请在你的作文中尽量用上本课所学的生词和句型结构。200–300 characters; please do your best to use the words and grammar patterns learned in this lesson.）

Lesson 8
美国校园为何枪击案频发